Final Days

Final Days

THE INSIDE STORY OF THE COLLAPSE
OF THE SOVIET UNION

❀

Andrei S. Grachev

with a Foreword by Archie Brown

Translated by Margo Milne

WestviewPress

A Division of HarperCollinsPublishers

English edition copyright © 1995 by Westview Press, Inc., A Division of HarperCollins Publishers, Inc.

Published in 1995 in the United States of America by Westview Press, Inc., 5500 Central Avenue, Boulder, Colorado 80301-2877, and in the United Kingdom by Westview Press, 12 Hid's Copse Road, Cumnor Hill, Oxford OX2 9JJ

First published in France as *L'Histoire vraie de la fin de l'URSS* © 1992 by Editions du Rocher

Library of Congress Cataloging-in-Publication Data
Grachev, A. S.
  [Dal 'she bez meniă—English]
  Final days: the inside story of the collapse of the Soviet Union
/ Andrei S. Grachev ; with a foreword by Archie Brown ; translated
by Margo Milne.
    p. cm.
  Also published in French as L'histoire vraie de la fin de l'URSS.
  Includes index.
  ISBN 0-8133-2206-5
  1. Gorbachev, Mikhail Sergeevich, 1931–   . 2. Presidents—Soviet
Union—Biography. 3. Soviet Union—Politics and
government—1985–1991. I. Title.
DK290.3.G67G7313 1995
947.085'4'092—dc20
[B]   95-16424
                                                                              CIP

The paper used in this publication meets the requirements of the American National Standard for Permanence of Paper for Printed Library Materials Z39.48-1984.

10   9   8   7   6   5   4   3   2

To my wife,
without whom this book
would never have seen
the light of day

Contents

Foreword

ARCHIE BROWN

Behind the monolithic facade that the Communist Party of the Soviet Union (CPSU) presented to the outside world until at least 1985 there was in reality a great variety of political opinion. Because it was generally expressed behind closed doors or in veiled or Aesopian form in books, journals, and newspapers, this was poorly understood in the outside world. But taking cognizance of this diversity of belief within a party that had preserved a monopoly of power for seventy years is basic to an understanding of the radical reforms and increasingly open debate of the Gorbachev era and of the ultimate demise of the Soviet system.

The "monolithic unity" that the Communist Party claimed as one of its greatest assets was a reality inasmuch as discipline was rigid; until the second half of the 1980s the Party spoke with one public voice. Yet the very fact that the CPSU had ruled throughout the entire lifetime of most Soviet citizens, that it was an integral part of the ruling structures of the society—a *party-state* rather than a political party in the Western sense of the term—meant that ambitious people of various views and of very different personalities and abilities were keen to join that party or were invited to join. Membership was a precondition of exercising political power or (with rare exceptions) even substantial influence within the society, and in almost every walk of life promotion to senior posts was reserved for the minority of the population who were within the CPSU. Although lip service was paid to the Party's supposed proletarian roots and care was taken to ensure that approximately 10 percent of manual workers were Party members, the CPSU became increasingly dominated by its "white-collar" component and, above all, by the full-time officials within the extensive Party bureaucracy. Even though talented professionals in, for example, the social sciences could be frustrated by the ideological constraints that Party doctrine placed upon their freedom of publication and action, the majority of them preferred to be inside the Communist Party than out. Indeed, the higher the education a person had, the more likely she or (especially) he was to be a Party member.

Party membership was, more often than not, linked to career ambitions. It was generally a sine qua non of holding down a position of executive responsibility. For some Party members it undoubtedly reflected a wish to be part of a ruling political class, although many rank-and-file members were far removed from the corridors of power. What Party membership did *not* necessarily indicate was a particular set of ideological convictions. That point can be illustrated by the fact that practically every member of the overtly anti-Communist administration of post-Soviet Russia was until quite recently a member of the CPSU.

In some cases they really were at one time Leninists by conviction, in other cases hardly at all. Boris Yeltsin—who would appear to belong to the former category—was a high-level Communist Party official in the Urals and, more briefly (under Gorbachev), in Moscow. His prime minister, Viktor Chernomyrdin, worked in the same Central Committee apparatus as the author of this book, Andrei Grachev (albeit a different department). Even Chernomyrdin's predecessor, the radical free marketeer Yegor Gaidar—acting Russian prime minister throughout 1992—was not only a member of the Communist Party but an economic journalist on its principal newspaper, *Pravda*, and its theoretical journal, *Kommunist*.

This diversity of view among "Communists" applied, then, not only to the mass membership, which for most of the 1980s consisted of some 6.5 percent of the total Soviet population and about 10 percent of those of working age (reaching a peak membership in absolute numbers of approximately 19.5 million people in 1989). The variety of opinion—albeit to a less dramatic extent—was to be found, too, within the Party apparatus. These full-time Party officials included also very different personality types and people of vastly varying intelligence and levels of education.

Even a single department of the Central Committee of the Communist Party could embrace people who wished to break with traditional dogma and those who feared all innovation. The International Department of the Central Committee—in which the author of *Final Days*, Andrei Grachev, gained increasing influence during the Gorbachev era—was very much a case in point. Although this department was long assumed in the outside world to be a citadel of Communist orthodoxy and a body constantly ready to place shackles upon the more pragmatic Ministry of Foreign Affairs, that was an oversimplification. If the long-term head of the International Department, Boris Ponomarev, was even more of a diehard than the almost equally long-serving minister of foreign affairs, Andrei Gromyko, the same Ponomarev was conscious of the need to recruit and retain the services of a nucleus of well-informed officials with a knowledge of foreign languages and cultures. Moreover, one of his deputy heads, Anatoly Chernyaev, gathered around him a group of highly capable younger men whose views were developing in directions that neither Gromyko nor Ponomarev—with all their talents for political adjustment and survival—could ever have shared.

One of the key figures in that group was Andrei Grachev, who, some time after his immediate superior, Chernyaev, was appointed principal foreign policy aide to

Mikhail Gorbachev in February 1986, himself became (in 1989) a deputy head of the International Department. By that time he was already an important contributor to the "new thinking" of the Gorbachev era. That thinking was genuinely new in the Soviet context and involved rejection of a Marxist-Leninist, so-called class approach to international relations, an acceptance of freedom of choice for the countries of Eastern Europe (including ultimate acquiescence even in the highly sensitive reunification of Germany), and the replacement of the timeworn Soviet view of East-West relations as a zero-sum game by an understanding that there were universal values and interests that transcended the traditional ideological divide and superpower rivalries.

This new thinking preceded the new political practice, and the role of the Party insiders who embraced it is, in a sense, even more important than that of scholars in the research institutes who helped elaborate the ideas. Although the latter had more contacts with their Western counterparts, their influence within the Soviet system depended entirely on support from inside the Central Committee building. For changes in doctrine and political practice as dramatic as those that occured after 1985 to take place, Party intellectuals within and outside the apparatus were even more dependent upon the receptiveness to new ideas of the general secretary of the Central Committee and on his willingness to lead in an innovative direction. More power was concentrated in his office than in that of any other political figure within the system, although even he did not have an entirely free hand.

A general secretary who challenged the fundamental norms of the system or who endangered the most important vested interests within it ran the risk of overthrow. Nikita Khrushchev discovered this in October 1964 when he was ousted from office, and Gorbachev—who far more thoroughly than Khrushchev shook the foundations of the system—had to display extraordinary political skill to avoid suffering a similar fate at the hands of the dominant conservative groupings within the Party apparatus, the government bureaucracy, the KGB, the military, and the Ministry of the Interior. In the end the leading figures in all of those bodies joined forces to place Gorbachev under house arrest on August 18, 1991; but by that time there were some institutional counterweights, and public opinion, moreover, was much less passive than in 1964. It is of considerable consequence that Gorbachev succeeded in postponing such a showdown for so long. As Andrei Grachev pertinently observes, "People seldom ask how many coups d'état Gorbachev managed to avoid in six and a half years of reform."

Boris Yeltsin, who had gradually been asserting his power and influence as the *Russian* leader at the expense of the *Soviet* leader, Gorbachev, throughout 1991, played a crucial part in the defeat of the August coup and this meant, among

other things, a temporary return to office for Gorbachev. Both the political base
of the Soviet president and the prospects for the preservation of any kind of
union—whether a genuinely federal state or a still looser confederation—had,
however, been fundamentally undermined by the putschists who, in their folly,
had helped to accelerate the breakup of the Union, which they claimed (and
doubtless believed) they were trying to avert.

Yet Gorbachev, as this book by Andrei Grachev so vividly shows, fought a rear-
guard battle to preserve some kind of union. His preference was for a federation,
but he was prepared to be flexible and was ready to settle for a confederal union of
independent states somewhat akin to the European Union. It is one thing,
though, for the countries of Western Europe voluntarily to join such a union—
whose evolution is reflected in changing terminology, from European Economic
Community to European Community to European Union—and subsequently to
deepen its links (even though that process is by no means uncontroversial in
Western Europe). It is quite another to establish confidence in analogous political
structures on the territory of the former USSR with its history of Russian empire
and of a highly centralized Soviet state, both of which were accompanied by
forcible suppression of the national aspirations of a variety of ethnic groups living in their historical homelands.

Gorbachev, nevertheless, profoundly believed in the necessity of preserving as
much of a political union as was compatible with political consent, although by
spring 1991 and, still more, in the postcoup months he had virtually given up
hope of persuading the three Baltic states to remain within such an entity, even
one called the Union of Sovereign States (USS rather than USSR). It is also the
case that Gorbachev, like most politicians, was understandably reluctant to abandon political office—the more so since he had bestrode the world stage more im-
pressively and with more acclaim than any of his Soviet predecessors. He had,
futhermore, influenced the course of world history in the second half of the twentieth century to a greater extent than any other politician, East or West, and he
had introduced reforms that were to have a more dramatic impact on Russia than
those even of the reforming tsar, Alexander II, over a hundred years earlier.

In the aftermath of the coup Gorbachev reorganized his political team—free
for the first time of pressure from conservative Communists, to whom he had
earlier (and in winter 1990–1991 well beyond the bounds of wisdom) made significant concessions. One of the people he invited to collaborate especially closely
with him was the author of *Final Days*. Andrei Grachev had accompanied
Gorbachev on virtually all of his foreign visits since 1985 as a quite senior and
particularly well-informed official on the staff of the Central Committee and as
an adviser on foreign policy. But the post he was offered now—as Gorbachev's

press secretary—made him a still closer political adviser with much more constant access to the Soviet leader. It turned him into an influential participant-observer in the domestic political struggles of the coming months while giving him at the same time a ringside seat from which to observe Gorbachev's conduct of international diplomacy.

Having to report and answer to the Soviet and world mass media as presidential press spokesman, Grachev was obliged to keep careful record of conversations and negotiations in which Gorbachev took part. Accordingly, he is now able to provide in far richer detail than has been available hitherto an eye-witness account of the final months of the Soviet Union and of the Gorbachev presidency. Grachev is not only a particularly acute and intelligent observer but also a gifted writer whose account of these fateful months is often enlivened by dry humor.

He gives an exceptionally vivid description of the demise of the Soviet Union from the standpoint of someone who stood close to Gorbachev and who had a privileged view of his relations with Yeltsin. These two politicians are skillfully portrayed, and although Grachev's sympathies are primarily with Gorbachev, he never resorts to hagiography and is not blind to some of Gorbachev's foibles. The reader is also free to conclude that the breakup of the Soviet Union has not led to such apocalyptic consequences as Gorbachev predicted—nothing on the scale of the disaster area that is the former Yugoslavia (and Bosnia in particular). Against that it may, of course, be argued that these are still early days and that the breakup of what was a unified state and an integrated economy, with an ethnically diverse population in all of the former Soviet republics, has added to the economic difficulties and has exacerbated the social strains to be found in the former USSR.

Different readers may come to different conclusions on the desirability of building a new and democratic union on the territory of the former (and far from democratic) Soviet Union—and, indeed, on the feasibility or unreality of such a project. But all can learn from the insights Grachev offers on the debates that occured between the August coup and the lowering of the red flag from the Kremlin on December 25, 1991. The most central of those debates concerned the future, if any, of the Union, but Grachev throws light also on Soviet and Russian relations with the United States and with other Western countries at this time of extraordinarily fast political transition.

The reader of *Final Days* will learn, too, more about the central characters in this great political drama—above all, the elusive but overwhelmingly important personality of Mikhail Gorbachev. This is not, of course, the Gorbachev of 1988–1989 who set the political agenda for his country and for the Western world. After the election of Boris Yeltsin as Russian president in June 1991, and especially following the attempted coup two months later, Gorbachev was politically much weakened in comparison with his earlier years in power. Yet even at this time, when his back was to the wall, he displayed—as Grachev shows—some of the political skills he brought to the earlier transformation of the Soviet political system. At the end of his final struggle as leader of a country that was ceasing to exist—as the first and last president of the USSR—Gorbachev could, with complete justice, claim: "I myself changed as the country did, but I also changed my country."

Preface

*L*ike it or not, Mikhail Gorbachev changed the destiny of our world. In his six and a half years in power, with courage, tenacity, and common sense, he succeeded in breaking down physical and psychological barriers that were believed to be indestructible and in moving the world away from a pattern of confrontation and its many attendant dangers. Through his actions, he sketched the broad strokes of a radically different concept of politics for the beginning of the twenty-first century.

And yet when on December 25, 1991, he relinquished the presidency of the henceforth defunct USSR, he left behind a splintered, ruined country, torn by conflicts and in doubt about its future, a country whose division may be a threat to world peace—a kind of Chernobyl on a global scale.

As the USSR toppled, it dragged its president down with it. Gorbachev's resignation marked a defeat and a tragedy: the defeat of a statesman forced out of power without completing what he saw as his mission and the tragedy of a reformer forced to abandon his plan before it had begun to bear fruit.

But this departure, paradoxically, was also a triumph. Gorbachev did everything he could to destroy the power that an aging Communist *nomenklatura*, wrapped self-protectively in the ideas of another time, had placed in his hands. And he succeeded. The single-party system vanished, almost without violence or confrontation, to give way to an approach to government based on democratic principles. His resignation was a legitimate and logical result of this change, and it was, therefore, the ultimate indication of how well his political agenda had succeeded.

By ending the reign of the party that had brought him to power, Gorbachev not only endangered his position as head of state, he also made it possible for the parliaments of the republics to affirm a new legitimacy. The emergence of strong local governments was a threat to the unity of the country. Gorbachev, however, could not imagine moving ahead with reform unless a unified state was preserved. It was undoubtedly in an attempt to save the union (not necessarily the USSR in name and with all extant bureaucracies) that, in late 1990, he formed an alliance with conservatives[1] who wanted to preserve the country as an integral whole. It soon became apparent, however, that the price of this coalition would be the abandonment of reform. And Gorbachev could not accept that either.

Inexorably, the situation came to a head. Gorbachev almost became a hostage of the right-wingers, whom he himself had appointed to key government positions and who were now steadily gaining confidence. The only factor on which he could rely to counterbalance their influence was the emerging power of the republics, especially since the conservatives also feared the consequences of abandoning reform. In April 1991, the Novo-Ogarevo process cemented the alliance between the President and the leaders of the republics with the formation of the new Union of Sovereign States. This irrevocable choice blocked the conservatives' strategy once and for all. In losing the President, the only person who could cover for them, they lost any chance of being able to retreat and regroup within the law. The only course open to them was to break it. This they did on August 19, with the attempted coup d'état.

It has been said that on his return to Moscow on August 22, after the dramatic days spent in isolation in Foros, Gorbachev landed in a country quite different from the one he had left behind. One thing is certain: The conservatives' defeat had the unexpected effect of closing off the path opened up by the Novo-Ogarevo agreement. The leaders of the republics had tasted sovereignty and had shaken off centralized control. The enemy they had feared so much before the putsch no longer existed. They no longer needed an alliance with the President or the union he supported. Gorbachev had only two options: to accept the conditions of these leaders, who were starting to act more and more like boyars, or to leave.

Gorbachev now found himself in the strange position of having to win back power that was still officially in his possession. Overriding his own natural inclination for balance and compromise, he threw himself passionately into the struggle for the preservation of a single state by flinging down the gauntlet of the union before the leaders of the republics. In so doing, he signed his own political death warrant, as well as that of the country he was trying to preserve. A second putsch, this time without tanks, became inevitable.

Gorbachev had been so successful at convincing the world that he could perform political miracles that he may have wound up believing it himself. He undoubtedly truly believed that in the aftermath of the August putsch he could mend the divisions in the Soviet Union, as one might glue together the fragments of a broken cup, and move forward with his plan for a democratic rebirth of the USSR.

For a few weeks it seemed that the miracle of this political resurrection would actually take place. But Gorbachev's "hundred days" lasted for four months and ended in a bathetic Waterloo with no heroic charges, no cries of "death before surrender." The setting for this bureaucratic defeat was Belovezhskaya Forest in Belorussia. There, in the best traditions of Stalinist justice, a troika of leaders whom Gorbachev himself had brought to power decreed the end of the USSR and sent its president into political exile.

Was this end inevitable? Were Gorbachev's fate and the fate of his country ir-
revocably sealed by the events of August 1991?

To answer these questions, we will accompany Gorbachev through his last
weeks of power, from September to December 1991—a hazy period, little docu-
mented and poorly understood, but heavy with consequences for the future of the
world.

On September 11, Mikhail Gorbachev asked me to become his spokesperson
and one of his aides, as the head of his press service. Shortly after the putsch, on
August 28, Vitaly Ignatenko, who had most recently held this post, had been appointed director-general of the news agency TASS. This was part of a move to replace officials of the public information enterprises who had supported the
putschists in any way. At the same time, another figure close to Gorbachev, the editor in chief of the *Moscow News,* Yegor Yakovlev, became the director of state television. Both had close ties to Alexander Yakovlev. During the putsch, Yegor
Yakovlev, already known for his independence and his radical temperament, had
become famous for organizing the illegal publications of the democratic press.

Gorbachev's offer caught me off guard. He had already asked me to join his
team of advisers on one occasion a few months earlier. Actually, I had been working for him almost since he first came to power, having joined his staff in October
1985. At that time I was part of the team handling the preparations for his first official visit to France. Since then, I had accompanied him on almost all of his trips
abroad. One of my responsibilities at the International Department (ID) of the
Party Central Committee was to coordinate the activities of the planning committee charged with working out and implementing the country's new foreign
policy. The most eminent members of this team, obviously, were Alexander
Yakovlev, who supervised the ID as the CPSU Central Committee secretary for
ideological questions; Anatoly Chernyaev, former assistant director of the ID and,
since 1986, Gorbachev's closest aide; Eduard Shevardnadze, minister of foreign
affairs; and Valentin Falin, former ambassador to West Germany, who subsequently took over the leadership of the ID.

After his election to the presidency of the USSR, in March 1990, Gorbachev
spent several months setting up a presidential apparatus separate from that of the
Party. His aim was to get the people he was used to working with to join this new
structure. The offer that he made me in January 1991, although an opportunity
for advancement, came at the time when he was just beginning to align himself
with the conservatives. It coincided with the bloody events of Vilnius, on January
12 and 13, 1991, a clumsy attempt to regain control of the Baltic states by which
the future putschists intended to tie the President's hands and make him their ac-
complice.

Under these circumstances, it was impossible for me to accept. Furthermore, once I had publicly expressed my distress and indignation, the offer would undoubtedly become null and void.

In September, the President, no longer under pressure from the conservatives, repeated his offer. People who had distanced themselves from him in recent months were returning to his entourage: major figures such as Eduard Shevardnadze, Alexander Yakovlev, and Vadim Bakatin, the former minister of the interior, who was charged with restructuring the KGB after the putsch. Perhaps Gorbachev had taken to heart the maxim that the only people you can lean on are those who resist. I no longer had any reservations whatsoever about the man himself, but I was still hesitating.

Guessing what was on my mind, he said to me: "Do you really think perestroika is over? I don't." Then he suggested that I think about it for a few days. "We'll both think it over, Andrei," he said to me, "each of us on his own."

Although this was very democratic of him, neither of us had any doubts as to who would be persuaded during the interval. When we saw each other again, on September 23, Gorbachev had not changed his mind, and I had decided to accept. I wanted to have a part in this last attempt to advance reform while preserving the unity of the country.

That is how I came to watch the demise of the Soviet Union from a unique vantage point beside its first and last legally elected president and to accompany him as he ascended his own personal Golgotha.

Andrei S. Grachev

Mending the Breach

Toward mid-September, Gorbachev became a real president again. Once again he seemed to have accomplished the impossible: He had lived through the most dramatic events that any statesman is likely to confront in the course of his career, and he was back on his feet.

The putsch, the tense days and nights in Foros, and the threat that had hung over him and his family were only an unpleasant memory now. The bitterness of betrayal by his closest comrades-in-arms had abated. His attitude toward them had faded to one of mingled contempt and vague satisfaction: Although they had seized the entire arsenal of coercion and all the levers of power, they had accomplished nothing. Moreover, he had warned them that they would fail. He had been right again. His dignity and self-esteem had taken a beating at the hands of a triumphant Boris Yeltsin and the members of the Russian parliament whom Yeltsin had set on him after the putsch, but these wounds were now beginning to heal.

Also behind him was the faint-hearted Congress of People's Deputies of the USSR—as frightened of the putschists and their ridiculous, blundering tanks as they were of the more realistic threat posed by the mob that had surged into the streets of Moscow. Tens of thousands of people, encouraged by the sudden power vacuum and drunk with the utter permissiveness that resulted, were ready to express their hatred and take revenge for the accumulated insults of decades of indigence, lashing out against anything that came to hand: the district committee buildings, whose windows were shattered, the Central Committee headquarters, monuments, party functionaries, government chauffeurs, and even the Union Parliament, which had caved in to the putschists' manifestos in such cowardly fashion.

In the days following the failure of the coup d'état, the risk that this uncontrolled human ebb and flow would degenerate into bloody chaos was greater than one might think today. True, there were no casualties during the expulsion of the officials of the CPSU's Central Committee and the sealing up of the building on Old Square. Nevertheless, at any time the excited crowd could have generated an explosion of violence comparable to that which occurred in Budapest in 1956.

Oddly enough, Gorbachev's presence at the funerals of the three victims of the putsch helped to allay the tension. People saw that the head of state was in his place—relegated to a secondary role, certainly, but restored to the privileges of office. And no one could dispute his moral right to be there. In Foros he had shown a strength of character the putschists had not anticipated, setting the stage for their defeat.

Gorbachev's return to power helped to channel the surging masses and convince those who were occupying the streets to go home. Also, in a way—although this may be stretching the point—it gave the breakup of the USSR, which had begun in the midst of this disorder, the semblance of a constitutional process. But for this a considerable price had to be paid.

Gorbachev was forced to accept the dissolution of the Congress of People's Deputies, the federal parliament he had worked so hard to establish and see elected in 1989. Now, disgraced by its behavior during the putsch and humiliated by the dictates of the leaders of the republics, it was no longer able to serve its intended purpose.

Some rather unflattering things have been said—and justifiably, for the most part—about this first and last Union Parliament. Elected by a process that might generously be called "semidemocratic," destitute of any experience or tradition, ignorant of the most rudimentary notions of democratic procedure, encumbered by an unwieldy two-tiered structure (the Congress of People's Deputies and the Supreme Soviet), it was a strange cross between a wild club of would-be anarchists and loyal Estates-General convening on the eve of the French Revolution.[2]

There would be no point in reviewing the ways in which this parliament was manipulated by its presiding officer, Anatoly Lukyanov. He was so skillful at playing on the deputies' weaknesses, fears, and self-interest that observers never knew whether to admire his virtuosity or be outraged at his cynicism. It is possible that this cleverness sometimes worked to benefit the cause of reform, especially since Gorbachev, Lukyanov's friend of many years, had such tremendous faith in him. The two first became acquainted while attending the Moscow State University Law School in the early 1950s. Both were Komsomol officials, but at that time Gorbachev took orders from Lukyanov.

Forty years later their roles were reversed, but the mutual understanding remained. At least, so Gorbachev thought. When push came to shove, however, Lukyanov betrayed Gorbachev, aligning himself with those who were afraid of the future. In the end Lukyanov became a sort of parody of Lucien Bonaparte, joining a coup d'état against a man who was like a brother to him.

Despite its unenviable image and its presiding officer, the Union Parliament did not deserve the shabby end it came to, that of self-dissolution. The Parliament was where the Soviet Union went to school to learn the basics of parliamentary government, and although it is now fashionable to claim otherwise, this two-headed donkey, always pulling in opposite directions, was in many ways more democratic than the famous czarist Duma.

I think future generations will realize that Gorbachev was right in imposing a number of quotas for party and social organizations on this first parliament. A normal ration of food can be fatal to someone who is dying of hunger. Future historians who analyze Gorbachev's strengths and weaknesses will undoubtedly see him as the true founder of the new Russian parliamentary system.

❀   ❀   ❀

After the putsch, the President found himself reduced to the status of hostage to the republics' barons. He was obliged to deliver speeches dictated by them and to give his blessing to actions that—as he saw quite clearly—were moving the country farther and farther away from the goal that he had considered within its grasp: a renewed union that would have preserved at least the outward appearance of a single state. Once again placing himself at the head of the inevitable, as de Gaulle put it, Gorbachev was forced to abandon the idea of actually governing this vast country of 280 million souls who identified power more with coercion than with the rule of law. Although his position was severely compromised, he still managed to preserve some of his authority. The fact that he was able to buy time in this way strengthened his hopes of halting the process of dismantlement of the Union. After the Congress of People's Deputies of the USSR adjourned on September 5, Gorbachev and the leaders of the republics managed to agree to resume negotiations on the Union Treaty. Boris Yeltsin consented to sign the new draft with Gorbachev.

Naturally, the outlines of the future union were even hazier now than they had been in the early stages of the Novo-Ogarevo process. But the most important thing, Gorbachev felt, was to stop the slide into chaos and to guide the political affairs of the country back into familiar territory where he could demonstrate his superiority: that of a gradual developmental process, taken in cautious steps and requiring daily compromises with reality and with individuals, combined with attention-getting appearances on the international scene. Within this context, he counted on being able to use his political gifts to gradually win back his former authority and channel the torrent of Soviet history back into the straight and narrow path of his reforms.

Gorbachev's greatest reproach against the perpetrators of the August putsch was not that they had dealt a death blow to the Union by legitimizing the ambitions of the republic leaders, or that they had humiliated him publicly by presenting him as a naive, myopic, credulous leader who had surrounded himself with sworn enemies. His main source of bitterness toward them was that they had cut his reforms off at the roots and pushed the unfortunate country into yet another revolution—a temporary and theatrical revolution, but a real one, bought with the lives of three young people. And its consequences had been the familiar repercussions of any revolution: an explosion of passions among the people, an orgy of extremism and revenge for social and personal grievances, intransigence toward the opposition, contempt for the law.

In their surge toward democracy, the people had wrested power away from the old *nomenklatura,* but they had replaced these officials with "second secretaries" who were even more ignorant and incompetent than their predecessors. Orwell was right when he wrote that a subordinate bureaucracy always tries to replace the higher bureaucracy and calls the achievement of its purpose a revolution.

Nowadays this resuscitated bureaucracy has changed its methods, but it is still defending its own interests. Corrupt, closely tied to the mafia that it created, it automatically sabotages even the most insignificant reforms instituted by the new government; its first line of defense is to block the establishment of independent enterprises and farms. The putschists and the republics' bureaucrats have all helped to demolish the Union in their own ways. But the bureaucrats have not brought the country a single step closer to democracy or to a civilized market economy.

The course of events that would lead to this situation began to take shape during the first few weeks after the coup. There were many signs indicating that Gorbachev was aware of what was impending. All the same, in September he felt that he had won the first round: The conservatives had been routed; the Party no longer hung on him like a dead weight; and the problem of clarifying relations with the increasingly visible republic leaders—especially the most combative of them, Boris Yeltsin—had apparently been put off successfully to the indefinite future. Besides, Yeltsin said that he was ready to cooperate actively with the "new" Gorbachev, proclaiming his high regard for Gorbachev's change of attitude since the putsch.

All signs pointed to a new window of opportunity opening before the President. Gorbachev knew that this chance was not likely to come again and that he would have to take advantage of it to present a fresh, untarnished image as a president who had no debts to the Party *nomenklatura* and the "socialist choice," one who could offer the country a program that would open up real prospects for the future. Essentially, he would have to create his electoral platform for the presidency of a renewed union.

❀   ❀   ❀

Since the worst was over—or so Gorbachev thought—it was time to repair the machinery of presidential power, which had been damaged when the President's chief adviser, Valery Boldin, had sided with the putschists in August.

Boldin's betrayal must have wounded Gorbachev even more deeply than Lukyanov's. Boldin was not only his closest adviser but also his personal confidant. They had worked together since 1981—a few years after Gorbachev had left the Stavropol area for Moscow, where he had been appointed to the Central Committee and the Politburo in November 1978. He had taken over the leadership of the agricultural sector of the Party, replacing Fyodor Kulakov, who had just died. Boldin followed Gorbachev throughout his rise to the highest echelons of power, assuming a position equivalent to that of a cabinet leader in the West. In March 1985, his boss's accession to the post of Party general secretary gave Boldin considerable influence over the affairs of the country. In particular, he controlled the circulation of all documents from the Central Committee's secretariat, and, later, from the office of the president. He also seemed to be obsessed with the power that he held. In March 1990, Gorbachev confirmed his confidence in Boldin by appointing him a member of the Presidential Council, which had just been created to assist the President in outlining policy. His position with Gorbachev was such that it fell to him to coordinate the new council's activities. Gorbachev, therefore, must have felt it as a real stab in the back when he saw Boldin with the delegation sent to Foros by the putschists on August 18, 1991, to obtain his resignation.

To replace Boldin as the head of the presidential advisory staff, Gorbachev called on one of his loyal followers, Grigory Revenko, whom he valued for his ease in dealing with people and his talent as an organizer. Revenko had been the Party secretary for the Kiev oblast at the time of the Chernobyl disaster and had been tremendously effective in his handling of the crisis. Like Boldin, Revenko had been appointed by Gorbachev to the Presidential Council, whose members were carefully selected to yield a balanced representation of the prevailing political trends.

Before the putsch, Revenko's organizational abilities had been a major factor in the success of the Novo-Ogarevo meetings. The choice of this man to head up the presidential apparat at a time when negotiations on a new Union Treaty were about to be reopened proved judicious. He had a difficult task ahead of him: to transform the former general department of the CPSU's Central Committee, inherited from Boldin, into an effective administrative body for presidential power—an institution that had never existed in Russia. In the end, he was unable to complete this task; but he probably did not have enough time.

Before turning back to politics, Gorbachev had to deal with some unresolved administrative problems: surrounding himself with an active, qualified team of advisers; obtaining decent offices inside and outside the Kremlin for the presidential departments; and, in conjunction with Yeltsin as the Russian president, making a final apportionment of the property that had belonged to the defeated Party and the former government—dachas, estates, clinics, garages, automobiles, and services of various kinds.

Revenko gave the go-ahead, and the administrators and officials of the office of the president, who had been chafing under their forced inaction, set to work preparing and outfitting the offices in the Kremlin. Even the President's security service, which was no longer an arm of the KGB but was placed under direct presidential authority, asked that the cumbersome, outmoded ZIL limousines be replaced with modern, more reliable Mercedes.

The political atmosphere became more relaxed. People were getting used to the sight of a second, Russian flag on the roofs of the Kremlin. The "cohabitation of two bears in the same den," as Gorbachev himself jokingly put it, looked as if it might last. Besides, Yeltsin, who had withdrawn to a sanatorium in Sochi, on the Black Sea, was mysteriously silent. Despite a few leaks from his press service hinting that he was writing another book, it was clear to everyone that he was recuperating in his usual way from the emotional stress of the events of August. This was confirmed by members of his own entourage who tried unsuccessfully to get through to see him. At the moment he did not appear to be a direct threat to Gorbachev.

This was confirmed by Western journalists who followed Yeltsin when he left the sanatorium for a few days on a trip to Azerbaidzhan and Armenia in the company of Kazakhstan's leader Nursultan Nazarbaev, in yet another attempt to extinguish the conflict in Nagorno-Karabakh and push the warring factions into concluding an "eternal" peace. On September 23 the umpteenth cease-fire was negotiated in Zheleznovodsk, in the northern foothills of the Caucasus, and returning journalists, lost in admiration, quoted Yeltsin's pronouncement that "great decisions are the prerogative of great politicians."

Be that as it may, the corrections to the new draft of the Union Treaty that Yeltsin made during his stay on the shores of the Black Sea were acceptable and relatively conciliatory in nature. It seemed fairly unlikely at that time that he would seek another confrontation.

Gorbachev knew that he should use this breathing space to good advantage. Acting as "the boss" but without circumventing Yeltsin, who would have to endorse the principal appointments, he completed his nominations to the key posts left vacant by the arrest of the plotters and the dismissal of their sympathizers. He appointed his adviser, Yevgeny Primakov, head of foreign intelligence (the First Chief Directorate of the KGB). This choice fell in line with the dismantling of the enormous structure of the KGB undertaken by Vadim Bakatin, whom Gorbachev had made chairman of the organization as a replacement for Vladimir Kryuchkov, one of the masterminds of the failed coup. The President also used the "valor" shown by Boris Pankin, then ambassador to Prague, as a pretext to appoint him minister of foreign affairs.[3] However, he did not oppose Yeltsin's nominations of Viktor Barannikov for the interior and Yevgeny Shaposhnikov for defense. These choices suited him completely at the time.

Gorbachev also had to form new ties with the free press and the creative intelligentsia and, through them, with the democratic forces in society that had triumphed over the plotters of the coup—a power base from which he had been cut off since the events at Vilnius. His emotional reconciliation with Alexander Yakovlev and Eduard Shevardnadze was intended to further this end. These two men, who were among his staunchest allies, had been alienated in recent months by Gorbachev's rapprochement with the conservatives. In December 1990, Shevardnadze had announced his resignation from his post as minister of foreign affairs in protest against this new political course and what he felt was a looming threat of dictatorship. Yakovlev had remained with the President until the end of July 1991, when the Party's Central Control Commission instituted exclusion proceedings against him. Wounded by Gorbachev's failure to stand behind him in this crisis, he resigned from his post as senior adviser. Gorbachev may have regretted the undeserved injury he caused Yakovlev by failing to support him. In any case, one of the results of the putsch and Gorbachev's unimpeachable conduct in Foros was to bring these three men back together.

Gorbachev's appointments of people close to Yakovlev to key positions of leadership in the mass media were similarly designed to boost his standing in public opinion. Yegor Yakovlev, the rebellious editor of *Moscow News*, who spearheaded the illegal publishing activities of the democratic press during the August putsch, was put in charge of state television; and Gorbachev's former aide Vitaly Ignatenko was named director-general of TASS. (It was around this time that Gorbachev offered me the position of aide and press secretary.)

Gorbachev made yet another symbolic concession to the democrats who had previously distanced themselves from him. He set up a political advisory council and populated it with the "big names" of the first phase of perestroika: Anatoly Sobchak, Gavriil Popov, Yury Ryzhov (later the Russian ambassador to Paris), Yevgeny Velikhov, Nikolai Petrakov, Grigory Yavlinsky, and Yegor Yakovlev. This move was intended to cement the reconciliation of the liberal intelligentsia with Gorbachev, a prodigal son who had returned to the fold.

In short, by the end of September, one month after the coup, the tattered front line had been restored and the President's main chess pieces were in place. It was time to begin the game. Gorbachev called a series of meetings with his aides to work out his strategy.

❀ ❀ ❀

It was at this time that Gorbachev's attention was drawn to Ukraine, although the situation in the second most populous republic of the Union did not seem to warrant serious concern. During the March referendum[4] the Ukrainians had voted overwhelmingly in favor of preserving a unified state, which Gorbachev naturally found reassuring. He believed that he had a more realistic understanding of the situation in this republic, which was as familiar to him as Russia itself, than did Ukraine's own leader, Leonid Kravchuk, who continuously vacillated between protestations of loyalty to Moscow and concessions to the Rukh nationalists.[5] In his efforts to convince everyone else that Ukraine was viable within its present boundaries only as part of a unified state, Gorbachev—as often happened—wound up persuading himself as well. He was convinced that neither the Crimea nor "the miners from Donetsk who recently came to see me" would allow the "Ukie separatists" to gain the upper hand.[6]

However, Kravchuk's ambiguous behavior and the doublespeak of his prime minister, Vitold Fokin, "who says one thing in Moscow, another to the journalists on the plane, and a third when he gets to Kiev," had begun to arouse Gorbachev's suspicions. True, these maneuvers of Kravchuk's could be interpreted as political tactics. Only recently, this zealous party ideologue had been castigating the nationalists; now, with the first open Ukrainian presidential election close at hand, he was suddenly a champion of independence. This transformation was generally perceived as a temporary strategy designed to enable Kravchuk to beat his principal rival, Viacheslav Chornovil, Rukh's main leader in L'vov, at his own game. Everybody was convinced that once the election was in the bag, Kravchuk would "return to ranks" and calm the separatist fervor of his republic.

The Ukrainian president carefully nurtured this impression, which protected him against any criticism from Moscow and reassured Ukraine's sizable Russian community. To them, he was the only candidate who would be able to contain the nationalists and preserve the natural union of their country with Russia.

Kravchuk explained his gradual adoption of Rukh's positions as the result of resolutions passed by the Ukrainian parliament, which he was "forced to submit to," although it was obvious that in most cases he had instigated them himself. This was true in particular of Kiev's "parliamentary" resolution "forbidding" the Ukrainian delegation to the Supreme Soviet to participate in any negotiations on the new Union Treaty before the referendum on Ukrainian independence that was to be held in December. A few days later, this prohibition was extended to all the activities of the new Union Parliament. The first session of the new Supreme Soviet was postponed for several days for this reason, in the hope that Kiev "would change its mind." In the face of this Ukrainian obstinacy, Parliament's work on the treaty turned into a legal battle that would drag on into December.

During a meeting with his aides, Gorbachev discussed his thoughts on the proposed union and exclaimed with unexpected intensity, "If we fail to preserve the unitary state, we're going to have another Yugoslavia on our hands. I bet my life on it."

When the question of Yeltsin's position came up, Gorbachev insisted, as if trying to convince himself, "We have no differences in regard to the union, Boris Nikolaevich and I. The republics have received our joint draft of the treaty. We've talked it over. He sent me some corrections that were generally acceptable, the most important one being that he does not want a constitution of union. He has also expressed misgivings about the election of the president by popular vote. But that doesn't matter, we have to keep on working."

This last-cited point bothered Gorbachev, and he couldn't mention it without reacting. "I believe that we need a president, and one who is elected by popular vote. There must be a mandate from the people. Otherwise, in the decentralized situation that we have now, it will be impossible to pull the country together. The presidential election must be organized as quickly as possible in order to halt disintegration. Yeltsin advises waiting until the end of 1992, but I think it should be held right away: as soon as the treaty has been signed, on with the election!"

He tried to make these remarks sound spontaneous, but they were obviously worked out in advance. It was also apparent that in addition to his understandable concern for the fate of the union, he felt—belatedly—an urgent need to equalize his status vis-à-vis the leaders of the republics, among whom he alone lacked a popular mandate.

The main effect of this courageous statement was to alarm his staff. His popularity had plummeted, and it didn't appear that he would be able to make up the deficit fast enough to have a chance of winning if the election were held soon. His aides, myself included, tried to convince him not to hurry. Our basic argument was that the leaders of the republics had to be given enough time to take concrete action; otherwise they would keep laying the responsibility for problems at the President's door, claiming that their efforts were being interfered with. At that time, they were still presenting themselves as heroes suffering under the whims of the central power. But as soon as they were confronted with real problems, the people would find out what they were made of.

Gorbachev reacted cautiously. Yeltsin needed support in order to speed up reform. At the rate things were going, the government would be forced to resign, and that would pave the way for a dictatorship. "Enough marching in place!" he exclaimed. "We should move forward immediately."

Such resolute words gave him the sense of having performed resolute acts. However, it was clear that he had allowed himself to be talked into postponing the presidential election. After that, he let the matter drop—although his subsequent moves were obviously aimed at broadening his base of popular support in the aftermath of the August putsch.

❀　　　❀　　　❀

On September 26, the President met at the Kremlin with the approximately thirty members of the future Enterprise Council, which he had decided to set up under his direct supervision. These were stockbrokers, newly minted business-men, and owners of private companies—in other words, individuals who would have been considered dangerous criminals and enemies of the people a few years before. As Arkady Volsky led these "fish out of water" inside the Kremlin walls, he told Gorbachev that they represented at least four-fifths of the new Soviet entre-preneurs and that he considered them worthy guests.

Gorbachev trusted Volsky, who was one of his closest advisers.[7] In 1989 he had chosen him to head the special administrative body he had established in Nagorno-Karabakh after the first violent confrontations there between Arme-nians and Azeris. Volsky had succeeded in restoring relative calm to the region, and at the time it had appeared that the conflict would be resolved very soon.

This man, who identified with the private entrepreneurs, was nevertheless a product of the Party and the state-owned industrial sector. During the first half of the 1980s, he had been an aide to Yury Andropov when the latter was general sec-retary of the CPSU. Volsky later was named head of the industrial department of the Central Committee. His experience was in "production," since he had man-aged a big factory in Moscow, and he had more influence than a mere appa-ratchik. Since the beginning of perestroika, he had solidly backed reforms while making every effort to remain outside the corridors of power. Most notably, he had refused to join the governments of Nikolai Ryzhkov and Ivan Silaev, or to go back to heading the industrial department of the Central Committee after the Twenty-Eighth Party Congress in 1990. That same year he founded the Scientific and Industrial Union, an association intended to gather together the country's major industrialists and to serve as a rough model for an employers' organization. (It would later become the Union of Industrialists and Entrepreneurs.) Due to his contacts with the economic sector and with leaders of the military-industrial complex, he was, and still is, one of the best-informed men in the world concern-ing the economic realities of the former Soviet Union. After the demise of the USSR he emerged as one of the most important figures in Russia, although he still preferred to remain in the background.[8] In any event, after the putsch Volsky was the man best situated to draw the country's economic decisionmakers—private entrepreneurs as well as government leaders—into Gorbachev's camp.

One of the first questions Gorbachev asked the businessmen present at the September 26 meeting in the Kremlin was—jokingly—whether they "were com-plying with the penal code." By way of reply, they proposed to him that the status of the entrepreneurs should be legalized as soon as possible and their rights de-fined. They also demanded the repeal of some of Gorbachev's own ukases re-stricting freedom of enterprise, which had been issued the winter before at the in-stigation of Valentin Pavlov, his former prime minister. In particular, they demanded that he renounce state requisitioning of hard-currency earnings and the "shameful" measures empowering the KGB to inspect their books and to determine their income and cash on hand. The President willingly promised to meet their demands but did not express any regrets about his part in the decisions made during the period before the coup.

The businessmen plucked up their courage and spoke to Gorbachev about their political interests. "We were afraid on August 19, and we don't want that to happen again," one of them explained. "If you want a stable society and stable presidential power, support and defend the property owners. Respect us the way the authorities respected the Russian merchants in the old days, and you'll see what we can do for this country." Replying to these remarks, Gorbachev said that he had intended this meeting to send a signal to Russian society as a whole. He promised to place "support for entrepreneurs" on the agenda of one of the upcoming meetings of the State Council and concluded by outlining the prospects for reconstituting a new unified state.

That same day, Gorbachev was informed that the representatives of all the republics except Ukraine had approved the text of the treaty on the economic community,[9] developed by a group chaired by economist Grigory Yavlinsky. The leaders of the republics were to meet at Alma-Ata on October 1 to sign the agreement. According to the President, eight republics had already come out in favor of adopting the new Union Treaty on the basis of the text drafted in cooperation with Boris Yeltsin. This good news strengthened Gorbachev's resolve. "We will begin the signing proceedings," he decided, "with any minimal number of republics, even if it's just two."

It seemed to him at that point that bright and reassuring vistas were opening up before him and the country. This was one month after the August coup d'état . . . and three months before the official liquidation of the USSR.

Reinforcements from
the Second Front

The drooping presidential flag also had to be freshly unfurled on the international scene—which was, moreover, where Gorbachev had had his greatest successes. Ironically, his policies, even in domestic affairs, were better understood and appreciated abroad than they were at home. Thus the support that he felt he needed in order to solidify his position had to come from the outside world, as it had the previous year, when he had been awarded the Nobel Peace Prize. Besides, there was no better way for Gorbachev to regain the sense of being the undisputed president that he was before the coup than by immersing himself in international affairs, receiving foreign dignitaries, and making trips abroad.

During this period in late September and early October, with Yeltsin away from Moscow, there were none of the ambiguities of politics and protocol that arose when foreign visitors got their schedules muddled and met with the two presidents one right after the other. On these occasions the protocol service would have barely enough time to clear the Catherine Room in the Kremlin, the only setting grand enough for diplomatic talks.

After the Cable News Network (CNN) broadcast a joint interview with Gorbachev and Yeltsin on September 6, the blunt, pragmatic American journalists kept asking the two of them to make television appearances together. The Western media even seriously discussed the possibility of the two presidents making joint trips abroad, either to participate in a NATO meeting together or to speak at the U.N. Gorbachev had to put up with this absurd situation, of course; but he had no intention of giving up his legitimately acquired position as a world leader or of sharing it with Yeltsin, who was energetic but, Gorbachev felt, ill-suited for the role.

There was another, purely personal reason behind Gorbachev's fondness for meetings with foreign guests, whether politicians or journalists. His training and abilities lay essentially in the area of oral communication, and he felt that he thought more deeply, reacted more forcefully, and formulated his ideas more precisely in a conversational setting, where he often hit upon the most convincing arguments, the perfect phrase, the most striking metaphors. This type of personal contact, which was gradually supplanting discussions with his opponents and

13

even his supporters, gave him occasion to contemplate the changing situation and to advance in his comprehension of it.

❀   ❀   ❀

Gorbachev's foreign colleagues, reassured to find that he not only had survived the putsch but had once again turned a difficult situation to his own personal advantage, joined forces with belated enthusiasm to open a "second front" in his support. The avowals of solidarity and expressions of personal friendship that reached him from many Western leaders were especially cordial because they were intended to compensate for the confusion and political conformism shown by these leaders during the first few hours—or even days—of the putsch.

The slow and sometimes ambiguous reactions of the major governments to the news coming out of Moscow on the morning of August 19 was, of course, due as much to the traditional principles of realpolitik as to any residual mistrust. No one could quite believe that Soviet society and the Soviet state had been radically transformed, even after five years of Gorbachevian reform.

There had been many signs of an impending revolt on the part of the Party and military bureaucracy; a number of Western leaders felt that this would be a much more organic and natural phenomenon than Gorbachev's optimistic promises of a smooth continuation of reform. That is why many Western leaders who considered themselves to be not only admirers but sincere friends of Gorbachev were, on some basic or even unconscious level, ready to accept the inevitability of a return to communism. The putsch, they felt, only confirmed their predictions. Their initial reaction was just what the plotters had counted on, and this reaction would not have changed if events in Moscow had not taken such a surprising turn.

The qualitative changes in Soviet society had withstood trial by fire in the streets of Moscow. Gorbachev, managing to remount the tiger, strengthened his image as a skilled tactician and as the prime mover of the irreversible transformation of his country. From that time on, the Westerners felt that Gorbachev deserved their strongest assurances of loyalty and support.

During one of his visits to Moscow, Secretary of State James Baker apologetically said to Gorbachev, "Only now, after the coup, do we really understand the difficulties and dangers that you were faced with every day, and the reasons for your tactics, which alarmed and disconcerted the West but were justified in order to neutralize the conservative forces in your country."

Gorbachev was gratified to receive these expressions of regret from the same Western leaders who, at the G-7 summit in London that July, had listened skeptically as he cited the danger posed by the conservatives. They had assumed that he was trying to pressure them into increasing their financial aid to Moscow. Gorbachev also saw nothing unusual in the fact that he was now getting good press, whereas three months earlier reporters had characterized his Nobel acceptance speech as "blackmail against the West."

On September 10, on the opening of the CSCE meeting in Moscow, he spoke as one of the leaders of the new "free world" that had emerged in Eastern Europe largely as a result of his efforts. Ministers of foreign affairs and ambassadors succeeded each other in the presidential reception hall. The former poise and ritual of top-level meetings were gradually restored. Yeltsin's vacation on the Black Sea, far from Moscow, helped to convince Gorbachev and, especially, these foreign dignitaries that the new leadership structure did not necessarily include the Russian president, as it had during the first few days and weeks after the failure of the coup d'état. At the end of September, the Italian prime minister, Giulio Andreotti, was received in Moscow. A visit by Egyptian president Hosni Mubarak was also anticipated.

During this period, however, it was "dear George," President Bush, who gave Gorbachev a political gift of real weight. On the morning of September 27, Washington's Moscow representative relayed some highly important information from Bush to Gorbachev through his assistant, Anatoly Chernyaev: the main points of a policy statement on nuclear disarmament that Bush was to make public that same evening. Before doing so, he intended to speak with Gorbachev by phone.

Bush was also preparing to call Yeltsin at his resort on the Black Sea. It was clear, however, that his initiative was addressed to Gorbachev and that he was waiting for a reply to his proposals from him, as president of the Union and commander in chief of the armed forces, rather than from Yeltsin.

The American initiative was unusual in that it included both unilateral decisions (the repatriation and destruction of tactical nuclear weapons based in Europe, the removal of those located on American naval vessels, a halt to the installation of Tomahawk cruise missiles on U.S. ships and submarines) and proposals for negotiations on the elimination of multiple-warhead intercontinental ballistic missiles, which the Americans considered especially dangerous and destabilizing because they could incite the enemy to a first strike.

An emergency meeting of Gorbachev's most important political and military advisers was held to help him prepare his response, and by the time Bush's call came through he was girded for battle. This conversation between "Michael" and "George" not only marked the end of the uncertain, ambiguous period in the relations between the two presidents that had begun in August; it also got the two-seated coach of Soviet-American strategic cooperation back on track.

Gorbachev supported Bush's initiative by temporarily refraining from making a detailed assessment of the various points it contained. The Soviet response, he promised, would be no less impressive—especially in its boldness and scope—than the unilateral proposals and decisions formulated by the Americans.

This conversation was taken as confirmation that the last leak in the presidential vessel had been stopped. The ship was no longer sinking and could venture into international waters again.

❁   ❁   ❁

That same day, Gorbachev received Egyptian president Hosni Mubarak at the Kremlin. Their discussion began, naturally enough, with the putsch and the reasons for its failure. According to Mubarak, this coup d'état had been patterned after the 1964 plot against Nikita Khrushchev, which had succeeded because of the lack of democracy in the USSR at the time. The instigators of the August putsch had not counted on the power of the democratic changes Gorbachev had instituted.

Gorbachev agreed with the gist of Mubarak's analysis and then commented, "Some people wonder why Gorbachev did not avert the coup d'état. Is it really possible that he didn't see it coming? Actually, it was easy to foresee such a turn of events, provided that one had a full appreciation of the scale of the transformations I envisioned. The goal of the process instituted in 1985 was to make a decisive change in the entire political structure, and thus in the country's system of rule. Power had to be taken away from the Party, which ruled as a monopoly without a mandate from the people. And how could the economy be liberated from the yoke of militarization without any impact on the armed forces, that is, without changing the situation of millions of people, including the vast corps of officers? The Party, the armed forces, the military sector of the economy for which 70 percent of the scientific establishment works—all this represents enormous investments and masses of people benefiting from better working and living conditions.

"In this situation, my job was to make changes gradually, by democratic methods, until we reached a level where any attempt at a reactionary coup d'état would be doomed to failure. If the putsch had taken place only one year ago, it might have succeeded.

"Unfortunately, this does not mean that the forces of democracy have solved all their problems by crushing the factionalists: They're starting to argue again and are all competing with each other to see who can sound the most 'democratic,' instead of uniting in a real cause.

"My other concern," Gorbachev continued, "is the behavior of the republics. The putschists played a crucial role in creating the present situation. After the coup d'état, there was a flurry of declarations of independence. The republics that want to break away, especially Ukraine, don't understand how dangerous this would be for them. They think the West is going to shower them with dollars. The leaders of the republics are enjoying their roles as heads of state, but the people sense the danger and are becoming increasingly concerned. While the supreme soviets of the republics argue, the masses lean more and more toward the preservation of the union. Ordinary people know, better than their leaders, that the present war between Croatia and Serbia is nothing compared to a potential conflict between Russia and Ukraine."

Mubarak observed that he had spoken with Yeltsin on the phone and had emphasized the importance of uniting with Gorbachev. He said that Yeltsin had brought up the subject himself by observing that he was working closely with the president of the USSR. "That's true," Gorbachev confirmed. "We cooperate to a high degree, although many people would like to sour our relations. But I feel that consolidating this relationship is a sine qua non for preserving the Union as a major power."

Gorbachev and Mubarak also addressed the economy and the most effective means of revitalizing Soviet agriculture. Referring to the Egyptian experience, Mubarak said that he was in favor of small landowners: "They will preserve and stabilize the country." Gorbachev was in complete agreement: "That's right, because if there is any turmoil they'll have something to lose." Mubarak told him that Khrushchev had once said to Nasser, "I advise against your following our path of collectivization."

Gorbachev replied emphatically, "It's good that that anecdote was not publicized at the time, because Khrushchev would have been thrown out of the Party for propagandizing in favor of private property." Returning to the present, he added, "My goal is to see an upswing in productivity. Then the people will follow the reformers and there will be no more room for the conservatives."

The conversation turned to the Middle East, where, after a long period of maneuvering by the parties in conflict, there finally seemed to be some likelihood of a peace conference. Gorbachev advised Mubarak not to stress the demand for creating an independent Palestinian state before the start of these negotiations. That would not be realistic. "We know that." Mubarak, a graduate of the Moscow Military Academy, gave this answer in Russian.

With regard to Saddam Hussein, Gorbachev expressed his concern about the Iraqi refusal to permit international inspection of certain military installations. He worried that the situation might escalate again to the point where the United States would think about renewing military action. "Speaking of which," Gorbachev added, "it's worth noting that only Saddam Hussein and Muammar Qadhafi supported the putschists." Mubarak concluded the conversation with these remarks: "We admire your victory. The new freedom has saved the Soviet Union."

Three days later, Austrian chancellor Franz Vranitzky arrived in the USSR to watch Austrian cosmonaut Franz Viehböck enter orbit on board the *Soyuz* spacecraft. Viehböck would also spend some time on the *Mir* orbiting space station. His meeting with Gorbachev gave the latter the opportunity to state his position on an important matter in European and world politics, Yugoslavia.

Gorbachev had two good reasons to be concerned about this problem. First, he felt that the USSR, as a major power, should take part in the international community's efforts to resolve the Yugoslavian conflict. The resources deployed by the European Community, especially Germany, and the U.S. attempts to join the process made the Soviet Union's inaction all the more flagrant. There was no doubt that its status as a world power was being diminished as a result.

The second reason was probably the more important one. Gorbachev wanted to take advantage of his statement on the Yugoslav crisis to strengthen his arguments for preserving a unified state at home. He felt that the appalling specter of a Yugoslavia times twelve or fifteen in the USSR would be certain to cool the zeal of the most impassioned separatists in the republics, diminish their bases of support, and remind local politicians of their responsibility toward their own people.

Gorbachev's statement was also meant to send a signal to other countries: By calling on other nations not to meddle in Yugoslavia's domestic affairs and not to encourage its dissolution, he was issuing a warning to any Westerners who might be tempted to stick their collective noses into the increasingly serious problems of the Union. This warning was aimed primarily at Germany, of course, because of its open support of Croat and Slovenian separatists. It would be hard to find a more convenient channel for this message than the Austrian chancellor.

In his conversation with Vranitzky, Gorbachev stated that he was solidly in favor of complying with the principles of the Helsinki accord and the Paris charter. He emphasized that "none of the parties involved in the confrontation within Yugoslavia should be able to count on outside support."

A few days later, Gorbachev called on the Yugoslavian political and military leadership to stop the bloody fighting and launched a personal initiative to defuse the conflict by inviting the Serb and Croat leaders to come to Moscow. However, this attempt to put out the fire next door so that it wouldn't spread to his own house failed to yield any practical results. The nightmare of Yugoslavia tormented him for the next two months, until it was thrust into the background by the crumbling of his own union.

❀   ❀   ❀

Gorbachev was haunted by the memory of the putsch. He came back to the subject time and again, especially because every visit by a foreign delegation gave him a logical opportunity to do so.

On October 1, Henning Christophersen, the vice president of the European Commission, was received by Gorbachev in Moscow. Once again, Gorbachev's first words related to the coup d'état: "A revolution took place in this country, with all the characteristics of a revolution, including the assumption of power by force. The reactionaries kept the idea of a putsch as a backup weapon for a while, but it finally did get used," he joked. "And now the West insists on waiting for the dust to settle before it will make any decisions about economic aid. God help us to preserve the political framework within which new economic structures can form—by this I mean the new unified state."

Gorbachev had been wrestling with the question of a link between an economic community and a political union for several days. Just after the coup he had been prepared to take a more gradual approach: first, the economic community, which would be politically neutral and profitable to everybody and might halt the process of disintegration of the state; and then, later on, the political treaty. Naturally, the two processes would have to be connected. Instructions to forge this link had been given to Grigory Yavlinsky, who was methodically trying to shape the economic community by getting his counterparts in the republics to face the reality of their own situations. Suddenly, with this accord in sight, the President abruptly changed course: "We must go straight to a political union. Without it we're at an impasse, including with regard to the economy."

It's hard to say what influenced him to change his approach. It may have been Nazarbaev's invitation to the leaders of the republic governments to meet in Alma-Ata, without the "center," to sign the economic treaty. The specter of an economic community without the President was beginning to loom on the horizon. Or he may have been responding to a signal from the opposite direction, in the form of Yeltsin's reassuring eagerness to support the idea of political union.

Both factors may have contributed. There may also have been a third that was even more important: the instinct of an experienced politician who understood that time was dulling his main weapon—the political initiative—a weapon that had always saved him before, even in apparently desperate straits.

By hurling himself into the battle for political union and the restoration of the crumbling state, Gorbachev felt that he was reinstating reform as a guided, controlled process. In addition, by invoking the results of the March referendum in support of his actions, he set himself up as the spokesman for the people's will while at the same time formulating a convincing election platform. This also made it possible for him to respond to Western diplomats worried about the threat of a new Yugoslavia and to wrest the popular idea of "saving the fatherland and the state" away from the discredited conservatives by giving it a modern, democratic slant. These actions were bound to exacerbate the rivalry between him and those on the next level down in the hierarchy, the leaders of the republics, who had tasted emancipation from the center and had no intention of giving it up. For these leaders, there was no going back to the preputsch days of Novo-Ogarevo, when they had entered into an alliance with the USSR's president against conservatives who favored the preservation of empire and who threatened the absolute power of the leaders of the republics. They had no further use for the Union now that the enemy who had so terrified many of them during the putsch was gone. Nor had they any use for their ally, the Union's president. He could either accept the conditions they imposed and agree to play the role of figurehead in the fictitious union or he could resign.

Thus, in challenging the bureaucrats of the republics by making a decisive choice in favor of preserving a unified state, the President signed his own political death warrant as well as that of the Union. A second putsch was now inevitable.

In early October, however, the outcome of this conflict was not clear to anyone, any more than were the balance of forces and the tactics that might be used. To preserve a unified state, Gorbachev was counting on popular opinion within the country and on political support from without. He believed that, faced with the looming threat of the disintegration of the USSR and the instability that would follow, the West would have to come to his assistance by making it a prerequisite for economic aid that the country maintain some kind of central political structure able to answer for the behavior of this dying monster.

During his visit to Moscow, Christophersen told Gorbachev what he was hoping to hear: "The West would like to see the advent in the USSR of a real political structure that would define the framework for economic reform. We feel that a union could provide such a framework." He went on to say that the G-7 and the European Community had studied the drastic situation and were ready to grant aid, with certain provisos regarding the principal ways in which it was to be used.

According to British prime minister John Major, then serving as coordinator of the G-7, and Jacques Delors, president of the European Commission, the aid was not to be purely humanitarian but would have to contribute to real economic progress. Christophersen asserted that this was the only way this unprecedented program could be "sold" to governments, legislators, and the public in the West.

The objectives of the program would be:

- Food aid to the major cities, some industrial areas, and, generally, the neediest strata of the population.
- Cancellation or postponement of current payments on the Soviet foreign debt.
- Financing designed to reestablish the economic ties, so casually broken, between the Soviet Union and its former fellow members of Comecon.[10]

This last step had the effect of channeling Western aid to the USSR through Eastern Europe. That way the European Community could kill two birds with one stone: The former satellite countries had been trying unsuccessfully to direct their flow of industrial and food products into Western markets; now this flow would be reversed and sent back to the USSR.

Some of the aid granted—more than one billion ecu—was to be allocated to 350 projects aimed at the modernization of Soviet agriculture.

Gorbachev nodded in agreement when the specific figures were read, but most of his attention was focused on another problem: how to use economic cooperation with the West to strengthen the trend toward integration that he felt was beginning to reemerge in Soviet society. To all appearances, the pragmatists of the European Community seemed disposed to help him. "We want to deal with you and with the structures that you direct, as well as with the republics, of course," Delors's representative assured him. "The G-7 and the Community consider the economic treaty and the plans for stabilizing the entire Union and the major republics indispensable to the implementation of the aid program." The West was obviously prepared to throw Gorbachev an economic lifeline by choosing to deal with him preferentially and having him ensure the proper distribution of the aid among the republics and regions of the USSR.

With the Soviet economic situation rapidly worsening and chaos looming just ahead, the G-7 and Gorbachev himself were trying to make up for the time lost during the summer, when both sides were still loathe to believe that a catastrophe was imminent. The President had arrived at the London summit on July 17, without Grigory Yavlinsky. As in the case of the 500-Day Plan,[11] he had tried to transform the new program that Yavlinsky had drafted in coordination with the West into a nonviable hybrid designed primarily to appease his prime minister, Valentin Pavlov.

By dodging the issue in this way, Gorbachev gave the leaders of the major industrial nations the impression that he was avoiding a hard and fast choice between a state-controlled and a free market economy. His declarations of good intentions drew only polite attention. His explicit and implicit allusions to the fact that Soviet society was not mature enough for this kind of choice and that it could neither embark on such a path nor continue on it for long had ceased to convince anyone but himself. Worse, they led to a decline in trust on the part of the West and simultaneously sent another message to Pavlov, who one month later would be one of the main plotters of the putsch.

Since his appointment in January, Pavlov had concealed behind his circumspect politics a determination to return to more traditional ways of running the country. He seemed to view Western aid as a kind of Trojan horse and had gained notoriety for denouncing a "plot by the Western banks against the USSR." When Gorbachev, realizing the mistake he had made the winter before, began to distance himself from the conservatives in order to initiate the Novo-Ogarevo process, Pavlov became more aggressive in his dealings with the President, even going so far as to demand, in June, that the Supreme Soviet grant his government extraordinary powers. Gorbachev managed to block this maneuver in Parliament, but he found himself forced to adopt a compromise position at the expense of Yavlinsky's plan.

The attempted coup d'état proved to the West that the threat posed by the right-wingers, which Gorbachev was trying to blunt with his compromises, was very real. Gorbachev, for his part, realized that his policy of mollifying the opposition in his inner circle was all the more obsolete because there was nobody left to mollify after the putsch. After this flash of mutual insight, Gorbachev and the Western leaders hastened toward each other. Unfortunately, their meeting of minds came too late to make a difference.

So it was that at the beginning of October, Gorbachev tried to persuade the vice president of the European Community that the republics would not achieve the necessary level of integration without the Union. "In order to succeed in introducing a free market economy," he explained, "we have to preserve a single market within the Union. The economic populism that some republic leaders are espousing in addition to political populism is harmful and shortsighted. It will lead directly to more barriers, customs duties, borders—and all that only makes the situation worse."

Gorbachev and Christophersen quickly reached the conclusion that without true coordination within the Union, none of the G-7 nations would agree to grant any aid whatsoever. They parted completely satisfied with their conversation, especially since, as "dessert," Gorbachev announced to Delors's envoy that "after final calculations," his government was ready to reduce the amount of aid requested of the West from $14 billion to $10.2 billion. He added that this would be adequate to keep the population's food supply "at the 1991 level."

Christophersen, thinking he had heard wrong, asked Gorbachev to repeat the figure. He then left quickly, before his host could change his mind. This decrease in the requested amount of aid restored mutual understanding between the G-7 and Moscow on economic matters and ensured international support for Gorbachev's plan for gradual reform of the USSR within the framework of a renewed union.

At that point Gorbachev undoubtedly believed that he could ignore the opinions of his adversaries in domestic political battles, the leaders of the major republics. But this was only an illusion.

Michel Camdessus, the director of the International Monetary Fund, arrived at the Kremlin on October 5 for the signing of the protocols of cooperation between his organization and the Soviet leadership in accordance with the fund's bylaws. The signing and the exchange of documents were intended to open the IMF's door to the USSR and give the country access to IMF loans. Since the USSR did not meet the strict conditions for membership in the fund, an exception was made and the intermediate status of "associate member" was created for it. (Note that this reservation was later lifted, without much hesitation, for the governments of Boris Yeltsin and the other former Soviet republics, even though the new states that they represented were no closer to meeting the IMF's formal criteria than their common predecessor had been. Faced with the rapid dissolution of economic and social ties, which threatened to plunge everyone into abject misery, the Western leaders no doubt decided to be good Christians and avoid being accused of a lack of charity.)

In his conversation with Camdessus, Gorbachev, by force of long habit, developed his line of thinking as he spoke: "It is in our interest that the reforms advance to a new level. To bring about radical changes, we will need the cooperation of the developed countries of the West. Only by working with you will we be able to achieve a real transformation."

Grigory Yavlinsky, who was present at this meeting, could not help but notice that his many earlier discussions with Gorbachev had metamorphosed into the President's arguments, and perhaps also into his convictions. For this young economist (he was not yet forty), the disappointments of the past seemed to be forgotten. In 1990, he and academician Stanislav Shatalin had developed the 500-Day Plan for economic reform. This plan was initially the result of a compromise between Gorbachev's and Yeltsin's economic experts. Yavlinsky was one of Yeltsin's aides at the time and was working for the government of Russia. Shatalin was an adviser to Gorbachev (he, too, was a member of the Presidential Council). Contrary to all expectations, Gorbachev tried to create an impossible synthesis between the grand ideas of those who favored rapid economic reform and the timid ideas of his prime minister, Nikolai Ryzhkov, who did not want to get ahead of schedule. Gorbachev's vacillating prompted Shatalin to distance himself from the President. Yavlinsky, by contrast, moved away from Yeltsin's inner circle and toward Gorbachev when he realized that it was impossible for him to work within the Russian government.

A year later, the situation was repeating itself: The economic plan that Yavlinsky, working with American experts, had developed for presentation at the G-7 summit was undermined by Gorbachev in his hazy, unquantifiable statement of intent, which, as noted earlier, left the Western leaders completely unmoved. Still, before he left for London Gorbachev had asked Yavlinsky to accompany him as a personal favor. "Do it for me!" he entreated. "The only thing I can do for you," Yavlinsky replied, "is not go."

After the putsch, Yavlinsky was finally free and was able to throw himself into the thankless task of negotiating a treaty of economic community on behalf of the President, who had decided to move ahead with it. On October 1, in Alma-Ata, he managed to "extract" from the representatives of the republics a cooperative agreement that was then confirmed by the State Council. This success restored Gorbachev's confidence, and in his meetings with Camdessus he was again able to show the conviction and persuasiveness that he had had before the August putsch. "As a matter of policy, we stand behind all of our international economic commitments. Instructions to this effect have already been sent to our ambassadors. I think that this will finally provide a clear answer to the question that the West is constantly asking itself and us: Whom do we deal with in the USSR? We have an interstate economic committee, headed by Ivan Silaev, with corresponding structures recognized by all the republics."

When Camdessus mentioned the continually contradictory positions taken by various representatives of the republics during their trips abroad, Gorbachev waved the argument aside. "I know that you in the West are astonished by the number of supplicants wandering the globe in the name of the USSR. This will pass. Our initiatives concerning the USSR's relations with the G-7 countries are coordinated with all the republics," he continued. "The economic cooperation agreement has been approved by twelve republics and has already been signed by the leaders of three of them. Today the text is being sent to Boris Yeltsin for Russia's final approval. I believe that by October 15 at the latest we will be able together to answer the principal question: How do we plan to build our future bridge, along the river or over it?"

To Gorbachev the answer was obvious, as was always the case in matters of common sense. A politician of his experience, however, should not have assumed that common sense was a universal attribute or, still less, have accepted what he wanted to believe without seeing any proof.

Yielding to the combined pressure of presidential faith and Cartesian logic, Camdessus responded with enthusiasm: "Our fund, which was created to aid countries undergoing transformative processes, has never had such a bold and impressive mission. It will take just a few years, not centuries, to solve your problems, after which your country will be in a position to become an economic superpower. For that you can count on aid from the rest of the world. All that the leaders of the major industrialized countries will need from us in order to decide whether to grant this aid is an analysis of the resources that you have available and confirmation that you are proceeding according to the guidelines. It seems to me that both can readily be provided."

Unfortunately, all Camdessus's vast experience as president of the International Monetary Fund, which had programs in place in 150 different countries, was not sufficient for him to foresee the turn of events that occurred two months later in this country to which he had promised such a brilliant future.

One explanation for this apparent paradox, aside from the interplay of political forces and ambitions that ultimately ran roughshod over political rationality, was that even though Gorbachev and Camdessus were using terms that sounded the same, they were not really speaking the same language. For instance, during the negotiations on the economic accords in Alma-Ata there was some discussion of creating a federal reserve system on the U.S. model. After the matter had been debated at length, a top official of one of the republics burst out, "Haven't we talked about the reserve system enough? Let's get to the main system, already!"

A similar disparity, this time in ethics rather than in understanding, emerged during negotiations between the new representatives of the sovereign states and their Western colleagues on the problem of the foreign debt of the former USSR. It took several days of meetings, plus a threat by the Westerners to break off all negotiations on the granting of aid, before the republic leaders finally agreed to examine the question of repaying previous loans from the West—not because one ordinarily pays one's debts but merely to obtain new credits.

Gorbachev was probably the only person still acting as a bridge across the chasm that separated (and continues to separate) the "lost world" of the USSR from the rest of civilization. He did not perform this task because of his office or out of a sense of obligation. Rather, he was inspired by an almost religious faith in the feasibility of finally joining these two separate worlds and a burning desire to bring this about. More than anyone else, he was conscious of the immense historical and psychological gap that this imaginary bridge would have to span. But even the immensity of this Herculean task did not destroy his optimism.

"Today we are on the eve of the most profound reforms in our history," Gorbachev said in concluding his conversation with Camdessus. "People must understand that we are a unique country with its own specific attributes: we all use the same notes, but everybody composes his own song. We are going to proceed with as much determination as our society can tolerate. We are not giving in to despair, and I recommend that you not despair either. Remember, just a year ago all somebody had to do was mention a market economy, without a word about private property, and right away he was a traitor in the eyes of many people. And today, millions of people in the USSR are already living according to the new laws of the marketplace. This means that a new social stratum is forming. The best objective indicator of this change in society has been its behavior during the coup. A year or two ago, the putschists would have been able to set up a veritable dictatorship."

"I certainly would not be here!" joked Camdessus.

"Nor I. I would definitely be somewhere else," replied Gorbachev. "My job was to bring this society to a point at which any attempt to restore the old government would be doomed to failure. We understand that the IMF has rigid rules and selection criteria, but we must not forget that reality is sometimes even more rigid."

"Each of the hundred and fifty countries we work with is different from the others," Camdessus countered. "Obviously, we are not proposing to straitjacket you with prefabricated solutions. However, don't forget that you do not have much time to work all your unique attributes into the program." He had no idea how close he was to the truth. Gorbachev immediately replied, "Time is what we have least of. If people do not see results very soon from the reforms that are being implemented, disenchantment will quickly follow. Of course, I am not trying to use the reality of the situation as an excuse for us to march in place again or to put off essential decisions. But we will have to maneuver, too. In any event, we do not intend to remain suspended between two systems, and we realize that if you leave one, you have to move on to the other."

Gorbachev and Camdessus exchanged the signed letters, shook hands, and the USSR became an illusory associate member of the IMF. Two months later it would vanish from the IMF's rolls, along with this category, invented especially for it and for Gorbachev.

❀   ❀   ❀

Gorbachev packed the first ten days of October with meetings, conferences, and negotiations. It was as if he wanted to demonstrate to the USSR, to the world, and perhaps even to himself why the country needed him and what could be accomplished by a modern, democratic, open-minded president accessible to the press and to the most diverse representatives of Soviet and foreign public opinion.

President Bush's nuclear initiative gave Gorbachev the chance to take up his position as the head of one of the world's two nuclear superpowers. It also afforded him the opportunity to appear in the role of commander in chief of the armed forces of the temporary governmental structure that the USSR had become after the August putsch.

A committee was formed to work out a response worthy of the U.S. plan. Chaired by Ivan Silaev, it included representatives of the minister of foreign affairs and the minister of defense of the Union, representatives of the KGB, and Alexander Yakovlev and Yury Ryzhov, political advisers to the President, who were to serve as "democratic counterweights" to the corporate interests of the military-industrial complex. A position was worked out "in consultation," that is, it was communicated in advance to the presidents of the four core republics of the USSR—Russia, Ukraine, Belorussia, and Kazakhstan. To this end, Defense Minister Marshal Yevgeny Shaposhnikov and Deputy Minister of Foreign Affairs Vladimir Petrovsky traveled to Sochi to call on Yeltsin.

Nevertheless, Gorbachev himself had already formulated the main parameters of the policy response to the president of the United States during a television broadcast taped on Friday, September 27, the very day of the American proposal. Gorbachev had shown up at his television "office" on the third floor of the government building at the Kremlin with no written text, only a few pages of notes taken during his phone conversation with Bush. I had thought that he was going to make a speech, but he decided merely to answer the questions I put to him, which we prepared in a few minutes' time.

Gorbachev was clearsighted about the political aspects of the matter: His response, although expressive of his high esteem for Bush's initiative, reminded the audience of who had actually reopened the negotiations on nuclear disarmament, which had been stagnating for many years, and who had been the first to evoke the prospect of a world without weapons of mass destruction, which until recently had been characterized as "utopian" and "a dream."

The program was not broadcast until the next day, Saturday, September 28. "Not too early in the day," Gorbachev had requested so that we would have a chance to address any last-minute changes Bush might make in his official statement. Because of the time difference, Bush's words would not become public in Moscow until the middle of the night. Gorbachev also had another reason to delay the broadcast: "Let's not get excited," he told me. "Let them think we're mulling it over."

I also suspect that he just wanted to get the taping done so that he could spend a quiet weekend. The situation was so nerve-racking that he wanted to avoid any unnecessary stress.

Throughout the following week, the President and his press service were besieged by journalists. The American correspondents were trying to put a negative spin on the Kremlin's delay in responding to the U.S. plan, portraying it as "indecisiveness" and linking it to resistance from the military. The Pentagon also exhibited some nervousness, and its director, Defense Secretary Richard Cheney, began to allude to the possibility of revoking some of the U.S. decisions for lack of an adequate Soviet response.

The Soviet press, instead of sinking its teeth into the military, technical, and strategic aspects of the new situation, used the Kremlin's silence as an opportunity to lunge for the President's jugular. *Pravda* accused him, before the fact, of being like "Ivan the Idiot" in the Russian fables and planning to squander the people's "goods"—in this case, rockets, submarines, and aircraft—just to please the Americans. The liberal press, for its part, skewered him for his evasive behavior and his delay in responding to Bush's historic initiative.

On October 5, the Silaev committee reviewed the text of the President's statement for the last time. Gorbachev wanted to give everyone present a final chance to express their points of view. He made some changes in the text during the meeting. Major differences of opinion surfaced between the military and the "democrats" regarding the eventual proportion of reduction of Soviet strategic bombers in response to Bush's statement. Gorbachev ultimately sided with Shaposhnikov. "We don't want to complicate life for the new minister of defense," he explained to me.

The possibility of another Soviet-U.S. summit meeting was also discussed. Someone proposed setting a time and place. Others objected, saying that the Americans were not ready for "another Malta":[12] It would look as if they were dropping Yeltsin. "Let's leave the specifics up to Bush," Gorbachev decided. "I'll call him right away."

The telephone operators and translators had trouble locating the U.S. president. "They're looking for Brent Scowcroft. Bush wants to have him on hand," surmised Anatoly Chernyaev, Gorbachev's aide for international affairs and defense. By thus emphasizing the importance of Bush's national security adviser, he was implicitly strengthening his own position.

Finally, Bush came on and Gorbachev presented to him the main points of the statement he was preparing to make, ending with a proposal to set up another summit meeting. Bush greeted the Soviet response warmly, calling it "remarkable," but said nothing about the summit. Actually, the United States did not respond to any of Gorbachev's proposals that exceeded the bounds they had set for themselves: not to his proposal to renounce the nuclear first-strike doctrine or to his call to join the new nuclear-test ban that had gone into effect in the USSR on October 5.

This October 5 moratorium was followed by a bizarre incident that did possess a certain logic. Only a few weeks later, Boris Yeltsin decided to suspend nuclear testing in Russia only. This decision was reported with elation in the international and even the Soviet press. The journalists, like the Russian authorities themselves, had simply forgotten that the moratorium Gorbachev had proclaimed was already in effect throughout the USSR.

❀ ❀ ❀

Gorbachev's "autumn offensive" was also waged on the domestic front. After meeting with the independent businessmen, he set up another meeting at the Kremlin, this time with independent agriculturalists, aimed at stepping up agrarian reform. He listened to the report from the Operational Steering Committee for the Economy[13] on problems of domestic supply and received the Committee of Soldiers' Mothers. He also sent personal representatives to various parts of the country: Anatoly Sobchak and Yevgeny Velikhov to Tadzhikistan to study the particularly tense political situation there; Alexander Yakovlev to Kiev, to take part in ceremonies commemorating the fiftieth anniversary of the Babii Yar tragedy.[14]

His strategy was theoretically quite correct: He was exploring, one by one, the spheres of public interest that deserved his attention and where he would have to exercise his power. There was only one problem, but it was a big one: It was much too late.

His attempts to reestablish contact with society in general and the forces of democracy in particular were being thwarted by prejudice, apathy, and mistrust. In addition, since August he had been deprived of the old instruments of power the country was used to. The liquidation of the central government structures—especially the all-Union organs of the Party—effectively transferred that power from the Union to the republics.

The effectiveness of Gorbachev's public diplomacy and his constant presence in print and on television definitely worked in his favor, enabling him gradually to shed the effects of the trauma he had suffered in August. But they also heightened the irritation of the republics' leaders and, especially, their inner circles, whose members had no intention of giving their newly acquired powers back to the "center."

Gorbachev seemed not to notice this. Or perhaps he believed that he could put the genie back into the bottle. He worked furiously to broaden public and political support for his proposal to create a new, unified economic and political entity in place of the USSR. The terms "community" and "commonwealth" put forward by those who wanted to reduce the role of the central government did not suit his purposes. He hoped to save "union," at least in name if nothing else.

❀ ❀ ❀

On October 2, Gorbachev had a phone conversation with Helmut Kohl on the occasion of the anniversary of German reunification. That same day, he received a delegation from the council of American organizations in support of Soviet Jews, led by Shoshana Cardin. In receiving the representatives of the American Jewish lobby, Gorbachev naturally intended to focus the attention of this group, and the vast pool of capital that it represented, on the acute problems of the Soviet economy. He expressed his satisfaction in finding that many Soviet Jews were beginning to understand that their country, the USSR, needed them. In his assessment, "Under the new conditions, they will have greater opportunities to find jobs in their fatherland that are commensurate with their talents and gifts. Of course, they are free to go wherever they want. That's a normal part of life."

Asked to comment on the danger of a rise in anti-Semitism in the USSR, Gorbachev answered that in his opinion, Soviet society, except for a well-known group of bigoted writers and ambitious, unscrupulous politicians, was free of this disease. He agreed, though, that it might be beneficial for him to condemn anti-Semitism more vigorously in his public statements. "By the way," he said, "read the message that I wrote for the fiftieth anniversary of the Babii Yar tragedy. I believe that it clearly expresses my attitude toward this repugnant phenomenon."

Economic aid was also the focus of a meeting between Gorbachev and the chairman of a U.S. pension fund, an extremely powerful investment finance group. The Americans again tried to obtain definite pronouncements from Gorbachev on how long it would take to get the economic breakdown of the USSR under control, on the transition to the convertible ruble, and on the creation of stable conditions for foreign investors. Once these matters were settled, they promised a staggering volume of investments, prompt most-favored-nation status for the USSR, and practical aid for the development of small- and medium-sized businesses.

In his response, Gorbachev assured them of only one thing: "It's not going to be easy. What counts is our desire for mutual profit and our willingness to work together. As for the rest, the risk is ours as well as yours. I realize that you have an extremely large amount of capital, which is very conservatively managed. The decision is yours. In spite of all our wealth, our economy is abnormal. Take the paradoxes of the ruble. Although people refer to it now as 'wooden money,' seventy rubles can still buy a ton of oil worth a hundred and twenty dollars. So one ruble equals roughly two dollars. And a modern MiG-29 fighter jet that costs thirty million dollars is estimated at two million rubles here. The Kamaz automobile factory here is worth between four and five billion rubles, but appraisers at the New York Stock Exchange value it at twelve billion dollars. However, at the current rate of exchange of one dollar to forty rubles, somebody could buy the plant for three hundred million dollars."

After dumbfounding the Americans with a few paradoxes of this kind, Gorbachev ended this part of the discussion by exclaiming, "That's why we so greatly need a market that will put everything back in its proper place."

He then moved on from calculations, which held little interest for him, to more general considerations: "I am worried about the weakness of our economic ties with the United States. If it weren't for grain, they'd be nonexistent. As I told Bush, we want you to depend on us as much as possible, and us on you. That will make each of us more predictable."

He ended the meeting with a quote from Pushkin: "'Youth feeds on hope.' Granted, I am no longer young, but I still have hope. And as long as there is hope, everything is possible," he said, as if to himself.

Gorbachev felt that he had made good use of his time. Once again he had inspired a group of influential friends of the USSR not to despair in the face of the bizarre spectacle taking place there.

But there would be no one to do the same for him.

On a Crumbling Verge

The October 11 meeting of the State Council was approaching. As the first real working meeting after the political turmoil of August, it was intended to confirm the decisionmaking ability of the new governmental structure, even if this structure should prove to be only temporary.

The message that this meeting was supposed to send to the public was obvious: The disintegration of the USSR had been halted. In addition, since the meeting was called by and, naturally, placed under the chairmanship of Mikhail Gorbachev, it would show that two levels of power really existed in the USSR, the upper level being occupied by the president of the Union and the lower level by the leaders of the republics. Yeltsin, who had just come back from vacation, was to sit on the republics' bench—on Gorbachev's right but not at the head of the table.

During the next few days Gorbachev was seized by a kind of "meeting mania." There was almost nobody he refused to see. It was as if he wanted to be in as many different places as possible and reach every audience at once (he was aided in this by television, where he was seen almost every evening)—in short, to fill up all of the political space with himself. These actions were more impulsive than considered. He failed to realize that his "omnivorous" choice of people to meet with and his constant presence on all the television news shows antagonized the public, devalued his image, and gave his increasingly implacable opponents the urge to "put him in his place."

It seems to me that Gorbachev had two reasons for wanting to see so many people. The first was rational: A propagandist and teacher by nature, he sincerely believed that he could convince everyone he spoke to, that he could persuade them to follow whatever course of action he felt was reasonable and sound. The second was irrational and subconscious and reflected the uncertainty, confusion, and anxiety to which he had fallen prey since the putsch. He was able to shed this inner weakness—which was something new for him—only when he was with other people, for whom he never ceased to be *the* President, the same as he had been before, though at the same time somehow changed and new.

On October 10 he received a group of leaders of the Moscow district soviets at the Kremlin. His advisers had tried in vain to dissuade him from meeting with these representatives of the old urban *nomenklatura,* who were clashing with the new authorities of the city (especially the mayor, Gavriil Popov), arguing that he was needlessly allowing himself to be dragged into this tangled internal conflict of city politics.

The district leaders were obviously coming to plead for Gorbachev's intercession against this satan-mayor who was methodically taking over all the positions of city government and appointing his own people. Relying on the support of the Muscovites who had elected him, he clearly intended to gain monopoly control over all the city's assets: its land, office buildings, and commercial establishments.

Apparently this democratic mayor considered the counterpoise to executive power embodied by the local representative organizations to be superfluous. Theoretically, it would have been the easiest thing in the world for him to get rid of them: All he had to do was proclaim that the local soviets were part of the old totalitarian system and accuse them of having supported the putsch because they had not bestirred themselves to defend the Russian White House.[15]

Such an accusation would have been well based in fact but misleading, since except for a few thousand democrats who had formed a living wall around the Russian parliament, the rest of Moscow, like the country as a whole, had stood by motionless during the coup, awaiting its outcome. And officials at all levels had done the same as everyone else.

Gorbachev listened to the district leaders' complaints about the mayor's arbitrariness but avoided siding with them. Popov, a member of the policy advisory council recently created to aid the President, was an important ally. In addition, since their college days he and Gorbachev had been bound together in a strange relationship of mutual attraction and repulsion that they could not quite bring themselves to terminate even at the most stressful points in their political lives. So Gorbachev scolded the leaders of the district soviets for their aggressiveness toward a popularly elected mayor, warned them against the possibility of letting themselves be used by "the forces opposing reform," and promised to speak to the mayor about the need to counterbalance the zeal of executive power with the elected bodies and the law. "I ask that you maintain a constructive attitude and not get yourselves into a confrontation," he said. That was the most that the complainants could get from him.

Since these were people who could broadcast his words throughout Moscow, Gorbachev took advantage of the situation to aim his propagandist offensive at public opinion in the hope that his listeners would come away from the Kremlin with a few substantial ideas that they would duly disseminate. He emphasized the following points:

- Positive, real change could be effected only on the path of democracy.
- Until only recently, our society had been the most militarized in the world. "It's atrocious, the size of our military-industrial complex!"

- The most important thing was to avoid civil conflict. At every meeting you heard cries of "Down with so-and-so! He should be shot!"
- It was clear that the putsch was organized by representatives of forces and powerful structures whose "most vital interests were threatened by perestroika."

Gorbachev recalled that it was precisely those forces that had stopped Khrushchev when he had been on the verge of implementing real reforms. "It's true that he himself belonged to the past to such an extent that he didn't dare break with it on several important points. Even in denouncing the crimes of Stalinism, Khrushchev didn't dare cross a certain boundary line and tell the whole truth. Because the whole truth was terrible. And most terrible of all was the fact that the people carrying out Stalin's orders were demanding that he increase the number of death sentences permitted."

Perestroika, he explained, implied a final break not only with the model of leftist-utopian socialism but also with the very psychology of voluntarism with which the entire society was infected. "This is the only way that we will arrive at true socialism. I continue to believe in socialism and talk about it, although I am booed every time I mention it. Nevertheless, I am convinced that we can attain it through freedom."

At this meeting Gorbachev got what he wanted: The leaders of the district soviets left mollified and satisfied to have had the President's ear. The daily problems that engulfed them again as they left the Kremlin seemed less dramatic now compared with the boldness and scope of the historic project undertaken by *their* president.

❁   ❁   ❁

The meeting of the State Council opened on October 11 in an atmosphere of nervous excitement. Until the last minute, no one knew whether all the members of the council (the leaders of the republics), especially Boris Yeltsin, would show up at the appointed time. The meeting was to take place in a hall on the third floor of the government building at the Kremlin where the Party Politburo meetings used to be held.

The critical nature of the situation prompted Gorbachev to invite an additional, last-minute participant he was counting on for support: public opinion. A television crew was called in without any advance notice, and the state broadcasting company was asked to stand by to telecast the meeting live.

The President decided to begin with an alarmist political gesture that was intended to remind the republic leaders assembled there of their responsibility to the country and to their own people. At the appointed time, everyone sat down at the table and cast sidelong glances at the television cameras and cables. Only Yeltsin's seat was still empty. Gorbachev waited for him for five minutes and then, assuming that he probably wasn't coming, decided to begin. The camera lights went on, and the President, addressing the television audience more than the hall, made his statement almost without glancing at his text. "I would like to say a few words to open this meeting of the State Council, which I consider tremendously important. I have been moved to speak by serious concerns regarding the trend in society and the actions we are taking to address both the current situation and potential future developments."

Gorbachev began by recapitulating the decisions he had made after the putsch, which had prevented "the worst from happening." He initially emphasized the mutual understanding between him and the leaders of the republics, which had made it possible to develop the economic accord and to reinitiate the process of signing the Union Treaty. Then he emphasized the risk of backsliding, which he felt was becoming apparent.

"We must be frank," he concluded. "We are all under tremendous pressure. There have been attempts to instigate confrontations between the members of the State Council, to sow suspicion, to delay approval of the documents that have been drafted, regardless of the cost. . . . And there is grave danger in this. People are almost out of patience. Their last hope is that the State Council, after the events of August, will take firm action, as we have promised; that it will make decisions that meet the vital needs of the country and the people. Our foreign counterparts see all this as well. People in other countries are confused and apprehensive about what we are doing. That is why this meeting is extraordinarily important. It is my feeling that the State Council has no right to close this session without making decisions on the principal matters before it."

Yeltsin entered the room just as Gorbachev was ending his address. He mumbled some vague explanations for his lateness and sat down. Yeltsin never smiled, but he looked even more sullen than usual at finding himself in the glare of spotlights that had not been cleared with him ahead of time.

At the end of his speech, Gorbachev asked whether they should continue the live broadcast. The members of the State Council, feeling themselves caught in a televised trap, shook their heads no, and public opinion was thrust out of the hall along with the television cameras.

After a bit of wrangling over the agenda, Gorbachev proposed discussing the Union Treaty, to the obvious displeasure of Yeltsin and Kravchuk. The meeting began with a discussion of the establishment of the economic community. The reporting committee chair was Grigory Yavlinsky, the author of the text approved by the twelve republics. He structured his address as a logical refutation of the arguments of opponents of the community or of those who doubted its feasibility.

Yavlinsky laid out his case in favor of a common economic zone, alternating between lyricism and matter-of-fact reasoning. He took the arguments of his opponents, most of whom were seated with him in the State Council meeting room, and turned them upside down with what was, he felt, irrefutable logic: "Some people say that it would be easier for the republics to get out of the current situation on their own than as part of a single country where the imbalances are so great. But calculations show that the price of isolation will be extremely high. And it is the people who will pay, not the politicians. Partitioning the country will result in a drop in production, accompanied by a rise in unemployment and disintegration of the monetary system.

"The greater the size and freedom of the union's internal common market, the easier it will be for the economy to tolerate reform, since there is no other all-encompassing market. The war among politicians in the republics will become a war against their own producers. Today, each republic feels that it is being plundered and is trying to determine who is living at its expense. But the system steals from everyone alike. With a common market, deregulated prices, and no customs barriers, there will be no more plundering.

"The new center will no longer be an instrument of totalitarianism. It will become a coordinating body, a mechanism for managing the ruble zone. Naturally, the community will place certain obligations on its members, but when nations make common cause together, international obligations must take priority over national resolutions. In the final analysis, each country has the option of defending its own sovereignty by political means without plunging into economic war."

Evidently recognizing that purely economic arguments would not be enough to convince his audience, Yavlinsky concluded his exposition with a more vivid turn of phrase. "We know," he said, "that even the most protracted wars end in peace treaties. Let's try for once to start out with a treaty instead of declaring war." He also invoked history in support of his arguments, pointing out that World War I had broken out after an economic accord was sabotaged in Austria-Hungary and that the creation of the Federal Reserve system in the United States marked the end of the Civil War.

Yavlinsky's eloquence made a favorable impression, especially on those who had no need to be convinced of the usefulness of the Union Treaty. The skeptics kept quiet, waiting to find out which way the Russian wind would blow. Everyone, Gorbachev included, watched for Yeltsin's reaction. He finally broke his silence with his usual peremptory tone: Russia would sign the economic treaty but would not ratify it until the practical provisions of the accord were ready. "And from now on," he said with index finger aloft, "we are going to stop financing the central organs of government, which are not provided for in this treaty."

This speech made it obvious what the results of the meeting would be. Gorbachev asked the participants to announce their decisions in turn. Kravchuk confirmed that Ukraine was prepared to sign on October 15 as long as its amendments were considered. Nazarbaev spoke on behalf of the three republics that had already signed the accord in Alma-Ata and took the opportunity to remark that he was "delighted at what he was hearing from Boris Nikolaevich." Nazarbaev added that if the leaders of the republics had not reached an agreement, they would have "been ashamed to leave this building. After all," he concluded, in essence, "anyone who is ready to sign should go ahead and do so. It doesn't matter how many of us there are—eight, five, or four."

The most important leaders had spoken and a tally could be made. But the president of Azerbaidzhan, Ayaz Mutalibov, took the floor to put forward his own conditions. The people of Azerbaidzhan, he said, "were in desperate straits" and would vote against any treaty that did not defend them against Armenian aggression. He felt that the situation in the Caucasus was not moving in a direction that would strengthen the new union. His republic's willingness to participate in economic and political treaties would depend on the allocation to Azerbaidzhan of "sufficient forces to organize its defense."

But neither his remarks nor the reservations expressed by Uzbekistan's leader, Islam Karimov, were able to affect the outcome of the discussion. All the members of the State Council initialed a document confirming that the heads of state and the government leaders of Azerbaidzhan, Armenia, Belorussia, Kazakhstan, Kirghizia, Russia, Tadzhikistan, Turkmenistan, Uzbekistan, and Ukraine[16] were called upon "to sign, before October 15, the treaty instituting the economic community adopted in Alma-Ata, taking into account the supplemental proposals put forward during the meeting of the State Council of the USSR." This meeting demonstrated once again that the strategic "alliance" of Gorbachev, Yeltsin, and Nazarbaev had unshakable authority within the State Council and guaranteed prompt approval of all decisions supported by the three of them in tandem.

Gorbachev announced a temporary adjournment, inviting the leaders of the republics to lunch in order to "consolidate the consensus." Discussion of the thorniest issues, especially the Union Treaty, still lay before them.

When the meeting resumed, the participants heard and discussed the report by Ivan Silaev, chairman of the Interstate Economic Committee, on the food accord for the end of the current year and the next. Apparently no one was troubled by the fact that the administrative logic behind this accord was in flagrant contradiction to the spirit of the draft treaty of economic community that had just been approved.

The meeting took on the busy atmosphere that always prevailed when advantages were being handed out—an ambience familiar to all former Party secretaries, including Gorbachev. There was talk of the republics' quotas, allocations to central stocks, and the volume of deliveries. Penalties for nonperformance were set. Stable, agreed-on prices were to be maintained. There was one new feature, the proposal that penalties should be collected in dollars. But the supply plan as a whole no longer reflected the former voluntarist power of the "center." It was only an imitation of power now.

Actually, all the republics were doing was rubber-stamping the accords they had already concluded among themselves. The forced character of this exercise finally became apparent to Gorbachev, and he proposed limiting further discussion to matters relating to centralized food imports and the volume of the Union's food reserves, needed primarily to maintain the army.

After the food issues had been discussed, Gorbachev called for the next item on the agenda, which was the most important one as far as he was concerned: organizing the work on the draft of the new Union Treaty. He suggested that the republics' comments be collected over a period of one week and a meeting of the State Council be convened for joint debate on the text. "Please give me your opinions on this," he said. An awkward silence descended. The republic leaders sat with their heads bowed. It was like an oral examination presided over by a strict professor: Nobody wanted to be the first to speak. Most were waiting for Yeltsin to set the tone, but he maintained an enigmatic silence.

Since the ball was at the republics' end of the court, Uzbekistan's leader, Islam Karimov, made a few attempts to keep it moving. He pretended that this was the first he had ever heard of the treaty and asked which draft this was: the one that had been discussed before August, or a new one? "That question was debated at the Congress of Deputies," Gorbachev replied curtly. "A decision was made. The draft that Boris Nikolaevich and I worked out together was sent to you. Let's discuss it."

Another silence. At this point none of the republic leaders were prepared to challenge the President, especially since this would have meant calling the resolutions of the Congress into question. No one but Kravchuk, that is. Without looking at Gorbachev, he announced that Ukraine's Supreme Soviet had decided not to participate in the work on the Union Treaty before December 1, the date it had set for a referendum on the independence of the republic. He said this apologetically, as if his parliament were depriving him of the opportunity to realize his fondest wish.

Kravchuk's attitude seemed to set him apart from the united front maintained by the other republic leaders, putting him in a more favorable position. It therefore irritated them. Gorbachev sensed this immediately: "Why not appeal to Ukraine on behalf of all the members of the State Council and ask it to reverse its decision? So many things were decided in the heat of the moment, after the coup! But now everything is getting back to normal. We only need to decide to whom we should appeal. To the people, probably, and not just the workers."

Suddenly Yeltsin broke his silence: "You have to address your appeal to the Supreme Soviet, to those who made this decision."

I sensed that he, too, wanted to strengthen the republics' consolidated front, but his remark instead lent support to Gorbachev's position. No one listened to Kravchuk when he objected that such an appeal might well have an effect opposite to that desired. Obviously, Gorbachev and Yeltsin together held a controlling interest in the State Council. The proposal to appeal to the Ukranian parliament was approved unanimously despite Kravchuk's glum silence.

After this discussion, the meeting moved on to less important subjects—the activities of Gosteleradio (state radio and television) and the reform of the KGB. The revolutionary proposal that the latter structure, so powerful until recently, should be melted down and recast was put foward by Vadim Bakatin. He was listened to politely, and his plan was approved after a cursory examination.

The KGB would henceforth be divided into three independent organizations: the Central Information Service (headed by Yevgeny Primakov), the Counterespionage Division (to be directed by Bakatin himself), and the Corps of Border Guards. This report, for the first time, gave the personnel figures on this monster nurtured by Stalin and Brezhnev, which had outlived several general secretaries and had almost cost the last one his life: There were 490,000 agents and employees, including the border guard troops (numbering 240,000). Bakatin pledged not only to decentralize the KGB's structure, bringing it into line with the new reality of the Union of Sovereign States, but also to depoliticize it, to keep it in strict compliance with the law, and, of course, to abandon its political surveillance activities.

Two months earlier, no one would have believed such changes to be possible. And yet they were treated as routine matters at this meeting. The press and the public barely took notice of the historic phrase contained in the October 11 resolution of the State Council, "to eliminate the KGB of the USSR." The explanation is simple: This decision, like many others, did not create change; it merely registered the intent to change.

Buoyed by the State Council meeting, Gorbachev decided to preserve the momentum he had built up. On Monday, October 14, he called his advisers together and described his plan for maintaining the political initiative. At this point it was clear that the economic treaty could not be signed on the 15th; the earliest possible date was the 18th. This did not make a great deal of difference, however. The important thing was to cast the event in a solemn and impressive light, since it marked the birth of the new union, although legal confirmation of the political treaty would still be necessary.

In the meantime, after several postponements and much temporizing, a session of the Supreme Soviet was finally about to open. The new Parliament of the USSR, whose members were elected on the basis of complex criteria established during the final session of the Congress of People's Deputies, was to present to the USSR and to the world at large the new image of an extraordinary nation: an assemblage of sovereign and independent states united by their unhappy past and their fear of an uncertain future.

In Gorbachev's view, this parliament, together with the president of the Union, should become a catalyst of the new democratic integration of a disoriented and disjointed society. For it to accomplish this, it would have to be presented with a concrete agenda.

Unexpected support for Gorbachev's position came from an article in *Nezavisimaya gazeta*. What the author had to say was what Gorbachev wanted to hear. He claimed that when confronted with the real problems of society, Yeltsin's administration, which was assuming the mantle of power in Russia, would not dare implement the plans for reform that it had loudly publicized because they entailed unpopular measures. Yeltsin was a populist by nature and would never risk incurring a loss of popular support. Such a situation would undoubtedly give Gorbachev, who "reigned" but no longer governed, a golden opportunity to recover his losses at the hands of the radical opposition and to speak on behalf of the people, who were insistently demanding changes.

Gorbachev was impatiently looking beyond the economic treaty, which had not even been signed yet. A coherent plan of action had to be proposed to all the republics. But the main thing, for him, was to maintain the initiative in the political process. As he explained to his aides (persuading himself at the same time), "The people are waiting for us to answer the question they're all asking: Where are we headed? We can no longer resort to generalities. And the best occasion for giving a clear-cut answer is the opening session of the Supreme Soviet. The president's speech should be specific, radical, and agenda-setting. The main point of emphasis should be the radicalization of economic reform. We must speed up the creation of a mixed economy, advance agrarian reform, support entrepreneurs. We've been marching in place long enough. The people must be told in all honesty that the road ahead of them demands some tough decisions that can't be put off any longer. We must seize the opportunity that was offered us in August."

In drafting this speech and preparing to appear before Parliament and the public in the new and unaccustomed role of a revolutionary reformer, Gorbachev never wondered how and by whom these radical changes would be effected. He assumed that matters would take care of themselves, through deliberations of Parliament, ukases issued by the republic governments, and a spontaneous movement of people reeducated by him.

He was still, first and foremost, society's consciousness-raiser, a man capable of changing the psychological, spiritual, and, of course, political reality of his country, but one who always stopped short of making material changes in the economy, in society, and in personnel. This was both his gift and his weakness as a reformer; and it was hard to say which type of skill was most needed at any given moment by this society that he had so electrified.

As was his habit, he continued to develop his new line of thinking while receiving his next foreign visitor—in this case, the Japanese minister of foreign affairs, Taro Nakayama. Gorbachev returned to his assessment of the consequences of the putsch, commenting: "After the coup was put down, some problems disappeared but others surfaced. The plotters gave impetus to the disintegration of the country, and there has been a whole swarm of declarations of independence since then."

Gorbachev explained to his guest that the centralized structures had crumbled but that society's self-defense mechanisms had worked. "With their help, we have succeeded in halting the country's disintegration." He went on to explain that the economic treaty would be signed on October 18. One week later, the leaders of the republics would give their verdict on the proposed Union of Sovereign States. Gorbachev described a new union with a drastic redistribution of powers to achieve a balance among the republics and the center. A new center, democratic but strong and effective, was necessary in order to perform the functions common to all the republics: to help create a single economy, to oversee the united armed forces. "We are now living through the most decisive days and weeks."

Nakayama nodded politely at each phrase from the interpreter. He then took out an envelope containing a message from his prime minister, Toshiki Kaifu. Nakayama was bringing two pieces of news: the announcement of $2.5 billion in aid, and another "slight nuance" with regard to Japan's position on the South Kuril Islands controversy. In his reply, Gorbachev showed the virtuosity of a diplomat able to make his negotiating partner think that he has taken a good-sized step in his direction even though he has not budged an inch.

The substance of his reply was that the Soviet Union wanted to speed up the work of preparation for the peace treaty,[17] but in order to accomplish this it would be necessary to create a new atmosphere on the issue of the Kurils. He emphasized that this was not a ruse or a pretext; it was just that the situation had to change gradually. "You yourself can see that this is a sensitive matter to our people."

Nevertheless, he said, he was convinced that the two countries, Japan and the USSR, had made more progress in the six months since his visit to Japan in April than they had in the previous ten years. As an example of what they might accomplish given time, he cited the recent successful resolution of the "German question." Who could have guessed that events would start moving so rapidly? He felt that the same thing might happen with Japan and that the process would be even faster than they had believed on his visit to Tokyo. The quantitative changes would necessarily lead to qualitative changes.

When Nakayama tried to pin him down regarding these reassurances, Gorbachev said jokingly: "Read your notes over carefully. You'll find the answer to your question there, in what I've said today. I feel sure that I will have something else new to tell you next time. My intuition tells me that Soviet-Japanese relations will soon be the most dynamic in the world."

The interview ended, and Nakayama, reassured more by the tone than by the content of the conversation, left to go over his notes. After saying good-bye to him, Gorbachev told us with a grin how last April, in Tokyo, he had had seven long working meetings with the Japanese that had revolved around a single word. He wasn't going to make that mistake again!

❀   ❀   ❀

The success of the State Council meeting bolstered Gorbachev's confidence and gave him new energy. He felt that his political strategy was beginning to show results. The country had seen its president in the role of the incontestable leader, with the heads of the republics performing on cue like so many circus animals in a ring. Even Yeltsin did not dispute Gorbachev's role as the president of the Union and ran through some prerehearsed "numbers" at his request, although grudgingly. "When you get together with him one on one," said Gorbachev, "you can come to an understanding on just about anything—though it might not last for long, once he leaves the room and falls under the influence of his entourage."

All the same, things still looked promising at that point. The treaty of economic community was in the bag. The text of the Union Treaty, in which Gorbachev had succeeded in involving Yeltsin, was being studied by the republics. The opening of the session of the Supreme Soviet was coming up, and no surprises were expected from that quarter. Gorbachev was reasserting his control over the levers of power with increasing energy.

It was time to send a signal to the outside world; the situation in Yugoslavia provided an opportunity. The European Community and the secretary of state of the United States had failed to put out the fire that had started there, and now it was time to make an attempt on the Slav side, especially since the German diplomatic machine, headed by Hans-Dietrich Genscher, was methodically ramming the gates of the Yugoslavian "fortress."

In mid-October, Soviet foreign policy, whose existence had almost been forgotten, returned to center stage. It was announced that the leaders of Serbia and

Croatia, Slobodan Milosevic and Franjo Tudjman, were due to arrive in Moscow at Gorbachev's invitation.

This initiative by the minister of foreign affairs was a surprise even to Gorbachev's aides, who had not been informed of the visit. The idea seemed risky. There was little chance of success, and failure could have dire political consequences for the President. In addition, with internal conflicts flaring up in Nagorno-Karabakh, Georgia, and other parts of the country, one might well ask why Gorbachev was giving priority to putting out fires in other parts of the world. But he had made his decision: The invitations to Milosevic and Tudjman had been sent through diplomatic channels, and—surprisingly enough—had been accepted immediately.

To ward off domestic criticism, it was decided to announce that the President intended to meet over the next few days not only with the Yugoslavs but also with the parties to the conflict in Karabakh, in the persons of Levon Ter-Petrossian and Mutalibov. For unknown reasons, this other meeting did not take place. Gorbachev said nothing about it, however, perhaps in the realization that nothing substantive would have come of it anyway. The Armenian and Azerbaidzhani leaders may have turned down the invitation because they felt that no one would have thought of them if the Yugoslavs had not been coming.

The initial plan was to set up separate talks with Milosevic and Tudjman. Relations between the two republics and their presidents were so strained that it was considered well-nigh impossible to hold a meeting with all three leaders present. Even the arrival schedules for the two presidents were a headache for the presidential guard and the protocol service, since the warring parties had to be "segregated" in the reception room, at the airport, and in the hallways of the Kremlin.

During a preparatory meeting, I asked Gorbachev if we should set up for a joint press conference in case the talks were successful. He waved his hands superstitiously and said: "Let's wait and see how everything goes. There will always be time to call the journalists."

Despite the difficulties, the meeting took place on October 15, and it was a minor triumph for Gorbachev. After hours of listening patiently to the claims of the Serb and Croat leaders, and then more hours of patiently exhorting them, the President obtained their agreement to a trilateral meeting. This meeting mushroomed into a formal dinner, which in turn stretched into a long Slavic repast with the two guests reminiscing about visits they had made to the USSR when they were young men, recounting memories of their Muscovite friends, and making confessional toasts.

By mixing diplomacy with the cordiality of a good host, Gorbachev adroitly warmed the atmosphere of the dinner, which was held in a mansion on Alexei

Tolstoy Street owned by the Ministry of Foreign Affairs. Surely he could melt the ice of alienation that separated the two adversaries seated across from each other. He recounted an episode from his own student days: "A Yugoslav—I don't know if he was a Serb or a Croat—" began earnestly to court Raisa Maximovna, and "he actually thought he had a chance with her!" His story created an almost familial atmosphere at the table.

Later, when they got down to more serious matters, Gorbachev's main arguments did not seem, at first glance, to have much to do with the situation in Yugoslavia. He spoke to his guests about perestroika, its dramas, conflicts, and failures. He also explained his political tactics, the difficulty of finding paths for compromise, the intolerance of his political opponents, and the aggressiveness of the republics' leaders. But all of this, by implication, was applicable to the Yugoslav conflict and might possibly have nudged Milosevic and Tudjman, however unwillingly, into a friendlier relationship.

The two leaders naturally had great respect for Gorbachev's prestige and authority, for the man who had succeeded, virtually without bloodshed, in reforming a state much more complex than Yugoslavia. When I repeated at table the question that had just been put to me at the press conference—"What advice could the president of the USSR, overwhelmed with his own conflicts, offer to Yugoslavia?"—the two Yugoslavs came to life. Each in his own way said the same thing: The experience of perestroika gives Gorbachev the moral right to advise us, and we are prepared to listen to his recommendations.

When the three men had drafted and signed a new cease-fire—which, unfortunately, would not be the last—Gorbachev, with a priestlike gesture, joined Milosevic's and Tudjman's hands in his own. "And now, let's go and see the press."

This is how the world learned that "a new chance" for peace in Yugoslavia had been created in Moscow. Unfortunately, it was to survive only for as long as the two warring parties were under Gorbachev's watchful eye.

On leaving the house, each of the three men went his own way: Tudjman to the airport, Milosevic to a meeting with Yeltsin, Gorbachev to his dacha. Gorbachev's conscience was clear. Once again, he had acted in a manner befitting a statesman of global stature. And it was doubtful that anyone could have done any better in his stead.

A President
Without a Country

One of the peculiarities of any political landscape is the impossibility of making out its true contours—the height of its passes and peaks, the steepness of its slopes, the depth of its abysses—until after the fact, when politics has become fossilized in the strata of history. To try to gauge events as they are taking place is a dangerous and not very productive occupation, like trying to sketch a torrent of lava as it flows out of a volcano.

None of the organizers of or participants in the ceremonial signing of the economic community treaty, which took place in the Hall of St. George at the Kremlin that October 18, realized that this would be the last triumph of the policy launched in March 1985. Without realizing it, we were bidding a solemn farewell to perestroika, both as a word that had found its way into the language of every nation in the world and as the last hope that the peoples of the Soviet empire might free themselves from their totalitarian past by the rational, cooperative solution of maintaining a unitary state undergoing a process of transformation.

Gorbachev's reformism had given historic impetus to the country's development, but this dynamic energy had gradually dissipated, and it was impossible for him to win in a confrontation with the darker social forces whose resistance and revolt he himself had provoked. After August, the driverless engine of the single state kept rolling along for another two months, running on the momentum of the political process started before the coup. It still seemed to be headed for an economic union—a voluntary, though truncated, one. In the end, though, the engine was stopped dead on the tracks by the bureaucracy of the republics.

On that day in October, however, Gorbachev was still unaware of any of this. He went to the Hall of St. George in the morning, well in advance of the ceremony, under the pretext of reviewing the protocol and rehearsing his part on stage, as it were. Actually, he just wanted to prolong the festivities and savor his well-earned triumph.

The Kremlin administration, the protocol service, and the press service reported to him on the arrangement of the room and the participants and showed him where the cameras and the flags of the signatory states would be positioned. The proper angle was selected so that the President would appear on the screen against the flag of the USSR. There was a discussion as to whether the flag of the Union should be larger than those of the constituent republics.

The question of whether the participants should be served champagne in front of the press and the television audience was also debated. Despite Gorbachev's doubts, he was finally persuaded that the importance of the event not only justified but demanded a festive atmosphere. Should normal emotions and rituals continue to be hidden, as they always had been in the past? Everyone was sensitive to this argument, and the champagne was approved. Then the administrators ushered Gorbachev into the Catherine Room, where the table was to be set up for the celebratory dinner.

The President made a few comments on the seating arrangement, criticized the chairs ("too official"), and left on foot for his office in another building. This gave him the opportunity to pass back through the courtyard of the Kremlin, this time through a crowd of Italian tourists who could hardly believe their good fortune, and "talk to the people," a group of tourists from the Ural Mountains region.

The ceremony was appropriately solemn and festive. When the treaty, signed by the representatives of the eight sovereign states,[18] had been passed around the table and had reached the President, Gorbachev signed it unhurriedly in order to give the journalists time to take pictures and record the moment for posterity. To many who were present, it was as though he were placing a period at the end of a long chapter of trouble and discord. The nine leaders who had just approved the economic union and were clinking their glasses of champagne seemed to have made a firm commitment to work together in lifting their dispirited country out of its crisis.

This impression was confirmed by the press conference that followed the signing. The leaders of the republics spoke with optimism of the need for integration and of the indissoluble bonds between republics and peoples and expressed the hope that other former members of the USSR would unite with them in the treaty of economic community. This occurred, in fact, a few days later, when Azerbaidzhan, Moldavia, and Ukraine joined in signing the pact. (Leonid Kravchuk was in Moscow on November 6, the day Ukraine signed the treaty, so he delegated that signal honor [or risk] to his prime minister, Vitold Fokin.)

The success of the economic treaty gave Gorbachev further encouragement to launch the political offensive he had planned for the session of the Supreme Soviet the following week. Despite the regrettable absence of Ukraine, this platform offered him a golden opportunity to solidify and expand the positions that he had gained. Gorbachev believed that his ascent would continue. But the very next day after his triumph in the Hall of St. George, he stepped onto a downward slope—imperceptible at first, but quickly becoming steeper.

His appearance before the Supreme Soviet, for which he had "plumbed the depths of radicalism," was a failure. In point of fact, it was no worse than his earlier performances; he even permitted himself to go farther than he ever had on certain points. He spoke of the need to discard totalitarianism once and for all, to make a real breakthrough to a free market economy, to change attitudes toward entrepreneurs, and to speed up "radical agrarian reform." He intended his speech to be understood as a national plan of action, and not just as an agenda for the session. He urged society, which was entering a period of tremendous economic and social upheaval, "to find ways to make these radical changes take place within the framework of the law, without dramatic conflicts and taking into account the interests of all strata of society, especially those likely to suffer the most from the rapid expansion of market relations."

But his noble appeal was not heard, nor could it be. The Supreme Soviet listened to him with a distracted ear, more concerned with its own fate than with that of the defunct state that it represented. And the people were not ready to believe that Gorbachev, the great compromiser, had transformed himself into a practical man and resolute leader capable of carrying society along with him rather than pushing it ahead.

Only once did he manage to project that image, when he succeeded overnight in metamorphosing a vague speech before the Supreme Soviet into a vigorous twelve-point program, accompanied by a precise schedule and obligations to be met. On that occasion he stood before Parliament as a latter-day de Gaulle, assuming the extraordinary powers and the responsibility of government. The members of Parliament, who were secretly hoping for a firm hand, responded with a standing ovation. But after the deadlines that had been set had come and gone and nothing had happened, he was unable to perform the same trick again.

In addition, although Gorbachev still had undisputed moral and political authority, he was no longer seen as the embodiment of power. First, during his six years in public affairs he had never assumed the character of a true "sovereign." Furthermore, after August, although he still had the crown, he had lost the orb and scepter, that is, the real instruments of power. From time immemorial, the mechanisms of authority and the true source of legitimacy of that authority in Russia, and subsequently in the USSR, had been coercion, subjugation, and fear—certainly not the Constitution, the law, and the ballot box. Because of his indecision at the time when the office of president of the USSR was being created in March 1990, Gorbachev held his mandate not by direct popular vote but only through election by a Congress of People's Deputies, which in turn had been elected on a "semidemocratic" basis.

Certainly one of his greatest triumphs was to free his country from the burden of fear. Because of this, however, when the putsch and its aftermath paralyzed the traditional mechanisms of coercion and control (the army, the KGB, and, more important, the Party apparatus), the republics took advantage of this opportunity to transform their declarations of sovereignty into real independence and to appropriate the remaining symbols of power: finance, personnel, and the media.

From then on, although the state still had a president, the President himself no longer had a country. No one realized this immediately: neither Gorbachev nor the citizens of the USSR nor the many foreign visitors who continued to meet with Gorbachev at the Kremlin and who saw him, especially after the signing of the economic treaty, as a phoenix of perestroika, in no danger from the flames he himself had fanned.

❀   ❀   ❀

A few hours after his appearance at the Supreme Soviet, Gorbachev received the Japanese minister of foreign trade and industry, Eiichi Nakao. In keeping with the etiquette of his country, Nakao extended profuse compliments regarding the "father" of perestroika and the revolution that had enabled the USSR to abandon the totalitarian single-party system. In Japan, according to Nakao, Gorbachev was considered to be not only a Soviet but a Japanese politician, and Nakao jokingly asked him not to run for chairman of the Liberal Democratic Party. (Toshiki Kaifu had announced his resignation, effective the next day.)

Gorbachev, as usual, replied in the same tone in which he had been addressed. "My impressions of my unforgettable trip to your country are as fresh as ever. It was an inspired idea to suggest that I visit Japan during the flowering of the *sakura*. Raisa Maximovna and I often look at our photo album of the trip together. I especially like the picture where she is learning the tea ceremony. I tell her that she has narrow eyes, like a Japanese."

After this exchange of compliments, they spoke briefly of the territorial problem of the Kurils and then moved on to the subjects that had prompted Nakao's visit. Nakao was already aware of Gorbachev's speech to the Supreme Soviet and had gleaned from it something that the people in the hall had little heeded: the President's determination to move more rapidly and irreversibly in the direction of a market economy.

Gorbachev confirmed the accuracy of his conclusions. "That is correct. I feel that I have more support from the country today than I did a year ago. This makes it possible for me to speak my mind more forcefully on the various aspects of reform." It was probably unconsciously that Gorbachev equated firmness in politics with the firmness of his political pronouncements.

The Japanese minister opened his briefcase and took out a voluminous computer-generated document containing several dozen proposals for economic cooperation between Japan and the USSR. Most of them related to the conversion of the military industry to civilian applications, the safety of civilian nuclear power plants, and the stimulation of small- and medium-sized private businesses. According to Nakao, demilitarization was the number one problem in reforming the Soviet economy. He proposed to Gorbachev a detailed schedule of Japanese measures for implementing the proposed projects.

The President praised the business sense of the Japanese and reiterated a common theme: "As I have said to George Bush, we should become more mutually dependent. That way we will be more predictable to each other."

Gorbachev had been trying to persuade the Japanese to familiarize themselves with the "vast Soviet market," saying that he was relying on their cooperation to help him break down the powerful stratum of state monopolies. "We will never be able to overcome this monopolism, this supermonopoly, on our own. It is impossible to break it up by the mere force of law. That is why we are counting on foreign support. We welcome capital investment, whether from Japan or from another country. Let the investors take the economy in hand, let them compete with each another and with our own entrepreneurs."

At the end of the conversation he returned to the subject of Soviet-Japanese relations: "Our relationship with Japan is of special importance to us. We want to open new vistas and develop genuinely close ties. We have already made significant and, I feel, irreversible progress that will ensure that those who come after us, whoever they may be, will continue what we have begun." This polite phrase, an appropriate one for ending the conversation, suddenly took on a note of farewell. But this went unnoticed by both Gorbachev and the others present.

❀   ❀   ❀

The next important foreign visitor was Hans-Dietrich Genscher, who arrived in Moscow on October 26. For some months, Gorbachev had been following the increased activity of the head of German diplomacy with jealous watchfulness.

Under Genscher's leadership, the foreign policy of reunified Germany was beginning to make inroads against the superpowers and was squeezing out the other members of the European Community. This had been especially apparent with regard to the Yugoslavian crisis. There were also signs of a major rapprochement between the United States and Germany in connection with the new NATO strategy as formulated in a joint statement by James Baker and Genscher.

Gorbachev had been irritated by the fact that Genscher had made reconnaissance trips to Kiev and Alma-Ata without once passing through Moscow, if only to observe the formalities. These travels were the height of political insolence to a president in office, and Gorbachev, after the successful "resuscitation" of his presidential power, decided to make this clear to Genscher.

Since he considered himself the true father of Germany's reunification, Gorbachev felt that he had the right to expect Kohl and his minister to conduct themselves with due respect toward him and the interests of the country whose leader he still was. After all, in the final analysis it was because of his efforts that Kohl and Genscher would go down in German history.

The conversation between Gorbachev and Genscher, who knew each other well, began with a comment by Gorbachev. Although made in a playful tone, it was hardly innocent. "Lately the vice chancellor prefers to travel across the Union without stopping in Moscow. Are we going to have to send out interceptors in order to have the pleasure of his company here?"

As an experienced diplomat, Genscher immediately sensed the appropriate response to this Soviet president who had obviously regained his former assurance. He observed that the purpose of his trip across the country was "not just to listen, but to talk" and to make the republic leaders, who were distinguished above all by their lack of experience, "see reason." It followed that, in a certain sense, he was helping Gorbachev.

Gorbachev answered briefly, expressing the hope that "the vice chancellor's excellent judgment will never fail him." He thus gave Genscher to understand that he accepted his apology and considered the matter closed.

The two men moved on to the main items on their agenda. Gorbachev brought up matters relating to perestroika within the new framework of a single, unified state. He took the opportunity to complain about his political companions: "In the transitional stage where we are now, there is much confusion, many rash acts are being committed, and all kinds of petty special interests are being promoted. My colleagues are often prisoners—of separatism in some cases and populism in others. But we have to figure out how to get this huge mass of people to move forward." (In other words, the President had to figure this out for everyone.)

To dispel the doubts that Genscher must have accumulated during his trip, Gorbachev explained that work on the economic treaty was almost finished. Ukraine had considered whether to ratify the treaty, and after two days of "shouts, uproar, and din," the supreme soviet of the republic had approved it by a vote of 284 to 39. President Ayaz Mutalibov "vowed" that Azerbaidzhan would also sign.

On November 1, Yavlinsky would present all the annexes to the treaty to the prime ministers of the republics, who would discuss them and send the final draft to their respective parliaments for ratification. "In short, after studying the situation, all the republics, including Russia, are now coming to the conclusion that they cannot get out of the present crisis if they break ranks."

Less than forty-eight hours later, Yeltsin would deliver his scheduled address to the Russian parliament, in which he would throw down a challenge not only to the center, represented by Gorbachev, but also to the other republics of the USSR that had just signed the economic treaty.

Yeltsin's address was undoubtedly already written when Gorbachev was reassuring Genscher. But on that day, in his office in the Kremlin, the President radiated such confidence and optimism and demonstrated such irrefutable logic that he could hardly be contradicted. Genscher adopted the same tone. This enabled him to suppress a feeling of discomfort that he had been unable to shake off since the beginning of the conversation. "In Kiev," he said, "I persuaded them not to turn back. We in the European Community are trying to make one market out of twelve, and the same goes for our currencies."

Gorbachev returned to this subject with obvious pleasure. "I have studied your experience, and I use it in my arguments with Yeltsin and the other republic leaders when we discuss a unified budget, joint taxes, and so on. You know, many people here are in 'elementary school,' just emerging from political illiteracy."

According to Gorbachev, practical work on the draft Union Treaty would be the next lesson. "There will be a single, unified state," he explained to Genscher, "with a single market, a common system of defense, and a common foreign policy."

Genscher nodded and echoed: "I hope Yeltsin will tell that to his foreign minister."

"Certain republics," continued Gorbachev, "feel that even the current draft treaty lacks force. Nazarbaev, for example, is demanding that some points be strengthened. On November 11, the State Council will meet to examine each article."

Everything seemed clear to Gorbachev that day: The path was open for the reconstitution in Eastern Europe of a powerful and now democratic state, closely tied to the new Germany by preferential economic and political relations. It was time to talk about a global European strategy.

Genscher strove to dispel Gorbachev's fears concerning the supposed changes in the West's strategy by explaining that his government, with the Americans, was trying to determine how to strengthen political security in a Europe where NATO was the sole remaining military-political structure. These deliberations contained nothing that was anti–East European. "It is time to consider a common security zone from Vancouver to Vladivostok," Gorbachev insisted.

The German minister elaborated on a multilevel security concept that would involve NATO, the future defense policy of the European Community, and bilateral structures something like the German-French brigade, which "would be raised to the status of a corps."

Genscher felt that the most effective formula for Europe would be to have multinational troops. "This is an idea you should find equally attractive, in view of the number of countries that want to set up their own national armies," he said, looking at Gorbachev significantly. "Integration in the military sector has tremendous political importance," he went on. "We realize that the purpose of integrating Germany into NATO is to maintain control over the German troops. Well, this is no burden for us. The Europeanization of Germany is precisely what we are striving for."

Gorbachev nodded noncommittally: "We will look foward to the results of your meeting in Rome.[19] But the very fact that NATO has begun to yield looks reassuring to us." He then led Genscher back to a subject which seemed very important to him at the time. "In view of the highly complex processes unfolding in our country, some people in other countries are losing their self-control and are becoming agitated. There is an increasing temptation to call the Helsinki principles—which were confirmed by the Paris charter—into question. Some people think that European boundaries can be debated again. Once that happens, the line between intervention and nonintervention vanishes. All of this shows that even experienced Western politicians frequently lack patience and the ability to recognize the historic nature of the changes in the East. But weren't we all longing for these changes? Obviously, not everything matches up with our early predictions, but which of us was really in a position to make an accurate forecast at the beginning?"

Genscher fended off these polite but pointed reproaches, assuring Gorbachev that for Germany, the inviolability of borders was still "a key element of security in Europe." Any change in the existing borders would be a serious blow to stability in Europe. Moreover, this problem could be debated ad infinitum, since "everyone has his own map."

Gorbachev developed the subject further: "I am in favor of eliminating borders, but only through the process of integration, not by redrawing maps." And he warned Genscher emphatically: "If the West is hasty in recognizing the independence of the republics of the USSR, there will be problems. Many of the borders between republics have no basis in reality, having been established by resolutions of the soviets."

He cited the example of Ukraine, which was a particular concern of his. This republic had been expanded several times by the Moscow authorities: first, after the revolution, by incorporating the eastern regions and the Donbass "to give the Bolsheviks more votes," and then, in 1954, because of Khrushchev's decision to add to it the "historically Russian" Crimea. None of these conventional boundaries caused any problems as long as people lived in the same state. But what if they started partitioning the state?

Genscher interrupted this emotional tirade to remark gloomily that problems of this kind "used to be solved by dynastic marriages." But then, perhaps having sensed that there could hardly be any question of such a union between Yeltsin and Kravchuk, he concluded more tactfully: "It is of the utmost importance, Mr. President, that you personally guide the process of negotiating the Union Treaty through to its conclusion."

The two men parted company with the usual compliments, but their old cordiality was not in evidence as they shook hands. Each was too skilled a politician not to be pondering questions that he knew would go unanswered even if they were given voice. Gorbachev was silently asking Genscher: Have you already forgotten so much of what you owe me—you personally, Kohl, and Germany—that you're not ready to help me now, when I need help so much? And Genscher, to himself: Will I ever enter this man's office in the Kremlin again? Isn't it time to bid him farewell as president, and even as a politician?

Each had difficulty banishing these thoughts from his mind, and so in their leave-taking they were formal and distracted. Although Genscher could envision Gorbachev's departure from the political scene at that time, one wonders if it ever crossed his mind that his own days as the head of German diplomacy might be numbered and that he would resign a few months after this meeting. The fact that Gorbachev did, actually, change the world may be the reason men like Genscher did not survive him politically and found themselves forced off center stage. They were too closely identified with the old world of East-West rivalry.

After Genscher had left, Gorbachev commented maliciously to Chernyaev, "I think 'the Elephant' understood everything, as far as Ukraine and Yugoslavia are concerned. That's why he started trying to justify himself. All the same, it's strange for a politician of his caliber to behave so shabbily."

The meeting with Genscher took place on Saturday. The following Monday, Gorbachev had to fly to Madrid for the opening of the Conference on the Middle East. He was also scheduled to meet with the president of the Spanish government, Felipe González, and King Juan Carlos, two people with whom he had good rapport. U.S. president George Bush would also be present.

He spent Sunday preparing for the trip, taking a bulky file with him to his dacha. That same weekend, he received a message from French president François Mitterrand, who invited him to stop over at his private residence, Latche, in the south of France, on the way back. This was a special mark of favor on the part of Mitterrand, who did not like to admit outsiders to his private domain. The gesture confirmed to Gorbachev that all doubts as to his abilities had vanished and that he was no longer viewed as Yeltsin's Siamese twin.

After the trauma of the August coup, Gorbachev was being officially reinstated in the club of world leaders. He prepared himself for these meetings with confidence and calm. The difficult, eventful months were behind him. The ship of the Union was under sail again, and he, as its captain, could rightfully accept expressions of respect and admiration for having saved it from foundering.

On the day he was to leave, he was scheduled to make another appearance before the Supreme Soviet to answer questions from the representatives concerning the extraordinary budget. Parliament, always given to insubordination, was refusing to authorize new loans to the USSR State Bank (Gosbank), although the Soviet government had to have these loans in order to finish out the year. Before taking off for Madrid, Gorbachev was also to receive the president of Cyprus, Georges Vassiliou. Neither event was expected to take much time.

A look back at that day, Monday, October 28, is enough to make one superstitious. There were so many bizarre details to which no one paid any attention at the time but that loom large in retrospect. First, the meeting with Vassiliou took place in Gorbachev's sham office, used for television broadcasts. The Catherine Room was unavailable: A meeting of the Russian parliament was taking place in the Grand Palace of the Kremlin, and Boris Yeltsin was about to speak. The inconvenience of the situation irritated Gorbachev, reminding him that there were two masters in the Kremlin and that he had to make the best of it. The sham office was equipped with a large worktable and a battery of telephones that had never been connected. Other furniture had been brought in for the Vassiliou reception, but the protocol service hadn't had time to check everything, and in the midst of the talks one of the doors started to swing open with a sinister creaking. Since it could not be closed securely and the noise drowned out the voices of the interpreters, a guard had to hold onto it from the outside throughout the meeting.

As if that weren't enough, at one point Gorbachev made a sudden movement and one of the lenses fell out of his glasses. No one could find it, and Volsky, who was seated next to Gorbachev, had to go out—making the door creak again—and ask the guards to fetch Gorbachev's extra pair.

Despite these frustrating mishaps, the talks were cordial. Vassiliou had long wanted to express his personal admiration for Gorbachev. He was proud of the fact that he had given a clear-sighted political appraisal of the situation during the first few hours of the putsch and had even predicted its failure, since "Gorbachev has made irreversible changes in his country."

The President had the additional pleasure of learning that Foros, the place where his dacha was located and where he had been detained during the three days of the coup d'état, means "lighthouse" in Greek. This gave him the opportunity to comment, greatly à propos, that the Crimea had ties not only with Russia but also with Greece, and therefore with Cyprus.

Relatively little time was spent on this ritual exchange of courtesies, as both men had in mind the fact that Gorbachev would soon be leaving for Madrid. The President promised Vassiliou that he would address the problem of Cyprus during his talks with Bush. "The new deal in the Middle East is paving the way for resolution of the stalemate in Cyprus," he said.

Vassiliou, for his part, proposed that Cyprus participate in the modernization of the port of Novorossiisk and provide aid to small- and medium-sized businesses in the Krasnodar region. "As president and as an economist, I am prepared to supervise these projects personally," he offered.

On leaving this interview, the President passed through the reception room and noticed a television screen that showed Yeltsin giving his speech. He asked for the text to be brought to him on the plane. In an unexpected move, Yeltsin would proclaim that Russia would undertake radical economic reform alone and that he himself would take the reins of his government as prime minister. He would also announce that the center of the Union would soon cease to exist. But Gorbachev did not learn this until he was on board the airplane, well on his way to Spain.

One Last Mission
for the Union

The presidential airplane was one of the integral symbols of the power of the presidency, which had begun to accumulate after Gorbachev was elected. Such symbols were intended to lend a certain luster to the office of president by creating an official protocol distinct from that of the era when the Party had been all-powerful. Some of the symbolism was inspired by other countries, especially the United States. This was true, for example, of the national flag hanging behind Gorbachev's desk. It also applied to the presidential jet, whose name, *Sovetsky Soyuz* (Soviet Union) was as clearly identifiable as the American presidents' *Air Force One*.

Unfortunately, Gorbachev was sometimes more preoccupied with this kind of ceremony than with the real apparatus of power. He knew, however, that this symbolism could not replace real, tangible support. He was well aware of the importance of a viable administrative mechanism to ensure that decisions were carried out and to monitor their implementation, and to maintain two-way communication between society and the president.

Gorbachev naturally felt the need for a "conveyor belt" of this kind, especially since the omnipotent, well-regulated Party apparatus was no longer serving this function. He occasionally made efforts to create a structure that could replace it. The last of these attempts was the introduction of the office of vice president, which was entrusted to Gennady Yanaev.[20] Yanaev was to direct a monitoring chamber responsible for following up on the execution of presidential decrees.

Efforts of this kind were usually impulsive, and Gorbachev was probably subconsciously aware that they would not yield any tangible results. Moreover, their success required persistence, organization, and a systems-oriented bent of mind—characteristics that were foreign to his nature—and he therefore took every opportunity to slip away from this type of work. It bored him to leave the heights of his historic reform project to descend into "the prose of life."

It was much simpler and pleasanter for him to concern himself with the outer trappings of presidential power. His staff was, of course, constantly approaching him on these subjects, proposing that he discuss the arrangement of his office or work out the fine points of diplomatic protocol for welcoming and leave-taking ceremonies on the staircase of the Grand Kremlin Palace.

Gorbachev's democratic nature did put up some resistance to this type of concern. During a visit to New York two years earlier, he had responded sharply to a Russian expatriate painter's offer to do his portrait: "If we get caught up in portraits and decorations, that will be the end of perestroika." But he was completely surrounded by staff, and they, observing the pomp of time-honored presidential welcoming ceremonies in other countries, persuaded him that the authority of those in power depended on protocol—especially in Russia. And he gave in, with some internal struggle, but also with a certain concealed pleasure.

It is significant that Yeltsin, who actively lobbied against the trappings of Gorbachev's "royalty" under the banner of democracy, nevertheless went farther and faster in this direction than his predecessor and began immediately to use the symbolism of ceremony to declare his power: The red flag was hastily torn from the cupola of the Kremlin, as if it were the Reichstag, and replaced with the tricolor; the plaque bearing Gorbachev's name was removed from his Kremlin office in the wee hours of the morning; the presidential guard expanded beyond the number of "escorts" that used to accompany Gorbachev on trips abroad; Yeltsin requested, on his visit to Paris, that he stay at the Palace of Versailles rather than the more modest Palace of Marigny. For Yeltsin, these were not merely symbols of victory but the very goals of the struggle, the chief trophies of his crusade against Gorbachev. In this atmosphere of intensified revenge, where protocol was a weapon, the presidential jet was immediately repainted in the tricolor and rechristened the *Rossiya*—indolent, dormant, eternal Russia, which accorded so ill with the outer appearance of the machine.

On October 28, 1991, however, the aircraft still bore a red flag on its tail and was still called the *Sovetsky Soyuz*.[21] The group of advisers and VIPs who were to accompany Gorbachev on his trip congregated in the presidential salon. Among them, the President was particularly occupied with his guest "from the Russian side," Vladimir Lukin, then chairman of the parliamentary commission on foreign affairs (later the Russian ambassador to Washington), and Yegor Yakovlev, the new director of state television, with whom he had made peace.

The atmosphere on board was animated. Fresh from the trenches in the war for a unified state, we saw the problems of the Middle East as little more than an obstacle course. What mattered most to Gorbachev was that he would soon be seeing Felipe González, whose spirit and world view were so close to his own, and, of course, "dear George," with whom he could discuss world affairs as they had in the good old days.

Gorbachev obviously wanted to transform his conversation with Bush, which was to take place on the fringes of the Madrid conference, into a major political event comparable to the unforgettable Malta summit—especially since he was to act as host again. During the Mediterranean summit meeting, in December 1989, a storm had forced Bush to leave his ship, the cruiser *Belknap*, and take refuge on board the Soviet steamer *Maxim Gorky*, anchored in the port of La Valletta.

It was on that occasion that the ice between the two leaders began to melt. Since his inauguration in January of that year, Bush had not seemed to place a great deal of trust in Gorbachev. But on the *Maxim Gorky*, with the storm raging outside, he became much more cordial. Perhaps it was because he had a certain attachment to the setting, having been a U.S. military pilot during World War II. Perhaps, too, he was grateful to Gorbachev for saving the summit by having anchored the *Maxim Gorky* to terra firma. At one point, Bush took out a photograph of his family and showed it to Gorbachev, commenting that everyone close to him was praying for Gorbachev and for the success of his reform policy. Later on, after the joint press conference that concluded the summit and just before stepping back onto dry land, Bush had his advisers join him in his cabin on the *Maxim Gorky* for a brief celebration of the successful meeting. Since their supplies had been left on the *Belknap*, he asked the Soviets to come to his aid once again. So it was that the U.S. president and his advisers drank their toast with a bottle of Georgian wine that had not been tested by the U.S. Secret Service.

In Madrid, the two presidents agreed that the meeting should take place at the Soviet embassy. This imposing building was more appropriate for a summit meeting than the U.S. diplomatic facilities. The "Moorish style" of the embassy building, as conceived of by its architect, artist Ilya Glazunov, was combined with frescoes in the Russian manner, painted by Glazunov (the image of Christ juxtaposed with a portrait of Lenin).

As was his habit, Gorbachev decided to work out the points he wanted to cover in this conversation ahead of time, on the plane. One of the main topics would be the reciprocal steps that the two sides would take toward the achievement of nuclear disarmament. Gorbachev, who had finally gotten the Americans' reaction to his romantic program of progress toward a nuclear-free world, clearly did not want to let the United States regain the initiative, nor did he want to see the disarmament issue turned into a diplomatic ping-pong game. He felt that we needed a joint disarmament strategy that would combine the process of disarmament with the preservation of global stability.

In the course of our discussion he suggested that we relay a memorandum to the Americans, in response to their latest proposals, outlining the steps the Soviet Union was prepared to take in reciprocation. Despite the lateness of the hour, he immediately telephoned the chief of the general staff from the plane to ask him for the necessary data. Some of the people he spoke to tried to get him to discuss the speech that Yeltsin had just made, but Gorbachev brushed their attempts aside—he had yet to read the speech through.

Nevertheless, the next day in Madrid when Gorbachev had assembled his closest advisers in the office of Ambassador Sergei Romanovsky, he began the meeting by commenting on Yeltsin's speech. It was apparent that he had read it over several times and wanted to make his assessment of it aloud, as usual. "This speech can be interpreted in various ways. On the one hand, you can see in it the desire to finally get economic reform moving. I can't refuse to support that [he seemed to say this in a questioning tone], since it's precisely what we are proposing all the time. Besides, people are tired of always waiting for real change. It's too bad, however, that all of this has been announced on a partisan basis without being coordinated with other republics. Even Russia can't bring about reform by itself. And as for the other republics, it's a real catastrophe for them."

He turned Yeltsin's address over and back again as if examining a coin. "Heads" was the economic side. On the whole, this aspect served his own purposes: first, because it matched his and Yeltsin's joint approach as they had defined it after the putsch; second, and more important, because Yeltsin was prepared to assume sole responsibility for implementing this reform package, heavy with shocks to the country's economy, thus taking Gorbachev out of the line of fire.

He was even willing to praise Yeltsin, out of gratitude: "The main thing is that he had the courage to speed up reforms." He realized that this had been a difficult and even traumatic decision for Yeltsin, who had built his entire career on his capacity for opposition and his talent for telling people what they wanted to hear. But now that he had the power, he had to take on the responsibilities. "It wasn't easy for him to reach this decision, and it's significant that he managed to do it."

A hint of envy could be detected behind Gorbachev's words. Was it for Yeltsin's ability to make decisions of which he himself was incapable? Or was it due to the obvious popularity of this "teflon-coated" leader, whom society allowed to take liberties of a kind that it would neither permit nor excuse in Gorbachev?

However, there was also the "tails" side of the speech, dangerous, although poorly articulated—the prospect of a break with the proposed union. Yeltsin merely alluded to it, saying that Russia would be the last to withdraw its support. Given the benefit of the doubt, this could be interpreted as confirmation of the concept of a unified state on which he and Gorbachev had agreed.

Of course, the speech could just as easily be read differently: The Russian leadership might be hoping to use the attitudes of the other republics as an excuse for renouncing the new union. Weren't the Russians pushing these republics into taking a more decisive position on the matter? If this were true, the signal was obviously intended primarily for Ukraine. In any event, it was picked up there immediately.

Gorbachev sensed this change in tone. He even tried to reason in Yeltsin's stead, as if hoping to banish the specter of this new threat. "Isn't it clear, after all, that Russia is the very republic that needs a new union? That is the only legitimate form that would enable it to assume a leadership role among the republics. The republics will never accept direct domination by Russia. That's why they are in favor of a union."

He saw very clearly that if the line of reasoning that could be made out in this speech resulted in Russia's isolation in independent statehood in order to crush the central government, this chain of events would have distressing consequences for Russia itself later on. But he could not believe, initially, that Yeltsin and his advisers were ready to pay such a high price just to eliminate the president of the Union. "No! He said in his speech that he would remain in favor of a union!"

Once again, he was trying to persuade himself that "everything would work out," that Yeltsin, after taking on the deadly risk of forcing the transition to a market economy, would leave Gorbachev in a position to enjoy the political dividends of a critical observer; that Boris Nikolaevich was reasonable and that you could still do business with him—all the while trying to forget that Yeltsin had already hoisted his own flag over the Kremlin and that he was counting the days until he would be the only leader there.

The start of the meeting with Bush was cordial and, in keeping with the ritual of American public relations, noisy. As the flashbulbs went off, the presidents smiled brightly and called out greetings to acquaintances on the other side. The dinner began. This was the first time Bush had seen Gorbachev since the failure of the putsch, and he asked him when the plotters would go to trial. Bush said that he was shocked by the treachery of Gorbachev's inner circle. Gorbachev explained their behavior by the fact that the changes in the USSR were having such a profound effect on people's basic interests that even personal friendship and ties of long standing faded into the background. "Lukyanov and I had been friends since our college years." To relax the atmosphere, he ended jokingly, with a nod in Scowcroft's direction, "You'd better keep a close eye on your generals, too!"

"If Scowcroft really wanted my office I'd gladly give it to him," Bush replied, catching the ball on the bounce.

"Not I," Gorbachev said in a serious tone. "Especially at such a difficult time. The country is ripe for radical changes. It even demands them." One could sense the specter of Boris Yeltsin looming behind him.

The Americans listened politely to Gorbachev's thoughts on the new stage of reforms and then moved on to what interested them: the control of Soviet nuclear weapons. They were especially worried by Leonid Kravchuk's ambiguous statements. Did the Ukrainians realize the importance of reducing the number of their nuclear weapons and safeguarding them?

Gorbachev made every effort to allay their fears: The press was exaggerating and distorting things a great deal. One shouldn't ascribe too much importance to the noise being made by the Ukrainian parliament. They were in the midst of an election campaign, when politicians tend to engage in verbal one-upmanship. "We'll have to be patient until December 1."

Another specter, that of future president Kravchuk, would have smirked with satisfaction at this point if it had been in the room. Apparently Gorbachev was mistaking his long-term strategy for clever election tactics.

True, Gorbachev could not have acted otherwise: He had to show his American counterpart that he was in complete control of the situation. He therefore spoke as the commander in chief of the armed forces: "The draft Union Treaty provides for a united armed forces of the union. There will be a unified command in which the republics will be represented, but there is absolutely no question of nationalizing the troops or of dispersing them to national quarters."

The caustic James Baker was not pacified. He was troubled by the Ukrainians' announcement of plans to create their own army of 450,000 and by the Russian authorities' allusions to the possibility of using nuclear weapons during conflicts between the two republics. Gorbachev swept aside these "irresponsible" statements: "Everything is under control now. You can all rest easy. Unified armed forces—that is our joint position, Yeltsin's and mine, as established in the draft treaty."

This conversation on the future of the army gave him the dramatic opening to put to the Americans the question that concerned him most—that of aid. "You see how complex it all is. We are in the midst of creating another state. We have not forgotten our responsibilities, and we are ready to coordinate the most important points with you, our closest partners. But we also are counting on your understanding of the exceptional nature of our situation, and on your extraordinary support. Now, all we hear from the West in reply is excuses, or references to our troubled domestic situation and to the problematic relationships between your own governments and parliaments. Don't you see that we are dealing with changes of historic scope here?"

Gorbachev ended this passionate appeal with a familiar parable. A passerby sees people working at a construction site. "What are you doing?" he asks. "Breaking our backs carrying blocks of stone," says one of them. But another replies, "Don't you see that we're building a temple?"

In this moving parable based on the building of the cathedral at Chartres, unexpected and a bit out of place in the pragmatic atmosphere of the diplomatic dinner table, one could hear echoes of the bitterness and solitude of this man whose partners had never fully understood or supported him.

Of course, the West had long since missed its chance to aid its sole potential ally in building the temple of a new, more predictable, more secure world order. During all the years when Gorbachev had made it clear that he was waging a domestic war and not a war against the West, the West still hesitated to serve as a base of support and to give him the material arguments he needed in order to win this nearly hopeless battle against horror and oppression in Russia's present and past.

As Gorbachev burned his bridges one after the other, blocking off any possibility of retreat for the people of the Soviet Union and hence for himself, as he made concession after concession to the West without a thought for the prestige of what had once been a superpower, hoisting the white flag of surrender in the Cold War, the Western leaders continued to mistrust, to hesitate, and to quibble about the price. They patted him on the shoulder as a sign of encouragement and goodwill and urged him to provide additional "proofs"—here, of loyalty to democracy; there, of devotion to the idea of a free market.

During this entire time the West made almost no perceptible effort to meet Gorbachev halfway, either in the realm of foreign policy or in that of economic aid. It gave him nothing he could use to show his people that democracy, a free market, pluralism, and the new foreign policy were justified and could change their daily lives for the better. From the high ground of its eternal safety and well-being, the West sympathetically watched a brave man who had taken on himself the risk of swimming across the river separating the two worlds and did not hasten to throw him a life preserver even when it became obvious that the strong current could carry him away.

In Madrid, Gorbachev intended to wring everything he could out of the opportunity—which he realized could be his last in an official capacity—for direct contact with the leaders of the Western world. He believed that it was necessary to appeal not to their generosity, but to their realism and their sound political sense, "because what is going to happen with the Union will have consequences for all of world history." He believed that it was not too late.

In his conversations with Bush, González, King Juan Carlos, and, subsequently, Mitterrand, Gorbachev wasted no time on protocol and diplomatic niceties. He went straight to the heart of the matter, asking the very questions about which they and their advisers had been racking their brains: Does the Soviet Union still exist? Whom does Gorbachev represent? And he tried to explain to them that the only way he could provide satisfactory answers was with their help.

Even when the discussion turned to other countries, to Cyprus and Yugoslavia, as it did in his talks with Bush, this theme still predominated. "Some people think that Yugoslavia no longer exists," said Gorbachev (and everyone realized what country he was really referring to). "Those who have hastened to encourage the separatists have done an ill service to peace in Europe."

Bush's analysis of this problem was in agreement with Gorbachev's. He also felt that Germany had moved too quickly. He reminded Gorbachev that the United States had tried to hold back the process of recognizing the independence of the republics; but Gorbachev was not to be placated. "In the final analysis, there's more at stake here than Yugoslavia. How can we pursue a united Europe if we are not able to solve such problems?"

And he returned to the disintegrating Soviet Union: "The central problem today is that of the state. If we do not manage to solve it, we will hit a brick wall."

As one example of inexcusable negligence that was likely to have costly, unforeseen consequences, he cited the statement that Yeltsin's spokesperson, Pavel Voshchanov, had just made concerning the possibility of reexamining the borders between Russia and Ukraine. "This really whipped up separatist sentiment in Kiev. People started talking about Russia's imperialist claims all over again. It is hardly surprising, under the circumstances, that President Nazarbaev of Kazakhstan has also spoken out against any territorial claims."

As Gorbachev discussed these subjects, it seemed that he still saw such "slips of the tongue" as the result of the incompetence or irresponsibility of the Russian leadership, of its populist origins and "pressure that certain people are exerting on certain people" (here he had Yeltsin's "evil genius," Burbulis, in mind), rather than as evidence of a willful and conscious intention to destroy the unified state. He could not quite believe that the power-hungry Russian neobureaucrats were willing to reawaken the volcano of ethnic nationalism in the republics in order to achieve their ends, especially when that would mean certain tragedy for Russia itself.

Gorbachev knew, of course, that some of the members of Yeltsin's inner circle were ready to go to such lengths. Moreover, against his better judgment, Gorbachev himself more than once quoted directly from the notorious memorandum by Burbulis, which had fallen into his hands, regarding Russia's need to throw off the burden of the proposed union and proceed on its own, appropriating the mantle of sole successor to the USSR. At the same time, his repeated discussions with Yeltsin had left him with the impression that the Russian president understood the extent of the dangers linked to this course of action. "It would cause tremendous difficulties for Russia and some years of great turmoil," Gorbachev told Bush.

Bush did not dispute this prognosis. He stated clearly that Washington preferred to see a central government maintained under Gorbachev's leadership. As proof of his sincerity, Bush justifiably alluded to his openly "pro-Moscow" speech during his visit to Kiev on August 1, in which he condemned the signs of heedless nationalism.

Nor did Bush show much enthusiasm for the prospect of having closer dealings with Yeltsin. One felt that despite the attempts he had made since August to elevate their relations to the same level of mutual trust that characterized his ties with Gorbachev after Malta, it wasn't working. Yeltsin's unpredictable behavior left the Americans baffled. They were not certain that the showy domestic policy measures that Yeltsin was energetically implementing had been carefully weighed or thought through. His improvisations in foreign policy caused them more embarrassment than amusement—even the "wholehearted" grand gestures designed to win them over, such as the proclamation that Russia was an "ally" of the United States and the announcement that Russian strategic missiles would no longer be aimed at American targets (without any mention of what they *would* be aimed at from now on).

Bush made no secret of his astonishment at Yeltsin's latest speech. He said that he had spoken with Yeltsin on the phone the night before the speech, and Yeltsin had not even mentioned the major points of his upcoming address, which was to elicit conflicting interpretations in the West.

"All of this raises the question of the solvency of the future Soviet Union," he told Gorbachev frankly. He indicated that his administration and the U.S. Congress would not grant the Union more substantial material aid until the relationship between the "center" and the republics, as well as that between Gorbachev and Yeltsin, was clarified.

Bush also made reference to public opinion, which he could not ignore on the eve of the election campaign, and to the experts, who, of course, had nothing comforting to say about Soviet solvency. Nevertheless, the principal conditions for increasing U.S. aid, which he laid out bluntly for Gorbachev, were to define the status of the "center" clearly and to get its legitimacy confirmed by the republics—especially Russia—which were contesting this legitimacy with increasing vehemence.

Gorbachev tried to explain that in the present difficult situation, aid itself could be an important factor for domestic consolidation and would be precisely what was needed to help solve the problems about which the Bush administration was concerned. However, all his efforts met with polite skepticism. The Americans probably thought that Gorbachev would try to use the fact of foreign aid to the central government as an argument to sway public opinion back home against the boyars in the republics and toward his own political agenda.

Probably in order to sweeten this bitter pill, after the meeting was over James Baker told Boris Pankin in a whisper to accept, "for the time being," the $1.5 billion in food credits proposed by the Americans instead of the $3.5 billion that had been requested. "Later on, we'll see," he said.

After the talks the two presidents went down to meet the press, which was weary with impatience. They tried to give the impression that Soviet-American relations had come out of the shaky postcoup period stronger than ever, but they did so more by their manner than by their answers to the journalists' questions. Bush played his part so conscientiously that the press, which had expected to hear

him refer to the absent Yeltsin, was disappointed and came to the unanimous conclusion that Bush was choosing Gorbachev and turning his back on Yeltsin.

One of the first questions posed by the Soviet journalists, however, reminded
Gorbachev that a significantly greater uncertainty as to his own future and that of
the USSR awaited him at home. "Mr. President, who is taking your place in
Moscow during your absence?" Gorbachev met the challenge implicit in the question. "No one is taking my place," he answered brusquely.

❀   ❀   ❀

That same evening, the frescoes of Ilya Glazunov, known for his advocacy of
Russian nationalism, looked down on a rather unusual guest for a Soviet embassy—Israeli prime minister Itzhak Shamir. His meeting with the president of
the USSR was, in its way, a far more significant political event than the bitter-
sweet conversation with Bush. It was the culmination of a long and delicate
process of rapprochement in Soviet–Middle East relations.

In this area of foreign policy the USSR had traditionally aligned itself exclu-
sively with the most radical Arab regimes and the Palestinian leaders who opposed
Israel and the United States. This shortsighted and damaging policy could not really be characterized as pro-Arab, since it was actually only one element in a global
anti-American strategy. In the minds of the previous Soviet leadership and Andrei
Gromyko, its inflexible chief of diplomacy, it was designed to illustrate the great-
ness of the USSR as the second world superpower. Still, the traditional policy was
unquestionably anti-Israeli, drawing on the powerful support of traditional anti-
Semitism in the USSR, which was cultivated by the *nomenklatura* in positions of
leadership. For broad strata of the population this sentiment was fed, paradoxically, by a certain envy of Soviet Jews: They were discriminated against, certainly;
but the other side of the coin was that they had the privilege of emigrating.

For all these reasons, it was probably even harder for Gorbachev to alter the
Soviet position and to reestablish diplomatic relations with Israel than it had been
for him to gain acceptance for German reunification. Even in this matter, however, encrusted as it was with social prejudices and age-old Russian anti-
Semitism, Gorbachev managed, in the six years history allotted him, to pay off
one of the last political and moral debts inherited from his predecessors.

The top dignitaries of Israeli diplomacy who accompanied Shamir, in their
black yarmulkes, wore a solemn but expectant air: One of the bitterest conflicts of
the postwar period was coming to an end right before their eyes. Shamir himself
made it clear that meeting Gorbachev in Madrid was almost more important to
him than being present at the opening of the Middle East Conference.

Gorbachev was cordial, and, as was usual for him, decided to be the first to break the ice on this "historic occasion." "I have always been in favor of contact between our peoples, and I have taken every means open to me to encourage travel to Israel. I remember that on his return from Tel Aviv, one of the members of the Presidential Council, Chingiz Aitmatov, told me that you could hear Russian spoken everywhere, even more than in some of our republics." He confirmed to Shamir that the question of the appointment of the Soviet ambassador to Israel would be settled over the next few days. (It would be Alexander Bovin, the commentator for *Izvestiya*.)

In discussing Soviet domestic policy, he complained about the tremendous number of problems: "Everything is all jumbled up." Fervent partisans of the ancien régime were suddenly beginning to look like the radical opposition. It wasn't easy to build democratic structures under these conditions, with all this populist rhetoric and irresponsibility. He saw some hope, he said, that the populist phase might be coming to an end; still, he reminded Shamir, the transition from opposition to responsibility has never been easy for anyone.

Shamir, looking for meaningful words to offer, began by expressing his gratitude to Gorbachev. "Our people have a long memory, and they know how to remember those who have done well by them. We recognize that it's through your good offices that laws have been adopted that guarantee the right to leave the country to anyone who wants to do so, and we are grateful to you for this."

Gorbachev explained that after the failure of the putsch, many people who had wanted to leave the USSR decided to stay there. "In general, there have been many positive changes. Today in Moscow there are twenty-two schools where the Jewish religion and culture are studied."

Responding to Shamir's thanks for his condemnation of anti-Semitism, he commented, "I have often been asked to take a definite stand on this matter, and I have always emphasized that I am against anti-Semitism, as I am against all manifestations of nationalism and chauvinism. The special character of the age we live in also must be taken into account: Decades of totalitarian rule have brought suffering to all peoples. Whole nations have been exiled, repressed, declared criminal. The Russians, too, have suffered much." However, he felt that on the whole, his society was not susceptible to infection by nationalism. "Even now, with the social tensions that we have, the temptation to look for scapegoats, we are not seeing any rise in anti-Semitism."

Gorbachev apparently wanted to preserve his official image: that of a self-assured, well-informed leader in control of the situation. This posture, which was one of the conventions of diplomacy, was not only natural for him, it was the only one he could assume under the circumstances. But in listening to himself—in being his own best listener—he persuaded himself more than he did other people. His real problem was not that he casually and calmly swept aside real, pressing issues during diplomatic talks but that he did the same thing in his internal dialogues with himself.

Having discussed Soviet-Israeli relations, the two leaders turned to the Middle East. "It's important that people have a chance to talk to each other!" For Shamir, this was the main reason for organizing the Madrid conference. With his characteristic insistence, gesticulating with his hands, Shamir strove to obtain Gorbachev's agreement for halting the delivery of Soviet weapons to the Arab countries. He also sought the President's support for his plan for subsequent negotiations with the Arabs: Israel wanted these negotiations to be held on a bilateral basis in the countries of the region.

Gorbachev heard out this impassioned speech, and his answer bespoke his training as a jurist: "As the Romans used to say, *auditur altera pars*"[loosely, "Both sides must be heard"]. He expressed the hope that Shamir's address the next day would start the conference off on a constructive note.

With that, the historic meeting came to an end. Shamir invited Gorbachev to Israel, and this offer, which would have been unthinkable a few years before, was graciously accepted. The journalists who had assembled in the vestibule of the Soviet embassy surrounded Shamir and spent twenty minutes extracting all the details of this conversation from him. It made headlines all over the world.

In the meantime, Gorbachev left to have dinner with King Juan Carlos, George Bush, and Felipe González. The ladies were not invited; this was to be a "men only" meeting.

And it turned out to be a real workout. The main subject, naturally, was the future of the Soviet Union. Gorbachev, as usual, tried to allay the other leaders' concerns: Yes, the struggle for a union was still going on; it was difficult, but there was every reason to expect that it would be successful; we understood our responsibility to see to it that this new unified state would play a constructive role in the world and become a powerful positive factor in the international arena.

But these general assurances were not enough. Juan Carlos, Bush, and González made no secret of their anxiety about what was happening behind Gorbachev's back and wanted to make sure that he thoroughly understood the threat to international order posed by a random, uncontrolled breakup of the community of peoples and states assembled in the USSR. This union, the "eastern rim," as González put it, was a center of influence and a factor in the maintenance of global equilibrium. "If this rim crumbles, it will leave a dangerous vacuum for Europe and the world."

Gorbachev responded with increasing determination, as though the concerns voiced by his counterparts fueled his resolve: "I am going to fight steadfastly to preserve full powers for the union. Our partners in other countries need this union as much as we do, since chaos and instability in a country as vast as our own would create a threat for everyone. I am going to do everything in my power to preserve the union, a renewed union, with greater rights of sovereignty for the republics and, at the same time, with a strong center to serve the unified economic space and to provide a coordinated foreign policy and a joint system of defense via combined armed forces. This union would keep everything intact that cannot be broken up: energy, transportation, communications, ecology."

But the men seated at the table with Gorbachev were political professionals who understood that statements of intent were scarcely sufficient. He was assailed with questions: "What are the real chances that you can carry out your plans? What are we to make of Ukraine's actions? How should Yeltsin's latest speech be interpreted?"

Gorbachev repeated the formula he had rehearsed on the airplane: Yeltsin's speech had been ambiguous, and it could be broken down into two separate parts. The economic program must be supported despite its libertarianism and the lack of any mechanisms for putting it into effect. Yeltsin was taking on the responsibility for painful, radical measures that could not be avoided. As for the political part of the address, it contained too many elements that were ambiguous and that appeared to deviate from the two presidents' preceding agreements on the design of the future unified state as established in the draft Union Treaty they had worked out together.

The foreign leaders were not put at ease. "How should we interpret the call to reduce the Ministry of Foreign Affairs of the Union to one-tenth its present size? Can you trust a man who promises one thing one day, and the next day says and does just the opposite?" And finally, the main question: "Doesn't he intend to clip your wings?"

Without much conviction, and thus with no hope of being convincing, Gorbachev defended the man to whom he had become chained by the force of events. He said that it was possible to find a common language with Yeltsin, that you could work with him. He explained the "surprises" that Yeltsin had sprung on him as owing to the influence of his entourage, which virtually had him in "tutelage." "Sometimes you work, you come to an agreement, and then you have to start all over again. That's the way things are." But at the same time, Gorbachev seemed to believe sincerely that it would have been a mistake to head into a direct confrontation with Yeltsin. This attitude was based less on the realization of his own weakness and his dependence on the Russian president, whose power seemed to be indisputable, than on the conviction that another conflict, a "divorce" of the two leaders, would have disastrous consequences for what, in the final analysis, was their common cause.

I am convinced that another factor was involved in the ambiguous relations between these two men. Gorbachev was loyal in friendship, and, in addition, he did not like to be in anyone's debt. For a long time, he must have felt guilty for having treated Yeltsin too harshly when Yeltsin was dropped from the Politburo and ousted from office as first secretary for the city of Moscow.[22] After the putsch this feeling was compounded with gratitude: Yeltsin had saved democracy and protected the institution of the presidency. These factors undoubtedly accounted for Gorbachev's "loyalty" and moderation toward Yeltsin. He felt that any rupture between them should not be caused by him.

This character trait of Gorbachev's had caused problems for him on other occasions. His relationship to the future putschists was mentioned earlier, but also before the putsch, he maintained personal relations with some members of his staff that could have hurt him politically. This was especially true with respect to Yegor Ligachev and Ivan Polozkov.[23] He had serious problems trying to break with these conservative hard-liners, who had helped him in various ways during his career. In addition, his approach to politics incorporated a desire to maintain ties in all camps, enabling him to "keep several irons in the fire." However, this desire to remain in the middle, and to keep his equilibrium even in the midst of disequilibrium, ultimately placed him in a vulnerable position.

This may still have been the case, to some extent, that evening with President Bush and the two Spanish leaders. "Tell, me, George," he asked Bush, "you were vice president for eight years, and this is the third year of your presidency. We have known each other all this time. Has there ever been a single occasion when I did not keep my word to you?" "No, never," Bush replied without hesitation. "Well," Gorbachev said, shaking his head, "I often find myself faced with the opposite phenomenon in my relationships with the leaders of the republics. Such are the times we live in."

The conversation moved on to the situation in the republics, the upcoming elections in Ukraine, the prevailing moods in the Crimea, the issue of national boundaries. Gorbachev stressed the immaturity of the politicians carried into leadership positions on the wave of perestroika. This immaturity explained a great deal: The former pillars of the regime were competing against each other to destroy what remained of the center—even though the old totalitarian center had long since passed away. He told a joke about a resistance fighter who was still blowing up trains in Belorussia twenty-five years after the war. Nobody had told him it was over.

In mentioning Belorussia, Gorbachev had no intention of criticizing Stanislau Shushkevich, the new president of the supreme soviet in Minsk. The complexity of Gorbachev's relations with Yeltsin and Kravchuk made the Belorussian leader look stable and predictable by contrast. He had assumed the leadership of the

Belorussian parliament as a replacement for Nikolai Dementei, who had compromised himself with the perpetrators of the coup. Shushkevich, a university professor and doctor of physics and mathematics, was no ordinary politician. In September he had won a decisive victory by recommending support for the new union, on Gorbachev's advice. For Gorbachev this was gratifying proof that the preservation of a unified state had the support of most voters at the grassroots level.

"But all the same," the other leaders kept asking him that evening in Madrid, "Do you think you will be able to win your fight for a union?"

He wanted so much to be able to reassure them! But he also realized that they were not waiting for him to provide soothing words but rather determined and productive action. "It will be difficult. The struggle will be hard, but I am going to work with each individual separately and all of them together. And if I see that the opposing idea is winning out, I will say so honestly and will not remain in the presidency." This was said sincerely and with conviction. And since this time he was making a promise he could keep, without any guarantees of success, he was believed.

"I have an awful year ahead of me, the election year," Bush commented as they were saying good-bye. "And yet, Mikhail, my problems don't even begin to compare with the gigantic task that you are accomplishing. It's a riveting drama. We're all following it with bated breath, and we wish you success." Fortified by these good wishes, Gorbachev left the court of the king of Spain and returned to what was still, for the time being, a Soviet embassy.

The Middle East Conference opened the next day, October 30, in the impressive setting of the Palacio Real in Madrid. The Great Hall of Columns had taken on an atmosphere of hushed excitement in keeping with the unique character of the event. The journalists, who were crowded onto a specially built dais, had more photo opportunities than they could handle: the Israelis and the Arabs seated at the same table, the two cochairmen of the conference, symbolizing the historic reconciliation of two opposite political worlds—ample front-page material.

To the great pleasure of those present, the overworked Spanish protocol service muffed the order of ceremony and brought Bush and Gorbachev out onto the "stage" twice before finally seating them on the more expansive presidential dais. The two presidents' experts and advisers were seated together in alternate order, forming the conference's second joint delegation, the Jordanians and the Palestinians being the first.

Finally, when everyone had found a seat, Soviet foreign minister Boris Pankin proclaimed the session open. Felipe González, as host, greeted the participants and the world at large and expressed the hope that this historic opportunity would not be lost.

Gorbachev and Bush then gave their addresses. Gorbachev spoke about the new political thinking and the difficulties of perestroika. Bush gave a lengthy exhortation to the conference participants. (The night before, during dinner with the king, Bush had warned Gorbachev that his speech would be boring and had asked him not to fall asleep. Gorbachev didn't nod off, but Shamir did.)

With the session now open, the two presidents left the hall with evident relief, leaving the delegates under the supervision of their respective ministers of foreign affairs. They parted company on the staircase of the Palacio Real: Bush had to catch a plane, and Gorbachev was going on to meet with González. In the haste of their leave-taking, it cannot have occurred to any of them that this was the last handshake between the leaders of the two superpowers and that this day, according to the prophecy of the American scholar Francis Fukuyama, would mark "the end of history."

The world at large and the participants in this historic apotheosis were not to discover the reality of the situation until later. At that point Gorbachev, in buoyant spirits, was on his way to meet the man with whom, as he himself said, he could speak more openly than with anyone else, anywhere, including at home in the USSR. He didn't just appreciate "Felipe," he loved him. I once asked him which politician he was closest to, and he answered, without hesitation, González. He immediately added that he had friendly as well as professional relationships with others, too: Bush, Kohl, Mitterrand, Thatcher, and more recently, Major; but "especially with González."

He liked everything about the president of the Spanish government: his temperament, his openness, his youth; his penchant for abstract, philosophical thinking. And especially his attachment to socialism, which provided further support for the Gorbachevian "socialist choice."[24]

Their conversations usually lasted for hours. González was the only person who could tell Gorbachev what nobody else dared to say to him: that in his opinion, Gorbachev did not realize how close he was to the end of his political career. But González seemed to believe that all he had to do was fan the flames of "Mikhail's" political will, determination, courage, and spirit of resistance—of his machismo, in other words—in order to put things to rights in the Union. His thinking was sound, logical, European. He had no way of knowing that looming behind Gorbachev was another, irrational reality, that of a country in turmoil, a populace enraged, and politicians devoid of scruples.

It was impossible, and useless, to try to explain it to him. Gorbachev simply tried once again to send a message to the Western leaders through González: They would make a "strategic error" if they continued to watch the disintegration and ruin of the Soviet Union without trying to come to his aid. But even González could offer him no reassurances on this score. "You realize, of course, that it's not up to me. I'm ready to back you all the way, regardless of the political costs. But Bush cannot allow himself to do this—what if he has to deal with Yeltsin and Kravchuk in the future? You'll have to solve this problem yourself."

González told his friend how, during the first few hours of the coup d'état in August, by common agreement with the king and despite the hesitations of his own advisers, he had worked out a position of firm condemnation of the new government. He had called Bush, asking him to demand that the putschists allow telephone communication with Gorbachev. "Above all, don't refer to Gorbachev in the past tense!" he had insisted to Bush.

"Now, Mikhail, it's all up to you," González concluded. "Our attitude toward a reality as vast as the Soviet Union cannot rest on faith in a single person. The only way to restore the confidence that was shaken in August is by real political progress. The West must be sure that it is dealing not just with a certain Mikhail Gorbachev but with the president of the Union, invested with full constitutional powers."

Of this Gorbachev was already convinced, but there was no one who could help him to achieve it. "Felipe, I promise you that I will die with my boots on in the battle for the union."

He was well aware that failure of the Novo-Ogarevo process would open up a direct path to chaos and dictatorship. Moreover, the disintegration of the Union would mean a new arms race, this time between the republics, which would paralyze international disarmament. If Ukraine and then Russia decided that they needed their own armies, who would explain to Kohl and Mitterrand that this was no concern of theirs? González agreed: Economic problems notwithstanding, governments can always find enough money to make weapons. "Mikhail, we cannot allow peace to depend on whether or not you have a heart attack!" Only someone who was himself suffering deeply could have said such a thing to Gorbachev.

It was time to end the conversation; the press was waiting outside. In meeting the journalists, Mikhail and Felipe expressed their confidence in future Soviet-Spanish relations and in the Middle East peace process.

❀　　❀　　❀

On the return trip to Moscow Gorbachev stopped at Latche, the private residence of François Mitterrand, located not far from the Spanish border near Bayonne.

The French president was obviously proud of his austere, secluded country retreat. The possibility of escaping, however briefly, from the tensions of modern civilization, of leaving the Élysée, his official residence in Paris, to immerse himself in the unspoiled beauty of southwestern France, enabled this refined intellectual to reestablish contact with his country's history and the natural rhythm of life.

"I'm going to warn you right from the start," he said in welcoming his guests, "from four a.m. on, you'll have to plug your ears because of the roosters crowing. Then the donkeys will start braying and the goats bleating, so there will be as much noise here in the peaceful countryside as there is right in the middle of town." His usually impassive face was lit with a shy, proud smile as he explained to Gorbachev, "I always spend my vacations here, never in the official residences. I only go to them to receive foreign guests. Perhaps my successors will get more use out of them."

The merest hint of disdain in this last phrase signaled Mitterrand's attitude toward his unknown successors, who by definition would be his inferiors in all respects.

Gorbachev was absolutely delighted. Mitterrand could not have offered a better setting to his guest, who had grown up in a *stanitsa*[25] in the province of Stavropol, in the Kuban. He loved it all: the purity of the air, the soft, resilient earth under his feet, the warmth of the fireside, and the beamed ceiling of the single-story "cottage." He was like Jack London's Martin Eden, going out onto the deck of his ship for the last time, finally able to unbutton the stiff collar of his uniform and breathe deeply again, as in his youth. During the last weeks of his presidency, Gorbachev often returned in conversation to the far-off years of his childhood. "Our *khata*[26] was the second one at the edge of the *stanitsa*; beyond it there was nothing but steppe for hundreds of kilometers. In the evening I would feed the cows their hay and go out into the courtyard under the stars, and I would be carried far away by my thoughts. I was very much a dreamer when I was young," he acknowledged.

Thus Mitterrand's farm immediately put him in a frame of mind for relaxed conversation. Night fell, and the guards carried Mikhail's and Raisa's luggage to the small room with shuttered windows that would be theirs for the night. "The members of my family are the only people who ordinarily stay here," Mitterrand said apologetically. Gorbachev was very touched by this.

The two presidents, each accompanied by two aides, followed a narrow path, visible only under the flashlights carried by the guards, to arrive at a narrow, barnlike building. This was apparently a deliberately maintained illusion; inside this stylized Old French peasant cottage we found an elegant salon. Seated on leather cushions, Gorbachev and Mitterrand began their conversation in this highly unofficial setting.

Gorbachev started off by recounting the opening ceremonies of the Middle East Conference. He made a rather clumsy attempt to congratulate Mitterrand by describing him as "one of the initiators" of the meeting. Mitterrand did not allow him to continue. Instead, he felt it necessary to reproach his guest—albeit in very polite terms—for the about-face made by Soviet diplomacy, which had bought into the American conception of the conference. Because of this, French diplomacy, which was used to maneuvering comfortably between the positions of the two superpowers, had been excluded from playing any practical role in setting up the conference agenda.

Gorbachev responded mildly to Mitterrand's pique, noting that "if we had not done that, the conference would never have gotten off the ground." Mitterrand generously wished success for the meeting, although he added that he was not very optimistic about its prospects. But the very fact that there would now be a place where the opposing sides could talk ("and every one of them loves to talk!") was a major accomplishment. And Mitterrand joked, since Gorbachev was cochairman of the conference, that if he didn't make much progress in Madrid this time he would have to go back, and that would give the two of them an opportunity to see each other again in Latche.

After this gracious comment, which completed their exchange of views on the Middle East, the two leaders moved on to the main topic of discussion: the situation in the Union. Gorbachev could not help but open up in the almost domestic atmosphere of his surroundings. After the traumatic events of August, he wanted simultaneously to explain himself, to justify himself, and to ask what advice Mitterrand, with his perhaps greater experience in political battles, might have to offer.

He began by describing the irreparable damage that had been done to his strategy for gradual reform. The critical stage had been reached sooner than he had anticipated. The plans for moving toward a free market and a new union had already been set in motion; so had the move to reform the Party, for which a new platform had been developed. That was why he had not stepped down as general secretary: His feeling was that he could not abandon such a formidable force in this uncertain situation. The putsch had ruined everything.

Like the manager of a supermarket after a fire, Gorbachev added to the list of destroyed merchandise a few items that may never have existed. But the main thrust of his analysis was as unassailable as it was desperate: The republics were breaking apart and the mechanisms of power were destroyed. This, in turn, would snap economic ties and throw the political process into confusion.

With the victory of democracy, contrary trends in society had intensified. Russia's "ill-considered" behavior had contributed substantially to this. Gorbachev had to use diplomatic circumlocutions, since unless he wanted to compromise his own prestige along with Yeltsin's reputation, he could not complain to the leader of a foreign power that the breakup of the unified state was being deliberately promoted by the Russian leadership in its struggle against the central power. However, he did allude to a statement by Gennady Burbulis, Yeltsin's éminence grise, to the effect that Russia was the sole heir of the USSR.

"And the other members of the new union?" Mitterrand commented. "Whose children are they? Are they orphans?"

Gorbachev strove repeatedly to modulate Yeltsin's position and thus his own attitude toward it. He stated that he was ready to support the most determined initiatives in economic reform but that he wanted to integrate them into a carefully considered system of measures that would, above all, be coordinated with the republics. "To act without coordinating our efforts would be to give up on politics and yield to despair."

The idea of breaking up the unified state was unacceptable to Gorbachev. He was haunted by a menacing number: 75 million, the number of people living outside their "ethnic" republics, and all bound together by the most stringent economic integration, under which geographical regions were fused with particular industries—not to mention their scientific, cultural, and personal ties!

His concern with these "micropolitical" relationships, as opposed to national and international "macropolitics," undoubtedly set him apart from the crowd of politicians who peopled the upper echelons of power, whether democrats or members of the *nomenklatura*. In the overturned anthill that the Soviet-Russian empire had become, this character trait of Gorbachev's was expressed by his innumerable doubts and hesitations and by his failures in managing his own staff. It led directly to a loss of effectiveness in practical affairs and a decline in popularity.

Gorbachev had agonizing difficulty in divorcing himself from the people in his staff, even those whose activity—or, in some cases, passivity—had a destructive effect on his politics and authority. He was hopelessly slow to make changes in top-level staff and almost never exercised his right to dismiss subordinates who opposed him, even when they confronted him with tougher and tougher political challenges, as in the cases of General Albert Makashov[27] and Prime Minister Valentin Pavlov. In August he paid for all of this with his crown and almost lost his head into the bargain.

Still, his psychological and ethical imperative "not to cut the people off at the knees," his obsessive hope that they "would understand on their own," and his suffering in the knowledge of the drastic consequences that the breakup of the single state would have for millions of individuals ("born in Ukraine, did military service in Armenia, married in Siberia—now what?")—all of this lifted him above the dull, pragmatic conduct of the country's affairs and made him a figure of truly historic dimensions.

He liked the formula that González had suggested, "national self-determination within the framework of a union." Any other path, tending to emphasize and stimulate nationalist ambitions, would, he felt, lead straight into conflict and catastrophe, to "another Yugoslavia, with consequences a hundred times worse for our peoples and for the world at large."

Mitterrand did not need to be convinced of the ruinousness of separatism, which would lead to the breakup of the centralized state. He said that France, "unlike some others," did not intend to encourage centrifugal tendencies in the Union or to use relations with this or that republic to its own advantage. Mitterrand's conscience was clear on this point, in terms of his relationship with Gorbachev. Indeed, the year before, when the sensitive issue of the Baltic states first arose, he had tried to restrain Bush from moving toward diplomatic recognition of the Baltics in order to give Gorbachev more time to complete his constitutional reforms. "Things have to be done in their logical order, step by step, *n'est-ce pas?*"

Mitterrand was basing his policy on European history and on his own political experience. It was clear to him that the existence of a centralized and influential power in Eastern Europe was in the best interests of France. If the breakup of the Soviet Union cast Europe back to the situation that had prevailed before Peter the Great, it would be a catastrophe of historic proportions.

Thus, Mitterrand's motivation for promising Gorbachev his support in strengthening the Union stemmed more from France's national interest than from sympathy for Gorbachev as a pro-Western democrat. Mitterrand felt that the best solution for the USSR and for Europe as a whole would be the reconstitution of a unified state, on a federal and democratic basis, in two or three years' time. Otherwise, all of Europe would move into a phase of unpredictable anarchy.

Gorbachev eagerly drank in these words from the patriarch of European politics. He would have loved to have Mitterrand use his armor-piercing arguments on the politicians at home—that flock of nouveaux riches excited by the smell of power and ready to discard the ABCs of professional politics, the lessons of history, and even the national interest. But he had to go back alone—back to his personal Athens, where, he suspected, a cup of hemlock was already waiting.

Still, he kept up the fight: "I consider it my duty to advance toward a new unified state through the Treaty of Union. However, I repeat to you what I told Bush: The situation is extraordinary. We must act not by the usual methods but with allowance for the unique nature of the process. And that applies to the West as well."

In practical terms, Gorbachev was asking Mitterrand to study carefully the results of the meeting of representatives of state finance of the G-7 countries, which had taken place in Moscow the day before.

Mitterrand nodded reassuringly. "I understand: To refuse you material aid at this time would be to endanger the whole process of reformulating the Union." At this point, the two presidents decided to break for a joint televised interview, to be broadcast live during the eight o'clock news on the French public television station Antenne 2. The barn and hayloft had been fitted out as a makeshift television studio. The cameras and lights, the tangle of wires, the bustle of the technicians, and a makeup corner at the entrance transformed it into a Hollywood set for half an hour. This illusion was broken only by the ghostly faces of the guards looking through the windows into the brightly lit room with its fireplace. Mitterrand's reason for agreeing to let his island of solitude be transformed into a media circus was fairly obvious: He wanted to appear on television with Gorbachev after his triumph over the coup.

This was not just another one of the joint press conferences whose tradition dated from Gorbachev's first official trip abroad—to France in 1985—as the new general secretary of the CPSU. Paris had received Gorbachev and Raisa with skepticism at that time. In December of the year before, Margaret Thatcher had said that Gorbachev was a man you could do business with, but this seemed a dubious recommendation to the French, who were waiting to judge for themselves. Nor would Paris recognize the certificate of elegance London had awarded to Raisa until it had seen her with its own eyes.

Gorbachev had literally sweated through this first press conference. Coming down from the dais where he had stood with Mitterrand, fielding the toughest questions without even consulting the notes prepared by his aides, he exclaimed with relief, as if after a physical workout, "My back is completely soaked."

But this time, in Latche, it was Mitterrand's turn to render accounts to the press. The French public had not been deceived concerning the Élysée's embarrassment on August 19 when the putsch in Moscow was announced. Mitterrand had been all too hasty to publicize the reassuring message that he had received from Gennady Yanaev, going on TV with it that same evening and referring several times to "the new leaders." This greatly diminished the effect of his subsequent condemnation of the putsch and expression of support for Gorbachev, who the plotters claimed was ill in Foros, although it must have been obvious to the whole world that he was being interned there.

In the long view, though, it is hard to blame Mitterrand for taking the coup seriously during the first few hours when such outspoken partisans of democracy as Kravchuk and Nazarbaev were ready to consider it an unpleasant but irreversible fact. Apparently the Soviet ambassador to France, Yury Dubinin, also did Mitterrand an ill turn by assuring the Élysée of the stability and legitimacy of the new authoritarian power in Moscow.

All of this had almost been forgotten when a spurious sentence that somehow found its way into the French translation of Gorbachev's book about the putsch[28] threw oil on the fire. In place of the original "I should have called Mother" was the sentence "Mitterrand should have called."

It was a surprise to no one when Christine Ockrent, the top newscaster from Antenne 2, who conducted the interview, began by asking about that passage. It was high time to dispel the rumors, and Mitterrand decided to take advantage of the presence of the number one witness in the case to confirm his alibi. Gorbachev was clearly happy to oblige him: "If that is in my book, then it's not my book."

Mitterrand, for his part, quoted from the English edition, which did not contain the sentence in question. There it was translated as, "I ought to have telephoned my mother. But I was unable to do it. I still regret that."

After the interview I asked Gorbachev what had really happened. "I don't know where that came from," he answered with a shrug. "You know how scrupulous I am in assessing how my own colleagues acted during the putsch. How could anybody think that I would have been so contemptuous toward a foreign leader? And toward Mitterrand, too—whose high regard I appreciate and value so much."

In my opinion, the explanation for this mystery lies in the haste with which the manuscript was prepared and translated. Although the English edition did in fact refer to Gorbachev's mother, the Italian and Finnish editions, like the French one, mentioned Mitterrand. I think I can provide a rational explanation for this.

It seems to me that the reason for this mix-up lay not in any failed phone call from Mitterrand but in the call to Bush mentioned a little earlier in the text. At Foros during the first few hours after the defeat of the putsch, Gorbachev was able to initiate calls but not to receive them. It was he who called Bush. When the book was being edited, it is possible that his advisers felt that it would not be very good for the President's image in the USSR to show that one of his first actions as a free man was to contact the president of the United States. Hence the deliberately vague wording of the sentence about his conversation with Bush, which does not specify who took the initiative and made the call. The sentence about there being no call from Mitterrand was probably then added to make the call to Bush seem more routine while at the same time suggesting that it was the foreign heads of state who had tried to contact Gorbachev.

The ambiguous nature of the passage, which could be (and was) read as an implicit criticism of Mitterrand, did not occur to the President's staff until the book was being translated. In mid-October, Gorbachev's personal interpreter, Pavel Palazhchenko, went to London to reread and correct the proofs. He changed the offending paragraph, replacing Mitterrand with the reference to Gorbachev's mother. It occurred to no one that the other publishers (the book was to be published simultaneously in several countries on October 31) might work not from the English translation but from the Russian original. Thus the correction was not made in all editions.

Mitterrand, reassured by the English edition, undoubtedly ascribed the sentence to a French domestic-politics maneuver involving the publisher in Paris, who actually had had nothing to do with it. The presence of the Soviet president at his side before the Antenne 2 cameras was the best way to set the record straight.

Gorbachev, for his part, was in a good mood. The logs were crackling on the fire. He knew Christine Ockrent well, having met her on several previous occasions, and was comfortable with her. It had been a long day, beginning with the pyrotechnics in Madrid and now winding down under the skies of southern France, so much like those of Stavropol.

After the interview, the presidents, their wives, their aides, and the Antenne 2 journalists went back to the main building. Raisa gathered a circle of ladies around her and began talking about her granddaughter, who referred to coins as "hard currency." Mikhail, after tasting a Château d'Yquem 1975 from the presidential wine cellar, told how in Stavropol they had cultivated vines that were resistant to cold temperatures.

During dinner, Danielle Mitterrand explained that she personally harvested the honey from the beehives near the house and offered to give one to Raisa. But Raisa exclaimed, "We wouldn't have anywhere to put it. Did you hear that, Mikhail Sergeevich? It's just like I've been telling you: It's time for us to set up a country place of our own, instead of all these state dachas."

The men, meanwhile, were talking about Europe, a subject on which they understood each other very well. Mitterrand's European "confederation" was a close equivalent of Gorbachev's "common European home." There was no need for a rehearsal to make this conversation proceed smoothly.

"There should be two fulcrums," Gorbachev said, "the European Community in the West and the Union of Sovereign States, which will replace the USSR, in the East. The cooperation between them should be based on the principles and standards of the Paris charter. The presence of the United States and Canada fits into this scheme very well."

Mitterrand pulled Gorbachev back to reality: For the present, there was only one fulcrum, the Western one, and it was closely tied to the United States. As for the other, in the East, no one had a very good understanding of what was happening there. Everything would have been much simpler, of course, if all the inhabitants of these republics were Gorbachevs. "Now, just a minute!" said Raisa with sudden coquetry. "At least half of them would have to be Mrs. Gorbachevs." Mitterrand smiled at this pleasantry. "I realize that my job is to strengthen the second fulcrum," Gorbachev concluded.

With the aplomb of a man who has accomplished the better part of what he set out to do, Mitterrand reassured Gorbachev: "You can be sure that France will never, under any circumstances, encourage the destruction of the Union. Despite the doubts of some of our allies, as well as those of our new friends in the East, I am certain that the future Europe will include Russia. Your problem is to determine what form Russia will take. All I want is for this to happen while I'm still alive. That's why I'm in a hurry."

After dinner, Gorbachev and Raisa were helped to get settled in their room. The setting obviously reminded the President of their youth and their college days at the students' dormitory on Stromynka in Moscow.

⸎ ⸎ ⸎

In the morning everyone was awakened early by the roosters, donkeys, and goats, just as Mitterrand had promised. When Gorbachev's staff, accompanied by photographers, arrived at the farm, they were told that the two heads of state had gone out for a walk. On their return from the woods, Gorbachev and Mitterrand posed briefly for the photographers and sat down to breakfast. The warm bread, fresh milk, and honey were an obvious pleasure to Gorbachev. Raisa did not come out; she was getting ready for their departure. At the table, the leaders were discussing the last few topics that remained, including practical, financial, and food aid to the Union, when the kitchen was suddenly invaded by curls of smoke. The lights went out: It was a short circuit. Raisa, disconcerted at finding herself alone in the dark, called to her husband. Gorbachev, abandoning the discussion on the conditions of aid to the USSR, rushed to his wife's side.

When the presidents came back out after their convivial morning meal, the sun was shining brightly. Accompanied by the lusty crowing of the Gallic roosters, the presidential motorcade left to convey Gorbachev and his party to the airport after a short stopover at the village of Soustons for one last press conference.

With its president on board, the *Soviet Union* took off for Moscow. During the flight Gorbachev sorted through his impressions of the trip. His main conclusion was that his Western partners were waiting for a clear-cut picture of what was going on in his country, and concrete action by him to save the unified state. Feeling that he could rely on their political support and that it was still possible to recover the advantage, Gorbachev again set foot on Muscovite soil.

On the Eve
of the Seventy-Fourth Anniversary
of the October Revolution

The meetings in Madrid and at Latche left Gorbachev charged with energy. Of course, it was important for him to feel that he was the president of a great country again, to find consolation in the honors of protocol, and to bask in the bright lights of the world's television networks; but it was even more important for him to be strengthened in the conviction that his political course met global standards. He had obtained the blessing of his Western friends for strong measures to save the union and, like the weak Czar Fyodor in Tolstoy's play, was preparing to strike the ground threateningly with his scepter before yielding his place in the Kremlin to "Czar Boris."[29]

Gorbachev spent the last few days before the crucial battle, which was to take place on Monday, November 4, in a sort of political warm-up. The strategy to be used in the battle for a union was clear; all that remained was for him to work out the tactics. He went over the arguments supporting his position with his advisers and dictated a draft of his opening address to the new session of the State Council—the blow of the scepter.

At the same time, Gorbachev hoped to create more favorable conditions for the new union. Like an expectant mother, he was impatiently counting the months and weeks that remained before the birth of his baby. His greatest concern was the economy. In talks with economists and the representatives of Western business interests, he no longer bothered with protocol.

Winter would be coming soon. In the final analysis, the future of his plan depended on how well the country weathered the season. Things were complicated by the fact that Yeltsin, who was urging the Russian economy along with both spurs, was leaving Gorbachev only a little space on the croup—just enough for him to be able to warn of approaching obstacles, and pray.

On November 2, Gorbachev received a delegation from the Deutsche Bank, the principal creditor and thus the potential savior of the dying Soviet economy. He could not let these German bankers leave without winning them over as allies, and he put all his energy into the task. "In Madrid and Paris, people are thinking, uneasily, that Germany is moving in on our market with increasing assurance," he said, telling the Germans what they wanted to hear, "but that doesn't worry us."

He found additional reasons to underscore Germany's special role in Russia's economic rebirth. "You understand us better than the Americans and our other Western partners, since you bear the heavy burden of integrating the economy of the former GDR with your own." At this point, the bankers, remembering that they were Germans first and foremost, expressed to Gorbachev the historic gratitude of the German people for their reunification.

"Now," continued the President, "in contrast to the GDR, which can rely on the economic might of the FRG, we have no one we can count on." Here he paused for dramatic effect. "Except you."

The Germans were touched, but they did not forget that they were bankers. They reminded Gorbachev of the minimum conditions for the allocation of aid. The most important of these was an unconditional pledge by the new union to honor the debts of the former state. Since this condition would be easier to meet within the framework of a unified state, the Germans willingly gave Gorbachev confirmation that they supported his efforts to reconstitute this state.

The second piece of advice, a natural one from prudent financiers, was not to hasten the process of reform and to implement measures in their proper order—in short, not to put the cart before the horse. One could sense that the Germans were dumbfounded by the swaggering assurance with which the Russian government was decreeing the advent of an open market.

Gorbachev was in complete agreement with his guests on this point. He complained about the Russians in an aggrieved tone, as if referring to the unrelenting harshness of the Russian weather. "The Russian government has not thought its plans through to their ultimate consequences. Freeing up prices in a totally monopolistic economy means subjecting people to unprecedented overcharges. Furthermore, this operation cannot be carried out without coordinating it with the republics. Ukraine and Belorussia had good reason to be frightened."

Nevertheless, he tried to allay the Germans' fears by giving them to understand that they were dealing with the driver rather than a mere passenger. "We still have to regulate the sequence in which the measures will be implemented. But we need your aid as never before. As you can see, we're jumping around like fish in a frying pan."

This stab at folksy, Teutonic humor, which sounded a bit awkward coming from Gorbachev, completed the process of charming the financiers. They still grumbled, however, for form's sake, "All the same, we'll need a detailed program and not just a request for a certain sum."

"These funds will be used primarily to pay our promissory notes that have come due, including those held by Germany," Gorbachev reassured them. "You know the volume of funds we are requesting. You can discuss the practical matters with your colleagues." As he said these last few words he resumed the bearing of a head of state. The Germans reacted to the change in tone, thanked him for receiving them, and took their leave.

❀   ❀   ❀

Monday came, and with it prayer time. The meeting of the State Council was to begin at noon, which left Gorbachev an hour in the morning in which to receive an imposing delegation of officials from several dozen American religious organizations who represented the Soviet-American Christian Bridge project.

The Americans, some of them Orthodox priests, stood about in the Kremlin's spacious Brezhnev office under the portraits of Marx and Lenin, taking pictures of the President from all possible angles and pouring out their expressions of admiration and deep respect. "Our meeting with you today is a confirmation of the existence of God," said the most ardent cleric to Gorbachev in Russian. "You know, Mr. President, you are the person most prayed for in American churches. You are an instrument of God: Thanks to you, there is much more freedom in the world today."

Gorbachev found the best way to conduct himself in this emotionally charged atmosphere: with exquisite politeness, tinged with a hint of irony. "I have long intended to meet with people who are more regularly in contact with God than I. I am a practical man, and I place particular value on the expression 'Prayer is dead if it is not reinforced with action.'" The Americans responded in concert that they were reinforcing their prayers with political action, influence, and aid to the President and to the peoples of his country.

"All of the changes in this country up to the present," Gorbachev remarked, "have occurred, as a rule, through confrontations, conflicts, and civil wars. My mission is to *humanize this country* for the first time in its history." He made this statement spontaneously, responding to the sincerity of these clergymen who had come so far to see him. And the strength of conviction that his words reflected immediately transformed the dreary office in the Kremlin into a sort of cathedral where the portraits of the founding fathers of Marxism and Leninism took the place of icons.

"The most difficult science," Gorbachev continued, "is to teach people how to practice democracy. For example, it is extremely important that the democrats not imitate the behavior of the putschists and give themselves over to vengeance, mistrust, and the settling of accounts. Otherwise we will forget our principal goal, to which all politics, including our own, must be subordinate: the interests of the living human being. Such is my prayer."

Gorbachev sometimes gave the impression that he would like to prove—more to himself than to others—that he was capable of doing everything just as well as everybody else, or even better. At any rate, he demonstrated to the Americans that he could be a fairly convincing preacher. Before leaving, they asked permission to say a prayer. Gorbachev was already late for the meeting of the State Council, but he couldn't refuse them. For about two minutes he stood with them in silence, his head bowed. Was he praying? Or was he preparing himself for the test that awaited him? And for that matter, is there really any difference between the two?

He entered the meeting hall of the State Council focused and tensed like a spring. Camera lights were trained on the presidents of eight republics and the two prime ministers who were standing in for the heads of state of Ukraine and Armenia. They were all seated at the table. The armchair to the President's right, which according to a now well-established tradition was reserved for Yeltsin, was still vacant. The participants blinked in the bright lights and kept quiet, just in case. The invitation to have TV cameras present was a "surprise" initiative by Gorbachev, who was hoping to use the medium to rally public opinion to his aid. The former leaders of the Party, terrorized by glasnost, did not dare contest this unilateral decision by their leader, and no one knew whether the live broadcast from the Kremlin had already started.

Gorbachev glanced over at Yeltsin's empty chair with mingled irritation and secret relief. He asked whether anyone had any news of Yeltsin and decided to begin without waiting for him—especially since he planned to make a change in the agenda.

The main reason Gorbachev had invited the television cameras in again was that he wanted to take advantage of the occasion to deliver a political speech to the country as a whole. His message, in a few words, was, "The fatherland is in danger!" Since this address was not on the agenda that had been sent out to the members of the State Council the day before, it was necessary to add an item blandly entitled "Current Issues." An objection on Yeltsin's part could have wrecked the whole scenario, but with him gone, this was not a problem. At least not yet. It would be another month before the leaders of the republics aligned themselves with a new magnetic north of power.

Gorbachev did not look at the members of the State Council as he read his speech, addressing himself instead to the citizens beyond the cameras. He began on a dramatic note: "We are in a situation that is difficult in the extreme. It is my impression that we have too easily and irresponsibly depleted the capital that we were given after the putsch and the resolutions adopted on the basis of the joint declaration of the leaders of the republics. At that time, we all had hopes of being able to master the situation and lead the country confidently along the path of reform and out of the crisis.

"We also felt very keenly that the disintegration of the state would be unacceptable. It was as if we had had a glimpse of the devil's abyss we could slide into if we were not careful.

"The first few weeks of teamwork strengthened this certainty. The people and the country supported this approach. But it was not long before the procrastination and the political games started up again. The birth of the economic treaty is agonizing. Work on the draft Union Treaty is progressing with great difficulty. The country is suffering from a lack of clarity on these essential questions. All this is very dangerous."

Having sounded the alarm, Gorbachev moved on to his assessment of the economic situation created by Russia's decision: "I hope that the State Council will support the initiative of the government of Russia to speed up the reforms. For my part, I confirm the general direction of the measures proposed by Boris Nikolaevich Yeltsin. However, I will say openly that this program's lack of clarity as regards the economic treaty, and its failure to recognize the necessity of working closely with the other members of the economic community, are sources of serious concern to me. I believe that this is a question of principle, since neither Russia nor the other republics will be able to bring the current drastic situation under control on their own. I have met with Boris Nikolaevich. We had a frank exchange of views. In answer to my direct question, he responded firmly that Russia would act within the framework of the economic treaty and, moreover, would serve as the initiator of this cooperation. In the complex set of circumstances prevailing in this country today, we cannot allow the common market to be destroyed, barriers to be set up, prices to be deregulated without coordination, and so on. I must say frankly that going back into a cocoon will not save anyone. That is an illusion."

Yeltsin came in just as Gorbachev was moving on to an assessment of the mistakes being made by the Russian government, which was repeating the errors of Ryzhkov and Pavlov, two former prime ministers of Russia who had caused a panic on the market by announcing future price increases. The President interrupted his speech to greet the new arrival and continued with a sense of relief, since the words that Yeltsin was likely to find the most disagreeable had already been spoken.

"This seems to me to be yet another miscalculation. We cannot deregulate prices without first solving the problem of stimulating producers, without demonopolizing production, and without making budget cuts. The situation is ripe for an explosion. We must act now, or people will soon be storming the private enterprises and cooperatives and then the state-owned stores."

Gorbachev's second major concern was, of course, the preservation of the unified state in some form. This time, after his meetings in Spain and France, he decided to include the Western leaders among his allies, using their opinions as support: "Everyone is afraid of the breakup of the union. People are trying to impress upon me the need to conclude the Treaty of the Union of Sovereign States quickly. They can't understand what is happening to us. Have we all lost our minds? Every day you hear statements over here that make the West shudder. And all those 'traveling ambassadors' of ours are spreading such discordant views of the Union's current situation and future prospects, all they can do over there is marvel at us.

"For two and a half days, they basically questioned me about the issue [of the union]. People over there have realized for a long time that it is in our interest as well as the West's to renew, to reform, but nevertheless to maintain the union as a basic fulcrum for the modern world. The question is: What are we politicians waiting for? This is a political matter: We should move forward more quickly to complete the process of drafting and signing the Treaty of the Union of Sovereign States. Comrades Yeltsin, Karimov, Nazarbaev, Shushkevich, and Saparmurad Niyazov, with whom I have been talking over the past few days, are all of the same opinion. [Obviously, anybody talking one-on-one with the President could hardly oppose him.] And if this is not the case, if the members of the State Council are changing their positions and renouncing what was decided at our last meeting, then we will have to decide all over again what we are going to do."

Gorbachev's speech lasted about forty minutes. Hearing the familiar tones of command, the members of the State Council grew quiet. Many knew this tone from having heard it a few months or years earlier, in that same room, when the meetings of the Politburo were held there. Only Yeltsin, having come in late, was still baffled by Gorbachev's address and the presence of the television lights. He was under the impression that someone had just played a dirty trick on him.

Even after Gorbachev's address had ended and the cameras had been taken out (the rest of the meeting was to be conducted in closed session), everyone remained silent. Those who were not looking at Yeltsin were waiting for his reaction. It was like the scene in *The Jungle Book* where the pack waits for the confrontation between the two strongest wolves to find out who will be their leader.

Yeltsin confined himself to grumbling that a political debate had not been on the agenda. But since he had come in late, he had to settle for Gorbachev's answer that this item had been included in his absence. Then Gorbachev proposed that the members of the council give their opinions on the questions he had raised.

Silence again. To comply with Gorbachev's request while Yeltsin was sitting there looking so sullen would mean to side with Gorbachev in the conflict that was brewing. Refusing to discuss the matter would be the same as siding with Yeltsin. Nazarbaev, who had never made a secret of his preference for Gorbachev over Yeltsin, saved the day. Without launching into a long dissertation, he merely said that they all had to make faster progress together and that they had "marched in place" long enough.

This put an end to the general discussion. The proprieties were observed and Gorbachev's speech received at least partial legitimation from the members of the

State Council, since they did not argue against it. In addition, when Gorbachev commented that Russia, according to Yeltsin, did not intend to act in contradiction to the economic accord, Yeltsin nodded his affirmation, although with a morose expression. As a result, this almost looked like a signal to retreat, and it relaxed the atmosphere and confirmed that the confrontation would be put off to another day. This relieved the members of the need to choose sides.

Gorbachev decided not to goad Yeltsin and, contenting himself with Nazarbaev's reply, went on to the next item on the agenda: Yavlinsky's report on preparations for the republics' ratification of the economic accord. Gorbachev had completed the task he had set himself: The country had heard his speech and had watched the members of the State Council listening to him on television. That should confirm that the President had regained the political initiative.

Gorbachev led the discussion of the other subjects on the agenda with the same energy and confidence he had had in the old days. Based on Yavlinsky's report, he formulated instructions for the government of the new union and for the republics, found a common denominator in the debate on the future structure of the Interstate Economic Committee, and reprimanded the mayor of Moscow, Gavriil Popov, who had slipped an off-color joke into his speech. Yeltsin remained silent throughout this part of the meeting. This gave Gorbachev the chance to win additional psychological points by strengthening the impression that he really was the boss.

After the break, it was time to move on to thornier problems: the fate of the army, the Ministry of Foreign Affairs, and the security organs in the future union. The minister of defense, Air Marshal Shaposhnikov, presented a dramatic picture of the breakdown in morale in the armed forces, which was threatening to turn into an acute internal crisis with unpredictable consequences on the international front. According to Shaposhnikov, the USSR might soon become a "conglomerate of warring principalities," and its gigantic armed forces might be dragged into the settling of political accounts.

The conclusion to be drawn from his speech was clear: With all due respect for the intentions of the sovereign republics to have their own armed forces in the future, civilized, rational solutions to these problems had to be found. Above all, the powerful, modern military potential of the second world superpower must be preserved from disorderly partitioning, nationalization, and privatization.

His speech clearly had the impact that Gorbachev was counting on. The irrationality of breaking up a state that had been in existence for hundreds of years not only became obvious to everyone but took on especially threatening overtones in the area of national defense. This was something that even the former Party secretaries who had difficulty assuming responsibility for the state could understand.

To general surprise, Boris Yeltsin, breaking his silence of several hours, expressed his staunch support for the minister of defense, and thus for the position taken by the president of the Union. Emphasizing that he was expressing not just his own personal opinion but also the official position of the leadership of the Russian Federation, he declared that Russia did not intend to create its own army despite the steps that other republics had taken in this direction. "We will not be the first, or the second, or the third, or the fourth," Yeltsin said solemnly. "This is our reply to those who fear that Russia might become a threat."

In so saying, he was borrowing the ideas Gorbachev had expressed on several occasions, even down to the phraseology he had used. "Since, despite the difficulties, we are trying to create a new state, a union of sovereign states, this state indisputably must have a single army, unified armed forces."

According to Yeltsin, the independence of the sovereign members of the Union in the military sector should not extend beyond matters relating to civil defense, the preparation of young people for military service, and measures to prevent coups d'état of the kind that occurred on August 19. The national guard units that each republic would set up for this purpose should "have nothing in common with the army" and should be no larger than "ten to twenty thousand men." He felt that these guards could be made up of troops of the Ministry of the Interior and a contingent of professional soldiers.

Yeltsin's next remarks seemed to suggest that he was debating against those in the hall who were in favor of partitioning the present armed forces, even though the Russian representatives could be suspected of similar intentions: He launched into a convincing sales talk on the reasons for preserving not only the strategic forces, the air force and the navy, but also the other branches, in a single army.[30] He explained that the army was such an integrated body that it could not be "cut to the quick." And he felt that even the Baltic republics, which had broken away from the Union, did not have the right to dismantle the elements of the national air defense system located on their soil at their own discretion. "That would be suicide. We cannot permit such a thing." The solution to the problem, he said, could be found within the framework of a special agreement that would define obligations in the area of defense, not only for the members of the future union but also for former members.

He ended his address by calling on all the participants to join forces to solve this important problem.

Gorbachev did not give any sign of the inner jubilation he must have felt, although it was clear that Yeltsin, in his characteristic peremptory tone, had just expressed Gorbachev's own position on the matter. He merely turned the floor over to the next speaker.

He had every reason to be satisfied with the meeting. For the first time since its near destruction in the August storm, the ship of state was beginning to respond to the tiller again. Gorbachev, as its captain, had succeeded in adjusting as complex, capricious, and ill-suited a steering mechanism as the State Council and getting it to work—no mean feat, since, very much like an international organization, it included the leaders of republics that had proclaimed themselves sovereign states.

Even more remarkable, he had managed to force this awkward imitation of the United Nations Security Council, composed of former members of the Politburo, to work to implement his own plan. During the meeting, he had succeeded in using his political comeback following the trip abroad as a backdrop for the proceedings. In addition, aided by the leaders of the other republics, he had also made use of this homecoming to pull a few excessively showy feathers out of Yeltsin's war bonnet. And finally, with Yeltsin's own assistance, he had used it to blunt the aspirations of the republic leaders in one fundamental area of national sovereignty, that of defense.

The leaders of the republics definitely did not have enough strength to challenge the united position of both presidents and the minister of defense. Even Ukrainian prime minister Vitold Fokin, whose fate was still uncertain pending the upcoming presidential election in his republic, preferred to lend his official support to Yeltsin's position on this question. Instead of the majestic *Mene, mene, tekel, upharsin*[31] the conformist motto "Let's agree to this for now, and time will tell" seemed to be written in invisible letters on the walls of the Politburo assembly hall.

The one topic that remained for discussion was the Ministry of Foreign Affairs of the Union, which was in a rather precarious position. On the eve of the Madrid meeting, Russian minister of foreign affairs Andrei Kozyrev had scornfully attacked this Soviet ministry, declaring that he did not see any special usefulness in its existence and that it should be reduced to one-tenth its present size.

The minister of foreign affairs of the Union, Boris Pankin, reacted immediately and with fury, since he felt that his own contribution to the victory of Russian democracy in August, when he had issued an open challenge to the Moscow junta from his embassy in Prague, was ten times more important than Kozyrev's. He refuted Kozyrev's statement, calling it a clumsy "slip of the tongue." The problem was that each of the two ministers justified his position on the basis of support that he claimed to have received from Yeltsin. So it was up to Yeltsin himself to clarify the matter in today's session.

The outside world was equally baffled by the question of whether a Soviet foreign policy still existed. Gorbachev had been questioned on this matter by U.S. secretary of state James Baker and King Juan Carlos in Madrid, who needed to know not only with whom they should deal in the area of foreign policy but also what the situation was with regard to the nuclear button, on which they were receiving contradictory signals. The latest cock-and-bull story on this subject had come from Italy. During Yeltsin's last visit to that country, the Italians had been given to understand that his finger had also been on the red button since August. Needless to say, this calculated "leak" had no basis in reality, but it did create a commotion in the West. Gorbachev was obliged to confirm, through me, that since he was commander in chief of the armed forces, he alone continued to bear personal responsibility for any use of nuclear weapons.

The sharing of foreign policy between the Union and Russia created many other problems and ambiguities as well. Boris Pankin, realizing that it was preferable to sacrifice part of his authority rather than lose all of it, explained to the State Council why the new union, the collective heir of the USSR, needed a single, coherent foreign policy that would combine the interests of all its components. It was especially important that the new unified state be represented on the United Nations Security Council and that the new union assume the obligations arising from the fifteen thousand or so treaties and accords signed by the USSR.

At the same time, he presented a plan for reforming the Ministry of Foreign Affairs, predicated on the merging of this ministry with the Ministry of Foreign Economic Relations, a drastic 30 percent reduction in the size of the apparat, especially the KGB workers "hosted" by the Soviet embassies, and, above all, the allocation to the republics of a sizable percentage of the posts at the Union's missions abroad, a move designed to satisfy the appetites of the republic *nomenklatura.*

When Pankin ended his speech, all heads turned toward Yeltsin. It was up to him to decide whether the ministry would be given a new lease on life or reduced to a mere symbolic appendage, the 10 percent Kozyrev had declared appropriate. The republic leaders' interest in Russia's position on this matter did not arise from any concern for Pankin's fate. They did not much care for the humble foreign relations role to which Moscow was relegating them, but they were willing to tolerate actions on the part of the central leadership that they would never have stood for from the Russian authorities. In any case, it wouldn't do for them to officially acknowledge that one of the republics was "more equal" than the others.

Yeltsin visibly enjoyed any occasion when his word was decisive. He even allowed himself to be magnanimous at such times. This time, however, he was irritated, and he launched into criticism of the Ministry of Foreign Affairs of the Union. Its personnel were corrupt, he said. These people had detached themselves from their own countries, and it was no coincidence that almost all the embassies had "saluted" the putschists. (The paradox of this attitude was that it emphasized Pankin's heroism and made it impossible to overlook his position.) Yeltsin also accused the embassies of often transmitting in code what had already been published in the press. Thus not only the diplomatic staff but also the number of cryptographers could be cut. More radical changes were therefore needed.

That said, Yeltsin finished by absolving the ministry of its sins. He stated that he respected the work the diplomats performed, which was useful. More important still, Yeltsin dispelled the fears of the foreign minister of the Union by saying that Russia "was not burning" to create its own embassies, since it "was counting its money."

All Russia wanted was to have its own representatives, posted at certain embassies as advisers or envoys. It would not consider setting up any diplomatic missions in the near future. First, Russia would have to develop direct ties with the countries concerned until a level was reached that necessitated official diplomatic relations. And in any event, this question would arise only vis-à-vis certain countries. "You will maintain contact with the others," Yeltsin said to Pankin in a conciliatory tone.

This episode merits closer examination. Yeltsin's statements on the single army of the future state and the need to maintain a central structure for foreign affairs confirm that only one month before the encounter in Belovezhskaya Forest, he had no deliberate intention of destroying the structures of the Union or of refusing to sign the new Union Treaty.

Otherwise he would have to be suspected of hypocrisy, and of brilliantly mounting an operation to lull Gorbachev and his colleagues in the other republics into a false sense of security. I feel that there is no basis for such an assumption. In early November, and even subsequently, as we will see, Yeltsin behaved as though he were following with conviction the joint strategy he had worked out with Gorbachev after the putsch. "I trust him now," were Yeltsin's words about Gorbachev, echoing Margaret Thatcher's. Of course, this in no way signifies that Yeltsin's entourage shared this opinion.

The agenda had now been covered, and the State Council could adjourn. Gorbachev had made a few major gains, this time without having to make any concessions of principle in order to get them. And most important, it had been agreed that the members of the State Council would meet soon to discuss the draft Union Treaty article by article. Gorbachev was stepping up his political and psychological offensive.

The light Gorbachev had been hoping for was finally beginning to appear at the end of the dark tunnel he had entered in August. And who, in his place, proceeding logically from the sum of information available to him at the end of this meeting, would have supposed that it was the headlight of a train bearing down on him from the opposite direction?

At the end of the meeting, one of the participants recalled that the anniversary of the October Revolution was coming up and that they should decide how to celebrate it. Gorbachev confirmed that the parade and demonstration in Red Square had been cancelled, as had the official meeting, with the reading of the customary report. It was still to be decided whether the traditional receptions should be held at the embassies and, of course, at the Kremlin, since this was also a festival of the state, not just of the revolution. Someone said that it would be better to put off any changes until next year. Another member of the council proposed confining the celebration to the usual front-page article in *Pravda*. (One month later, incidentally, these same officials were doing their best to convince people that they had never had any relationship with the Soviet Union at any time during their political careers.)

Rejecting the *Pravda* proposal, since "they'll write plenty!" anyway, Gorbachev asked again, "What are we going to do about the receptions?" Yeltsin replied that they should cancel them but should come up with serious arguments for this decision. There was the critical financial situation, for example. People would understand that "there isn't enough money for sausage."

"Well then," concluded Gorbachev with a smile, "all I can do is offer you my congratulations on this anniversary of the revolution!" And that was how the national festival of the Union of Soviet Socialist Republics was commemorated for the last time, during a closed-door session of the State Council—unbeknownst to the country, which was making preparations to celebrate the seventy-fourth anniversary of its great revolution three days later. The USSR was just one year short of its seventieth birthday.[32]

The Mirage
of a Confederal State

Gorbachev had won the first round in the battle for a unified state, and he turned with redoubled effort to his preparations for the second: the approval of the treaty. He spent long hours with his political advisers, working out what he felt to be irrefutable arguments in favor of union, considering avenues of compromise. He worked without pause.

And this was unfortunate, because if he had lifted his attention from his work he probably would have felt the electric charge in the air that heralded the coming storm. The circumstances that had preceded the August coup were slowly but surely coalescing again. Absorbed in his efforts to win tactical victories, he failed to realize that these gains brought him ever closer to strategic defeat.

A memorable speech, a successful interview, favorable results of a poll, gave him a false sense of security and created the illusion that he was clearing all obstacles, like a runner leaping the hurdles, and was on the point of winning the race. Actually he was the only one on the track, since his opponents, realizing that they were unable to beat him in this event, had decided to play cards for the gold medal.

All the same, I feel that he would not have abandoned the race even if he had sensed that something was wrong, because he believed that it was possible—especially for a man like him—to emerge victorious despite all odds. He seemed to be guided by Kozma Prutkov's aphorism, "If you want to be happy, just be happy." He probably felt that all he had to do in order to become president of the new union was to act like the president. This was apparent in his work schedule and his agenda.

On November 5, the day after the meeting of the State Council, he received the assistant secretary of defense of the United States, Donald J. Atwood, who was in the USSR on a research mission to study ways of speeding up the conversion of the military-industrial complex to civilian applications. Gorbachev gave Atwood a cordial welcome and, as he so often did, raised the conversation to such a level of candor that his visitor felt compelled to respond in kind. "The Soviet economy is overburdened with military spending, probably much more so than the American economy," he said to Atwood. "If the only thing I could accomplish in my lifetime was to give these resources back to mankind, I would be completely satisfied."

By the time he paid his visit to the Kremlin, Atwood, with Volsky's aid, had already had a look at several military enterprises in Moscow, St. Petersburg, and Kiev. Gorbachev asked him what he thought. Atwood diplomatically praised the leadership of the Soviet military-industrial complex, which, he said, showed a strong interest in conversion, and noted the positive attitude of the workers "with whom he had stopped to chat." The technology in some areas, such as optics and electronics, was as advanced as it was anywhere in the world. "In short," he said, "all the elements for success are there."

Gorbachev nodded approvingly, but his reply was intended more for the man sitting next to Atwood, Ambassador Robert Strauss, who would pass his words on to President Bush. "When a runner finishes his race, he has no further need for blood doping. I'd like to see the United States move into our economy quickly. Let Americans buy stock here and vie for profits. I have often said that I am in favor of mutual dependence between the United States and ourselves, since that will make us more predictable to each other and will add a measure of security to our relations as partners."

He also said he had no intention of responding to the hysterical accusations of opposition forces back home that he was selling the country out by flinging the doors wide to foreign capital. "This capital—it's not even faintly visible on the horizon. These accusations are a reflection of the slave mentality that we developed during all those years spent behind the Iron Curtain."

Ambassador Strauss, as a businessman of broad experience and expertise, readily agreed with what Gorbachev was saying. The United States, he said, had gained its own wealth from the influx of foreign capital—English, French, Dutch, German. "They made money and we got rich."

The three men decided not to go into the practical details, apparently to avoid lowering the tone of mutual understanding that they had achieved at the meeting. Gorbachev expressed his satisfaction at seeing the nuclear disarmament proposal he had developed "jointly with Bush" go into effect and walked the Americans to the door of his office. It was time for him to plunge into his study of the new amendments to the Union Treaty.

As busy as he was with this task, he still found time the next day, November 6, to receive the representatives of a number of the Union's religious communities. This meeting had been on the President's schedule for a long time. Gorbachev believed, justifiably, that the religious *nomenklatura*, whose faithful inhabited every corner of the Soviet Union, could become his active ally in strengthening the Union.

Given the rapidly increasing fragmentation of the country, this meeting, like a number of others, was reduced to a mere exchange of compliments. The religious leaders knew that the President did not have the resources to solve their problems, which were basically financial, so they didn't ask for anything. The interview gave them the opportunity to thank Gorbachev sincerely for having allowed religion to emerge from "the underground." The representatives of the small churches, who really were feeling the fresh breeze of tolerance, were more eloquent in their gratitude than the dignitaries of the partially state-controlled Orthodox Church, who had lost through perestroika at least as much as they had gained.

Gorbachev, for his part, was grateful to these perceptive clergymen for not assailing him with specific demands. In addition, he approved of the work they were doing to strengthen the moral principles of a society that seemed to have lost all others.

The free days that were gained with the cancellation of the festivities celebrating the anniversary of the revolution[33] would supposedly give Gorbachev a chance to gather his forces before the next session of the State Council, scheduled for November 14. As it turned out, however, he was unable to isolate himself from current affairs.

On November 7, the ever-unpredictable leadership of the Russian republic, steering the country left and right with an unsteady hand on the tiller, declared a state of emergency in the Chechen republic (at the time, officially known as Checheno-Ingushetia), which was demanding independence from the Russian Federation. Yeltsin sent an ultimatum to Chechen leader Dzhakhar Dudaev, and then promptly made himself completely inaccessible, as he had often done in the past.

Naturally, no good came of this high-handed approach except that it provided some free publicity for Dudaev, an obscure and hitherto unknown general in the Soviet air force. But the issue was taking on alarming proportions, threatening to turn into another bloody and unresolvable Afghan war. In fact, a division of the Russian Ministry of the Interior had already started its movement toward Grozny when Gorbachev on his own initiative ordered the troops to stop and immediately approached Russian parliament speaker Ruslan Khasbulatov, urging him in the absence of Yeltsin to cancel the president's decree. The decree was rescinded, the fuse put out, and Russia's image preserved. But although Gorbachev acted with the best intentions, he only managed to irritate Yeltsin. Yeltsin's annoyance was increased by the (carefully considered) remarks Gorbachev made on November 12, during the press conference on the publication of his book *Avgustovsky putsch* (*The August Coup*).

Gorbachev took great pains preparing for this media encounter: He repeatedly went over his opening address as well as the guest list, which included not only the journalists but also the country's leading political figures and members of the diplomatic corps. Everything went as planned. The hall was packed. The President's invitation had been accepted by Russian vice president Alexander

Rutskoi, the diplomatic corps, and, of course, all the top Muscovite and foreign journalists. Compared to Gorbachev's previous appearance in the same room, after the coup that was the subject of his book, the contrast was striking. This time he looked confident, gave precise answers to the journalists' questions, and made no attempt to duck the more treacherous ones. He felt that the main reason for the failure of the coup was the fact that the plotters were "lagging behind their own country." As late as August 1991, they were still trying to replay Khrushchev's removal from office in October 1964.

In response to a question about Lukyanov's role in the plot, Gorbachev said that they had been friends for forty years and that Lukyanov's betrayal had been especially painful to him. He felt that there were two people who could have put a stop to the coup: Anatoly Lukyanov and Vladimir Ivashko, the deputy general secretary of the Party Central Committee. Obviously, neither had done so, which meant that they had not wanted to.

Few questions were asked about the book itself, which was, after all, the reason for the press conference. That may have been because many of the people who were present had not had time to read it. However, despite the haste with which it had been written, it shed considerable light on the character of its author. It described the circumstances of Gorbachev's arrest at Foros and gave a chronicle of the putsch that had endangered both his life and the fate of his political agenda. It included an argument in favor of a union and an appraisal of future prospects, together with a long article that Gorbachev had written with his aide Anatoly Chernyaev before the coup, in which he examined the potential for reform in light of the conditions that prevailed immediately before the attempted takeover.

In the book, Gorbachev acknowledged that those three days in August had brought about a change in both the country and its president. At the same time, the book was clearly written by the same person who launched an unprecedented program of reform in 1985, perhaps without imagining all the consequences of his decision. And Gorbachev himself has affirmed that he never regretted inaugurating this turning point in the history of his country.

After the August coup, some people claimed that 1985 was neutralized by 1991, which was when the real revolution began. The book confirms that these events were both different stages in one and the same contradictory process: a program of reform that needed a revolution in order to bring it to fruition.

People often ask whether there wasn't some way that Gorbachev could have foreseen and thus prevented the coup. Both his friendly competitors in the democratic camp and foreign colleagues such as Bush and Baker had informed him that the reactionary forces were becoming dangerously active. In my opinion, the question might better be worded, Was there any way to avoid this clash between reactionary and democratic forces? Was there any reason to hope that those in the

Party and state leadership who would not agree to democratic reform would peacefully and voluntarily leave the political scene? Probably not. Besides, it was precisely the escalating scale of the transformations brought about by perestroika, the fact that the changes were moving from the slogan phase toward the actual redistribution of power and property, that prompted the opponents of reform to resist and pushed them into their desperate and irrational attempt at revenge.

People seldom ask how many coups d'état Gorbachev managed to avoid in six and a half years of reform. Any of these potential coups could have occurred under much less favorable circumstances, when Gorbachev's position in the Politburo and the Central Committee was such that he was virtually isolated from the Party of which he was the leader. There had been rabid opposition to him on the part of conservative political bodies and the conservative public. Tanks would not have been needed to halt the process of reform—a simple closed-door vote by the Party leadership would have been sufficient.

When people discuss the reasons for the August coup, they usually cite the sharpening of economic, social, and political contradictions in a society that had started down the path of radical and highly traumatic reforms. Several other factors must be added: the reaction of the conservatives—on the whole, an understandable one—to a process that posed a real threat to their political status and their vital interests; the destabilization of the country triggered by the actions of nationalist and separatist forces; internal differences of opinion among the democrats, who often looked for their worst enemies in their own camp. And one should not gloss over the inconsistency, indecision, and often inexcusable slowness to act of the "center," and thus of the President.

However, any list of the factors that led to the putschists' defeat (Gorbachev cites the democratic gains of perestroika, the new atmosphere in foreign relations, and the stance taken by the Russian leadership) should include the President's courageous refusal to bow to dictatorship. It was this refusal, in fact, that marked the beginning of the end of the putsch. It sabotaged the putschists' plans, since they had been expecting Gorbachev to capitulate, and it forced them into elaborate contortions intended to give their actions a semblance of legality.

A detailed analysis of the elements that led to the defeat of the reactionary movement would have to include the atmosphere of glasnost in society, the courage shown by the media, and the changes that had taken place in the army, which refused to serve as a blind instrument of reactionary politics. Paradoxically, the factionalists themselves acted—probably unconsciously—like people who had been schooled in perestroika. This, and not just their incompetence and professional inadequacy, explains why they behaved in such a contradictory and inconsistent manner. They were trying to give a constitutional veneer to a crime against the state. They were more concerned with explaining their motives to the press than they were with actually making a move and using brute force. That is why the President's refusal to cooperate with them was the first step in the chain of events leading to their defeat.

Gorbachev had a choice: By agreeing to the plotters' ambiguous conditions, he could keep both his official status and his freedom. But in so doing, he would have made himself the hostage of men who were preparing to destroy his life's work. He preferred detention at Foros, and thus true freedom. He has been suspected of using the actions of the putschists to promote his own secret agenda. To be convinced of the opposite, however, one need only read the article he wrote at Foros the day before the coup. In it he stated, with a combination of reasonableness and passion indicative of the depth of his conviction, that the only way to prove that one is right is to act within the law, by democratic methods. He also called the plans to declare a national state of emergency an "underhanded scheme."

Gorbachev will probably continue to be thought of both as the man whose hesitation made this "underhanded scheme" possible and as the one whose resolve caused it to fail. He was both the victim and the vanquisher of the putsch. After all, it was his own work that had brought about the very changes in the country that enabled it to defend its newly won democracy by its own efforts, and thus without him.

On Monday, November 11, the day before the press conference at the Kremlin, Gorbachev met with his inner circle as usual. These meetings were ordinarily attended by the people who worked most closely with the President: Chernyaev, Shakhnazarov, Alexander Yakovlev, Revenko, and myself. Sometimes the group was expanded to include Vadim Zagladin and Vadim Medvedev, who advised him on international and domestic affairs, respectively.

The business at hand that Monday was to evaluate the last session of the State Council and to formulate plans for the future. Gorbachev began with the fact that the republic leaders had agreed in principle to work together. He noted with pleasure that they had reached a consensus on having a joint foreign policy and that "Ukraine [Vitold Fokin] had supported Boris Nikolaevich on the issue of unified armed forces."

He also believed that everyone now recognized the need to have a government for the new union in the form of the Interstate Economic Committee. This confirmed his principal conclusion: The structure created should be not an amorphous union of sovereign states but a unified state subject to international law with single citizenship and a single territory.

His sense of responsibility toward the world community, which had been intensified by the trip to Madrid, clearly tended to make him more unyielding in his concept of the future union and how long it would take to set it up. "A state's foreign policy must be predictable, whereas some of our republic leaders go barging into world affairs like booted muzhiki into the Assembly of Nobles."

We also discussed the upcoming session of the State Council, which was to be attended not only by Russia, Belorussia, and Kazakhstan but also by representatives of the Caucasus (Mutalibov) and Central Asia. Ukraine was still on the sidelines, preparing for its upcoming presidential elections. This republic's drift away from the new union was a matter of growing concern to Gorbachev, who was beginning to realize that "these were not just preelection maneuvers." However, he still believed that the magnetic attraction of the other members of the future union would pull this rebellious republic back into line.

The discussion also turned to the need to have ongoing contacts with various segments of society and more regular meetings with the media. Serious consideration was given to the idea of publishing a "presidential gazette." But all these plans were soon to be buried under the political avalanche that came crashing down on Moscow from Minsk.

Gorbachev had talks scheduled with two more foreign dignitaries before the session of the State Council. He received a visit from Umberto Vatani, the diplomatic adviser to Italian president Giulio Andreotti, who informed him of the results of the meeting of the North Atlantic Council that had just been held in Rome. NATO had decided to send an unmistakable—although slightly belated—signal of support for Gorbachev's foreign policy strategy.

Gorbachev put a positive construction on the results of the Rome meeting, viewing them as a rejection of Cold War stereotypes and a gesture of solidarity with domestic reforms in the USSR. In his opinion, this meant that NATO was beginning to change gradually under the influence of the transformations taking place in Eastern Europe.

The President also received the deputy prime minister of Czechoslovakia, Pavel Rihetsky, who passed along another invitation to him from Václav Havel. The kind of personal chemistry that Gorbachev relied on as the basis for a candid working relationship with other statesmen had been slow to develop in his dealings with Havel.

The reason for this is hard to pin down. It may be that Gorbachev had a prejudice against or a guilt complex toward the Czech democrat, whose past as a dissident who had gone to jail for his activities made him so different from such Communist reformers of the Prague Spring as Zdenek Mlynar,[34] for whom Gorbachev had a greater affinity. Or it may have been caution on Havel's part: He may have had difficulty believing that a leader of the *nomenklatura*, a newly spawned—although possibly sincere—democrat, could really adhere to the principles of democracy.

They had been scheduled to meet in Paris in November 1990 during the Conference on Security and Cooperation in Europe (CSCE), but the meeting was cancelled because Havel had expressed too much support for the Baltic states in his speech. The coolness in their relations may also have been due to a concealed rivalry kindled by their respective claims to the Nobel Peace Prize.

Now that the two were on equal footing, not only in terms of public office but also in their concern for preserving the unity of their respective states and the democratic values they had come to by different paths, the ambiguity of their relationship obviously weighed heavily on them both. That was why Gorbachev initially said that he wanted to accept Havel's invitation and go to Czechoslovakia. He felt that after a period of mutual alienation and efforts to live separate lives, the Soviet Union and Eastern Europe were beginning to realize that this kind of isolation, although possible, was not very profitable.

Ambassador Slansky, who had accompanied Rihetsky, signaled his approval of Gorbachev's statements with a nod. He was the son of the general secretary of the Czechoslovakian Communist Party who had been executed by hanging under Stalin's orders in 1952,[35] and he had come to be a very popular figure among the intelligentsia in Moscow. In welcoming him as he came into his office, Gorbachev asked Slansky whether he should address him as "comrade" or "mister." The ambassador answered without a second thought, "Just Rudolf. That'll be fine."

The deputy prime minister began with the usual diplomatic compliments, but in this case they seemed to reflect personal sentiments and his own recent experience. "Mr. President," he said, "our country will be eternally grateful to you for allowing it to return to freedom and democracy. How we utilize this potential will depend on us alone. In any event, we have already had proof that it is more difficult to preserve democracy than it is to win it."

He readily agreed with Gorbachev's view that Eastern Europe would choose to cooperate actively with the renewed union, since "after all, the West does not look on us as full-fledged partners." He also expressed his admiration for Gorbachev's brilliant work in drafting the new Union Treaty. "We are persuaded that federation is the best way for different peoples to live together. All we have to do now is convince our opponents, who keep harping on nationalist themes."

Gorbachev did not need to be convinced of the truth of this assumption. "I know that the breakup of the unified state would not end with the republics. Some of my close friends, including some university comrades [he was referring to Mlynar], assure me that nothing serious would happen. They advise me to adopt a structuring plan for the state similar to the one proposed by Solzhenitsyn. But that road leads back to the previous century!

"Even the West understands this, as the recent NATO meeting shows, and has come out in favor of reforming rather than breaking up the Union. No, I will oppose that line of action to the very end!" Gorbachev's tone, rather than his words, made his resolve clear.

He decided to soften the harshness of this last statement. "In general, I am not in favor of quick decisions and improvisations. You know, I recently read a phrase that I liked very much: What grows too quickly lacks endurance."

The Czech dignitaries were also interested in Ukraine, their immediate neighbor. What could they expect in the future? Gorbachev could offer few reassurances. "The situation there is complex and contradictory. At the top, you have a bunch of loudmouths who say they are in favor of separation. But at the grass roots, the popular mood is in favor of preserving a union." Gorbachev cited polls and drew on history and the economy. His final argument, as usual, was his own ancestry: "I am half Russian and half Ukrainian. How am I supposed to partition myself?"

He apparently succeeded in convincing the Czechoslovakians; it was too bad they weren't Ukrainians. The reasoning of the deputy prime minister as he denounced Slovak nationalism was also very persuasive.

The conversation ended where it had begun, with the possibility of Gorbachev making a trip to Prague. The two visitors offered an additional reason for him to go: The Czech government wanted to sign two treaties immediately, one with the Soviet Union and the other with Germany. It would be a good idea to start with the USSR, they said, since the Czechs couldn't forget its role in their liberation. Gorbachev shot back, "And if you ever did, the Germans would be sure to give you a quick reminder!" He ended the conversation with a promise to come to Prague as soon as he had "even one free day."

Gorbachev never did find this free day during the remainder of his time in office. Or rather, none were available to him, and so he missed a timely meeting with Havel. Nor would there be time for the many other meetings and tasks he had planned, none of which would have sufficed to keep him at the head of the state whose salvation was his chief purpose during the last few months of his presidency.

He did get the chance to see Havel five months later, when the Czechoslovakian president came to Moscow at Boris Yeltsin's invitation. By that time, Gorbachev was president only of the foundation that bore his name. The meeting between these two remarkable men, who had passed into European history in their own time, took place without protocol in a cordial and informal atmosphere.

❀   ❀   ❀

The November 14 meeting of the State Council, held in Novo-Ogarevo, opened to rumblings of thunder.

The decision to hold the meeting at the same villa in Novo-Ogarevo where the Union Treaty had been drafted during the last months before the coup was obviously intended to create a sense of continuity. When Gorbachev had begun his rapprochement with the democrats in April and was looking for a place to host the negotiations on the renewal of the union, he had settled on this state dacha. Once allocated to Georgy Malenkov by Khrushchev, it was situated on the Uspenskoye causeway west of Moscow, at least ten minutes by car from the president's official residence.[36]

In making the decision to hold the meeting at Novo-Ogarevo, Gorbachev certainly had no idea that it would begin with a psychodrama. On the day of the meeting, Yeltsin, as usual, was the last to arrive. He was scowling as he strode into the ground-floor room where Gorbachev had already assembled the other participants. His expression made it clear that this meeting was not going to be smooth sailing.

The cause of his ire soon became apparent: He had been infuriated by a report that Gorbachev, during his press conference, had criticized the Russian leadership's handling of the events in Checheno-Ingushetia. "Since you're criticizing Russia, let me respond," he flung at Gorbachev. "Our new relations have lasted all of three months, and now they're over."

Gorbachev was thunderstruck. The situation was especially embarrassing because he had to respond in front of the republic leaders who were present.[37] The latter, realizing that they were de trop in this domestic altercation, slipped out of the room one by one.

Gorbachev tried to mollify Yeltsin by telling him that he had never intended to make Yeltsin's position more difficult. Moreover, he had tried to express support for Yeltsin's stance on the indivisibility of Russia—and he would prove it by showing Yeltsin the transcript of the press conference.

Despite Gorbachev's conciliatory tone, it took Yeltsin a few minutes to calm down. He grumbled about "Gorbachevian" television, which was repeating the President's critical remarks about the Russian leadership, and expressed outrage at how these leaders were being discriminated against in the allocation of vacation homes and resort facilities. Finally he had let off enough steam and the meeting could begin.

It had barely started when the discussion of the wording of the future treaty became snagged on the issue of how to define the structure of the new state.

Gorbachev made a stand on behalf of a "unified state," with a new center that would have powers transferred to it by the members of the new union.

Yeltsin, backed by Shushkevich, said that he was against a unified state, much to the surprise of the other leaders, who thought that the draft they were discussing had already received his endorsement. Seeing Gorbachev's perplexity, Yeltsin reminded everyone that he disagreed with the principle of a single constitution for the entire union, as he had indicated in his amendments.

Gorbachev proposed that they concentrate on this main point. "We have to define precisely what it is that we are going to create," he said. "After August we rejected the idea of a federation, but certainly not so that we could set up something amorphous in its place."

Nazarbaev gave Gorbachev energetic support: "We must confirm that those who are present here today at least have the intention and the will to form a political union, with a single army, territory, and boundaries. If we don't do it, others will—those who succeed us or take our place. Let's use foresight, for once, and not just hindsight."

Nazarbaev was the youngest of the republic leaders and certainly one of the most capable; if he had not been Kazakh, he would undoubtedly have been a candidate for the presidency of a future union. Before gaining the presidency of his republic he had been the leader of the Kazakh Party. Of all the first secretaries of the republics, he was, at that time, the one Gorbachev trusted the most. He obviously shared the Gorbachevian ideal of the peaceful evolution of the USSR and preservation of a unified state. Later on, after the "soft" coup of December, Gorbachev said that he and his colleagues in the Central Asian republics had proven to be more "European"—that is, civilized—than their Slav counterparts.

The opponents of a new union began to discuss the possibility of confederation, citing Switzerland and Canada as examples. Gorbachev resisted: "If we reject a unified state, we will have something that is indefinite and nonbinding, something that serves no useful purpose whatever." He added that even the international community would prefer to deal with a union as an accountable state, if only because of the issue of nuclear weapons. Again he tried to bring the term "union" back into their discussion, arguing that it was the most acceptable wording because it encompassed all sorts of ties: those of a federation, a confederation, and even an association. He ended on an emphatic note: "In the end, the decision is yours. I am convinced that we must preserve a unified state. If we do not, we'll bring ruin on our country and on the rest of the world."

Yeltsin tried to tone down this stark portrayal of the situation: "You exaggerate the position of the West." But Gorbachev was adamant. "If we fail to preserve a unified state, you'll have a disaster on your hands. That is the main issue."

Shushkevich jumped into the debate by observing that a confederation could have unified armed forces. Yeltsin added the transportation system, the space program, and the environment to the list. But Gorbachev would not back down. "If there are no effective state structures, what good are a president and a parliament? If that's your decision, I'm prepared to resign."

"Now you're getting carried away," Yeltsin remonstrated.

"Nothing of the sort. I'm too exhausted for that."

So saying, Gorbachev got up briskly from the table. He did not look exhausted. And it was obvious that he was not about to give in. "I don't want to take responsibility on myself for some sort of amorphous entity, and I will not. If you're looking for a figurehead or a doormat, count me out. The country needs a strong leader elected by the people, someone who can counterbalance the new level of decentralization we're heading toward. I am sure we'll have the people's support. But, I repeat, I do not aspire to such a position."

Gorbachev turned toward Yeltsin, every muscle taut, poised like a tennis player waiting to swing. "Boris Nikolaevich, you must realize where they're leading us— the people who suggest that Russia should leave everyone behind in the dust and proceed on its own."

He was referring to Yeltsin's shadowy adviser, Burbulis, who had ambitions of being the Russian version of the American vice president, and Burbulis's notorious "memorandum" in which he called for the speedy formation of a Russian state as the chief legal heir to the USSR. This man, whose lack of charisma relegated him to the position of power behind the throne, had engineered a strategy to oust Gorbachev by dismantling the center and thus the Union. Once the USSR was destroyed, Burbulis undoubtedly expected to be able to reorganize the empire around Russia.[38]

Even Yeltsin had difficulty resisting the force of Gorbachev's personality. Or perhaps he wasn't ready to challenge him publicly quite yet. When the three Slav leaders, Yeltsin, Kravchuk, and Shushkevich, met deep in their forest in December, they lacked the courage to announce their verdict to Gorbachev's face, instead judging him in absentia. But today Kravchuk was not there (besides which he hadn't been elected president of Ukraine yet), and the balance of forces was not in Yeltsin's favor: The only person he could count on was Shushkevich, against a "united Moslem front" with a very determined Nazarbaev at its head.

"I don't support extremists," Yeltsin mumbled in a conciliatory tone. "Let's spell it out: 'a confederal state.'" This was an obvious improvisation, but it confirmed that at that point he too was seeking a compromise.

Sensing a slight weakening in Yeltsin's attitude, Gorbachev immediately decided to reinforce his own. "I'm willing to go the whole distance," he said. "It's all the same to me. The difference is that I am guided by principles, whereas the first thing you think of is what other people will say. You have to realize that a state is more than just a union of sovereign nations. It has its own specific qualities. And our world has been in the making for more than just the past ten years."

He made repeated efforts to demonstrate the need for a center that could administer the joint system of defense, carry out strategic missions, implement a united foreign policy instead of "eight or ten different policies," and push the country in the direction of a market economy. "We already have proof that the economic treaty cannot function without the political treaty. I'm telling you," he said, raising his arm in admonishment, "this excessive liberty, this license, will be our downfall. I won't be responsible for some flaccid arrangement that carries no obligation for anybody to do anything, like some kind of retirement home. Especially during the transition period."

He spoke with conviction. Everyone realized that he had meant what he said when he threatened to resign and leave them all faced with a mountain of problems they didn't know how to handle.

"I don't know," Yeltsin suddenly said. "Maybe you're right and I'm wrong." This sounded almost like an apology. Accepting it, Gorbachev replied in a conciliatory tone, as if the matter were closed, "I'm surprised that you put me in such a spot, Boris Nikolaevich." And he immediately proposed a compromise of his own, which was both a peace offering and a way of saving face: "Maybe we can do without the single constitution."

The legal experts who had been invited to the meeting, the academician Vladimir Kudryavtsev and Professor Venyamin Yakovlev, who had been keeping their own counsel, suddenly came to life. "There would be no problem replacing the constitution with a treaty on the structure of the state and the human rights declaration," said Kudryavtsev. "The confederal state is already a compromise," Yakovlev said, meaning that it was a compromise between politics and the law.

Gorbachev, with a victor's generosity, tried to bolster Yeltsin's position on the still slippery platform of compromise. "We have to find some way to make sure that the treaty supports the indivisibility of Russia and aids its leadership in conflicts with the republics and the independent regions," he said, by way of apology for his intervention in the Chechen crisis. "If Yeltsin loses in Russia we all lose, since we are all bound together by a common goal."

Yeltsin, satisfied with this obeisance, returned to the subject of Ukraine. "We have to provide something for them. A way to join. If they establish their own armed forces and their own currency first, they're not going to come back."

"But Ukraine could join a confederation," mused Shushkevich. Then he proposed an even more flexible compromise: "Let's start with a confederation, and move to a federation later on." To this Nazarbaev rejoined that Ukraine's constantly shifting position was just one more reason why all the others should unite.

Yeltsin and Gorbachev each proposed a different version of the first chapter of the treaty, and then everyone left the table for a break. As the aides were having the two drafts of the treaty typed up, they had the idea of omitting the author's identity in each case. The documents were marked anonymously number 1 and number 2, as in competitive bidding, to avoid any further ego conflicts. It was already clear what concessions would be made: There would be a single, confederal state (as Gorbachev wanted), without a single constitution (Yeltsin's preference).

Over lunch, Gorbachev read aloud from the transcript of the press conference that included his statements on the subject of Checheno-Ingushetia. Yeltsin saw nothing offensive there and was appeased once and for all. He even seemed to be in good spirits. "You see how badly we started out today, and how well everything has turned out!" he exclaimed, as if amazed at it himself.

❦   ❦   ❦

After the details of the compromise wording had been worked out, everything went much more smoothly. There was some quibbling, but there were no fierce arguments, and agreements were reached on other points of principle: The president would be elected not by a parliament but by the citizens of the future union, through an electoral college system; the parliament would be bicameral, with deputies elected from republics but also from territories other than those with the status of republics; there would be a government and a capital (which the authors of the Russian amendments initially wanted to christen the "place of residence of the central organs"), and so on.

The main sticking point was the procedure by which the president, the parliament, and the vice president would be elected. The latter office came under fire from Yeltsin, who demanded categorically that it be "eliminated." "I cannot support this office after it has been held by Yanaev," he said.

When it came time to discuss the office of head of parliament, he stipulated, "We have to find someone trustworthy." "But even among Jesus' twelve disciples, one traitor turned up," Gorbachev parried. (Since there were only seven disciples at the table in Novo-Ogarevo, it was assumed by those present that there was no Judas there.)

It was also decided that membership in the future political union should be linked with economic benefits. Yeltsin decided to put this wording into practice immediately. "Back when the economic accord was signed," he said, "we calculated that if all the reciprocal obligations between Russia and Ukraine were tallied at world market prices, there would be a difference of some eighty billion dollars in our favor. If Ukraine agrees to join the new union, we can forget about this little debt. Otherwise, they can pay up!" He grinned slyly, satisfied with the effect he had made.

It really did not seem that Yeltsin was playing a game or trying to allay the fears of the President and the State Council regarding his real position on the future union. At that point he was acting as though he were a true partisan and defender of the union. Perhaps he felt it was possible that he might have to work with Gorbachev for some time to come. Or he may have been assuming that the Union would soon have a new president—a Russian one, for example—who would, of course, need Ukraine. The most likely explanation, however, is that like so many Russians, Yeltsin had two different and contradictory personalities—equally real and often at war with each other.

During this discussion, Gorbachev frequently got up from the table to pace around the room. In one excited moment, he even knocked over the briefcase containing the nuclear codes, which was always with him and which, as usual, had been placed just at arm's length.

The meeting was drawing to a close. The participants agreed to incorporate the approved amendments as soon as possible, so that they could be submitted to the parliaments of the republics without any loss of momentum. Shushkevich proposed that another meeting be held so that each member of the State Council could approve the final version and pledge to defend it with all his authority before the members of Parliament. This was agreed to. If this was a delaying tactic on Shushkevich's part, it was a very subtle one.

The deadlines for signing the treaty were also discussed. Everyone agreed that it should be done before the end of the year. "But this time, let's not tell anybody the date!" joked Nazarbaev.[39] The others appreciated his humor, and there were some faint smiles.

The debate on the treaty ended with an unexpected twist. One of the participants asked about the future of the State Council. "I don't know," said Gorbachev, spreading his arms in a theatrical gesture. "I have deliberately refrained from proposing anything because I get the impression that these meetings are a burden to you. You have to be begged to come. In short, it's up to you." He later admitted that this was a calculated move. "I decided to let them bring up the issue of the State Council themselves," he told me.

The leaders of the republics demanded as one man that the State Council be added to the draft treaty. "And let the membership be by name rather than office, so that we ourselves must participate rather than sending our delegates," someone said. This comment contained echoes of years past, when most of the people assembled in that room were members of the Politburo.

Late in the evening, after the last break, the council discussed the governmental structure. By the combined efforts and entreaties of several members of the council, Yeltsin was persuaded to give some of the doomed Union ministries—notably the ministries of finance and the economy—a two-week extension, if only in order to draw up an extraordinary budget. Otherwise, they would have ceased to exist the very next day. Yeltsin, obviously disgruntled, agreed to "one last reprieve." "If we don't make this the last one, though, they'll all be resuscitated," he added.

The meeting finally broke up, and the participants were met at the foot of the stairs by a crowd of news-hungry journalists. Behind the media one could sense a public grown weary of uncertainty, waiting to hear these eight leaders announce what it would be called from now on: a union, a commonwealth, a confederation, or some other, even less comprehensible appellation.

Gorbachev shepherded the Magnificent Seven out in front of the lights and the cameras with practiced composure. He let Boris Nikolaevich answer the first question. As the country—a most demanding audience at this point—watched and listened, Yeltsin solemnly proclaimed, "We have agreed that there will be a union: a democratic, confederal state."

Gorbachev had just won another round. After Yeltsin's statement, the other members of the council and even the media felt more at ease, and the customary biting exchange between Gorbachev and Yeltsin was almost looked on as a friendly dialogue. "We don't always understand you," said Yeltsin to Gorbachev. "That's all right," Gorbachev replied, "as long as you eventually catch on."

"A Free Man
with Nothing to Fear"

For the first few days after the meeting of the State Council, Gorbachev was unable to calm down. He kept describing the ups and downs of the meeting to anyone in his inner circle who had not been there, reliving all the dramatic moments of the confrontation, the clash of ideas and personalities, and the keen sensation of danger and victory.

"I was completely calm," he told Chernyaev and me. "I had no fear of losing, so I didn't feel that I was under any pressure. I was just following my convictions, and I told them so. I explained to them that they, however, were not free if they had to worry about other people's opinions, moods, and ambitions. And they realized that I was going to leave if they didn't accept my arguments.

"You see, I am willing to build any kind of union—federal, confederal, whatever—but build it, not destroy it. And when they realized I was serious, they all got flustered and immediately asked to take a break." He turned to Chernyaev. "I really would have left, you know; and you would have lost your president and his press secretary at one blow."

Gorbachev obviously relished the new freedom that he had gained. It was the freedom of a man who not only had made a choice in his own mind but had placed his fate in the balance, uncompromisingly and with determination, in order to achieve his goals. For years he had tacked into the prevailing political winds, invented ingenious maneuvers, and, at times, struck dubious compromises. He considered these moves to be the inescapable lot of any responsible reformer, and the price that had to be paid for progress. But now he had discovered—late in the game, unfortunately—the pleasure of openly expressing his thoughts and feelings. He found with astonishment that risk-taking and candor could yield greater results than political strategems. He probably arrived at this sense of inner freedom at Foros in August, when he refused to cooperate with the putschists, preferring seclusion and freedom to power with his hands tied.

Gorbachev also shared his impressions of the meeting of the State Council with his foreign guests. In a conversation with India's minister of foreign affairs, Madhavsinh Solanki, he said, "We had a tough discussion, but in the end we all came to the conclusion that it was imperative to construct a united state with a

common economic space, territory, and citizenship." He felt that the most difficult year still lay ahead, and "the situation would have to be kept in hand" at all
costs.

The meeting with the Indian minister, like the interview with the emir of
Kuwait, Jabir al-Sabah, who came into the President's office immediately afterward, gave Gorbachev the opportunity to call on these countries to consider
granting aid to the USSR in its hour of need and to confirm that the Union's foreign policy—or at least that part of it for which he remained responsible—was
still operating according to the same priorities. This was especially true with regard to India, since "without its cooperation we would never have made such
great strides and could not have made a real breakthrough in global politics."
With regard to the Arab countries, Gorbachev said that friendly relations with
them would remain a cornerstone of the union's foreign policy.

As usual in such meetings, he was talking half to his partner in conversation
and half to himself. "Three different processes converge in our perestroika: property reform, that is, the destruction of the state monopolies and a return to normal economic stimulation; political reform, which replaces the exclusive reign of
the Communist Party with a pluralistic democratic system founded on respect for
human rights; and finally, the transformation of a multinational unified state into
a voluntary union of peoples exercising their right to self-determination and sovereignty. Each of these 'minirevolutions' has stirred up political passions and conflicts of interest, and partisans of extreme opinions on either side are lifting their
voices. To reconcile them, or at least to prevent an open confrontation, requires
the skill of Jesus Christ—or rather, Allah," he corrected, remembering that he was
speaking to the emir of an Arab country.

"These processes are moving forward with great difficulty," he complained
suddenly and spontaneously, to draw attention away from his momentary lapse
and to end with an appeal to the emotions. "The time has come for politicians to
assume responsibility and to take action."

His guests listened respectfully. They expressed their admiration for his "heroic
efforts to save the Union" and demonstrated their solidarity with the position of
the central authorities by condemning the separatists. Each in his own way, based
on his own interests, confirmed his desire to see the Soviet Union remain the
great, influential, friendly power that it had been. The emir even expressed his
conviction that sooner or later the republics would realize that secession was not
in their own interest. He informed Gorbachev that he had decided not to make
any visits to Central Asia, to avoid giving the impression that he supported the
separatist leanings of some of the republics there.

Gorbachev was very moved by this fervent and characteristically Eastern expression of solidarity. Responding in a lighter vein, he reminded his visitors of

something he had once said to Syrian president Hafiz al-Asad: He was almost sorry that Prince Vladimir of Kiev had not chosen Islam as the future religion of Russia when he made that decision in A.D. 988. He told the legend, embellishing it with details: how Vladimir and his Moslem guests were about to celebrate their spiritual union over a bountiful repast when the prince found out that the Koran forbade alcohol. That put an end to what would have been the accord of the millennium.[40]

In taking leave of the emir, Gorbachev said, "I salute your desire to see a unified state in the Soviet Union. I think that that will come about sooner than the creation of a united Arab state."

This may still be a valid prophecy.

❀   ❀   ❀

After winning his round with the State Council, Gorbachev unexpectedly decided to consolidate his advantage by making a long-planned but always postponed trip around the country. The immediate precipitating factor for this move was the announcement that Yeltsin would be making an official visit to Germany over the next few days. Gorbachev knew from experience that Yeltsin's rugged face would be seen on every TV screen and front page. So he decided to beat Yeltsin at his own game by finally making his own trip into the "provinces." Then, too, with the decisive battle for the new union coming up, he wanted to sound out public opinion and see for himself what people thought of his program for renewing the unified state, of the realities of a market economy, and of him personally. This was actually a rehearsal for the future presidential election campaign, whose result, he hoped, would be the popular mandate he so desperately needed.

The itinerary chosen was not an easy one: the heart of Siberia (Irkutsk and Lake Baikal), then the new Kirghizia, which had been so full of surprises lately, and its president, Askar Akaev, an extraordinary man who had been reelected as the leader of his republic one month earlier, this time by popular vote. Akaev, a self-effacing person with a ready smile, had a degree in optical physics and was a former president of the Kirghiz Academy of Sciences. He had been one of the first republic leaders vigorously to condemn the August coup.

The trip was such a last-minute decision that the President sorted out the schedule for his first day in Irkutsk on the plane. He was planning to make changes in both his image and his modus operandi. It was for this reason that the press was invited on board the presidential jet—for the first time and, he later vowed, the last. The journalists could hardly believe their luck. It was a long night flight to Siberia, and shortly after takeoff they were invited into the President's cabin. During the revealing two-hour conversation that followed, Gorbachev uttered a phrase that could have been the motto for his political career: "My conscience is clear. For the first time in the history of this country, an attempt has been made to humanize it by civilized means."

The members of the press were witnesses to one unexpected event that occurred during the flight: Gorbachev received a phone call from Vadim Bakatin, who told him that a helicopter with twenty-three passengers on board had crashed in Nagorno-Karabakh. There was a possibility that it had been shot down, and the President ordered a detailed inquiry.

Much of Gorbachev's conversation with the journalists that night revolved around him personally. Toward the end, someone asked him what his mother thought about his work. "Her reaction is probably what any mother's would be under the circumstances. How many times has she said to me, 'Why in heaven's name did you ever take all of this on?'"

In meeting with the journalists, Gorbachev believed that, as always, he was speaking to the country through them. Sadly, this was no longer the case.

He gave careful thought to the final address he was scheduled to give at Bishkek,[41] trying to decide on a central theme. He went over all the proposed versions with his aides and rejected every one. Finally, up and pacing the floor, he said, "What if we put it like this: The main thing is that the phase of destruction is over. The democrats have gained the upper hand. We are now entering on a period fraught with greater responsibility and difficulty, that of creation." And he began to list the points that should be addressed: first, second, third. "But where are you going to say all that?" someone interrupted with astonishment. Gorbachev stopped talking and smiled wanly. "Nowhere," he replied.

❀   ❀   ❀

And that was, in fact, how the trip worked out. His speeches to workers, deputies, and military personnel in Irkutsk and to researchers and herdsmen in Kirghizia barely reached Moscow. The newspapers gave only brief accounts. The press made no secret of its suspicions as to the real purpose of the trip, viewing it as a follow-up to the political test of strength between Yeltsin and Gorbachev. A headline in *Izvestiya* summarized the situation: "The Battle for Moscow: Yeltsin in Germany, Gorbachev in Siberia, the People in Line."

The contest was still going on when the two presidents arrived in Moscow. Gorbachev's jet, coming from Bishkek, landed in Vnukovo barely one hour ahead of the plane bringing Yeltsin back from Germany. The very correct German chargé d'affaires had come out early to greet Yeltsin and didn't know where to hide himself in order to avoid Gorbachev.

It was cold at the airport; the heating system had broken down. The usual briefing with the President's closest advisers (which until recently had taken place at a session of the Politburo) was hurried and unfocused. Due to the cold and the inexorable approach of Yeltsin's plane, the aides listened distractedly to a Gorbachev animated by the results of his trip and then left with relief.

Two days later, the new optimism that Gorbachev had acquired in Irkutsk and Kirghizia underwent a crucial test: the session of the State Council at which the Union Treaty was to be approved. Unfortunately, the Union was approaching disintegration rather than reconstitution. Reassured by the results of the last council meeting, Gorbachev considered the new treaty a done deal. The departments of protocol and special events worked frenetically to arrange just as sumptuous a public ceremony as had been held for the signing of the economic accord. The round table that had been used on the previous occasion was shipped to Novo-Ogarevo and decorated with miniature flags of the republics. The TV cameras were set up and the journalists invited in.

By the morning of November 25, everything was bathed in a glow of solemnity. This date might become the political birthday of the new union that was to succeed the former empire. Everything had been arranged except for one troublesome detail: the lack of political will on the part of the founding fathers, especially the Russian leaders.

These politicians, who had been thrust into power by the August revolution, decided not to yield their newly acquired privileges to the president of the Union or share their power with him. Once this basic position had been taken by Yeltsin's inner circle, all that remained for them was to work out skillful tactics for implementing it.

Ideally, of course, Russia would have to find an excuse for its attitude toward the fate of the proposed union—or create one. That is why Yeltsin had come to the previous session of the State Council with relatively "mild" amendments to the draft treaty. The purpose of this move was to obtain the desired result without inflicting too much damage on Yeltsin's prestige and reputation.

The attempt had failed. Yeltsin was unable to bring about a definitive break with the concept of the union based on the amendments that had been suggested to him: rejection of the single constitution and election of the president by popular vote. Gorbachev's tactical skill was such that he was able to preserve the concept of a unified state. Furthermore, it was Yeltsin himself who made the public announcement of the plans to set up a confederal democratic state.

This fiasco inevitably tended to strengthen the position of Gorbachev and his team (which now included two "giants" of the initial phase of perestroika, Alexander Yakovlev and Eduard Shevardnadze). In the aftermath, Yeltsin's entourage probably decided to raise the stakes and give the Russian president a

mandate to recoup at the next State Council meeting everything that he had con-
ceded to Gorbachev at the previous one.

Shevardnadze's unexpected return to the office of minister of foreign affairs of
the Union may have been a more important factor in this sequence of events than
it seemed to be at the time. This move on Gorbachev's part was like one of those
incredible shots at billiards where three balls are dropped into three different
pockets.

Shevardnadze had made a dramatic exit in December 1990, predicting the advent of a conservative dictatorship for which Gorbachev would be indirectly responsible, or which he might even conspire to bring in. His return at this point
had to mean one of two things: the implicit realization that he had been wrong to
abandon his friend and ally during this difficult period; or confirmation that the
"new" Gorbachev had become an incontestable and indispensable element in the
process of defending and consolidating democratic gains. During the coup,
Shevardnadze had made some fairly transparent allusions to Gorbachev's ambiguous relationship with the plotters; by now accepting Gorbachev's offer to re-
claim his former ministerial post, he was indirectly apologizing for his former
suspicious attitude.[42]

Another important aspect of this appointment was its impact on international
relations. It was clear to everyone that the return of a figure of Shevardnadze's
stature to the international political scene meant the resurgence of the USSR as a
superpower and the relegation of all republic ministers to the provincial level, beginning with the pretender to the Russian diplomatic throne, Andrei Kozyrev.

Finally, a third aspect of Shevardnadze's return may have been the most crucial
in terms of domestic politics: By resuming his former post, this veteran of the
Soviet *nomenklatura,* well versed in the artful maneuvers of the *apparat,* was
sending a clear signal to all public officials. His decision indicated that it was time
to choose where the power would actually reside from now on.

Any one of these three factors would have been enough to corner the republics'
bureaucracies, which were still waiting for their first real taste of power, and make
them aggressive and dangerous.

"A Cloud in Trousers"

The November 25 session of the State Council opened with the sensational announcement by Boris Yeltsin that due to new elements in the Russian position, it was impossible for him to sign the draft treaty in its present form. "Discussions within the committees of the Supreme Soviet indicate that the Russian parliament is not prepared to ratify the concept of a unified state, or even a confederal state. Defining the union as a confederation of democratic states would have suited our purposes better. Let's reopen the debate on this issue, or else note Russia's opinion in a separate official statement."

Gorbachev couldn't believe his ears. "But that would wipe out everything we've already agreed on. We debated all of this language for hours last time. Then we announced to the country what we had worked out together. It's irresponsible to start over again, not to mention the fact that we have a very specific mandate from the Congress."

Shushkevich rushed to Yeltsin's aid. He had originally proposed that the presidents sign the draft treaty to make sure that it would get through the various parliaments without any trouble, but now he took a different tack. "Since we haven't had time to show the draft treaty to the parliamentary committees, some of the committee members may be irritated. Let's postpone the proceedings and sign the draft later on."

Gorbachev finally realized that he was facing coordinated opposition from at least some of the republic leaders, and he decided to take up the challenge. "This little game of yours," he said to Shushkevich (although his words were intended for Yeltsin), "is not just a postponement. You are rejecting what we agreed on. You are destroying the very foundations of the future document."

Alliances formed around the two opposing positions. The first to voice his support for Gorbachev was Eric Assanbaev, vice president of Kazakhstan, who was attending the meeting in place of Nazarbaev. "We are in favor of the language that was decided on at the last meeting," he announced, "that is, a unified confederal state, and not 'a cloud in trousers.'"[43]

On the other side, in Yeltsin's camp, Uzbekistan's leader Islam Karimov made his allegiance known. "We cannot sign this text until it has been discussed by the parliamentary committees." It was amusing to see how quickly the former Party autocrats had learned to use the complex machinery of democracy to bolster their positions vis-à-vis the center.

As at the previous session, seven republics were represented, but they were not all the same ones. The leader of Azerbaidzhan, Mutalibov, had decided not to make the trip because of the tension between his republic and Armenia. But Karimov, who had not taken part in the treaty negotiations, was now on hand—undoubtedly so that he could back Yeltsin, as we have seen.

Gorbachev decided to stake everything on one throw of the dice. "If we come out of this meeting without a text that everyone has signed, the consequences may be irreparable. The country is in chaos and here you are, engaging in intrigue."

Shushkevich, the leader of Belorussia, tried to lower the level of the dispute from large-scale politics to humble technical issues. He said that the whole question could be reduced to the desirability of postponing the signing of this draft, which would not undergo any substantial changes in any case, "for about ten days." After that, "Belorussia will sign and ratify the agreement without any problems." It is difficult to say whether Shushkevich was already aware of the fact that ten days later the very existence of the Union would be called into question at a meeting in Belorussia between him and his two Slavic colleagues, or that he himself would temporarily become the chief administrator of the new structure set up in its stead.

Even Yeltsin backed off slightly, explaining that nobody wanted to reject the draft that had been prepared: It would be perfectly acceptable to send it to all the republics, accompanied by a protocol giving the new comments. It seemed that his concern was simply to carry out his mandate, whatever the cost.

Gorbachev, sensing the insecurity in his opponents' position, immediately raised the stakes, as he always did under such circumstances. "In that case I feel that I am no longer necessary here, but I warn you that you are doing serious harm to the country and to the state."

Faced with this unforeseen turn of events, the members of the council—Yeltsin included—began to try to mollify Gorbachev. "We shouldn't get overheated and dramatize the situation too much. After all, the text submitted to the parliaments of the republics will be the same!"

Before allowing himself to be convinced, Gorbachev stated his conditions. One and the same document would have to be submitted to the parliaments and to the country. Furthermore, the members of the State Council would have to pledge to defend this version of the treaty while it was under discussion. Only under these circumstances would he consider replacing the signing of the treaty with a joint resolution of the State Council.

Negotiations to hammer out the details of the compromise began. Yeltsin proposed having the resolution of the State Council say that the treaty was "approved in principle," with the fine points to be worked out by the plenipotentiary delegations of the republics.

Shushkevich decided to reinforce the democratic note that had been struck: "After all, we in the council are not dictators." Gorbachev retorted acidly, "Dictators don't come in groups of nine."

Yeltsin marshaled an argument from his "strategic reserve." "It is not a well-considered action to sign the text without Ukraine," he said. "That might push them into making decisions that would wreck the union once and for all."

Gorbachev had been waiting for someone to bring up Ukraine. His argument was simple: To avoid encouraging the separatists, the members of the council must themselves take an unequivocal position. Besides, nothing new had happened in Ukraine since the last session. Everybody already knew that a referendum would be held on December 1. And he repeated, like an incantation, "Unless you change your minds, you'll have a disaster on your hands." He also said that he had no intention of having his name linked to the chaos that would ensue.

Shushkevich was still trying to appease Gorbachev by vowing that the treaty, which he would sign without any major amendments, would be ratified by Belorussia in ten days. "Technically, it's just not possible to do it any sooner."

It is tempting to see Shushkevich's position here as an almost Shakespearean example of political treachery. This interpretation does not hold up, however. As the situation stood, there were so many uncertainties that even Yeltsin, for all his inborn decisiveness, must have had a hard time making a final break with Gorbachev.

The most important factor, of course, would be the outcome of the upcoming Ukrainian referendum. Kravchuk seemed to be assured of victory, although to the very end he pretended to see some danger that he might be defeated by the extremist candidate of the western Ukrainian nationalists, Viacheslav Chornovil. He used this grossly exaggerated risk both in his relations with Moscow and in the final salvos of the electoral campaign in Ukraine, where he presented himself to the large pro-Russian and Russian-speaking population as an ideal candidate who would be able to build relations with Moscow on a new foundation.[44]

Although Kravchuk's election was assured, it was not clear yet whether he would win an overwhelming majority of votes. More important, no one knew whether the electorate would give as strong a show of support to an independent Ukraine as they did to his presidency, thereby giving him a free hand to choose the form that the newly independent state should take. So the outcome of the election was difficult to predict—which is why the republic leaders, led by Shushkevich and Yeltsin, were procrastinating.

Gorbachev realized that this was a critical situation and thus displayed a firmness and even intransigence that were foreign to his nature. He was a man of extraordinary emotional resources. During these sessions of the State Council, the tension sometimes ran so high that his aides' nerves were completely frayed, but he showed a disconcerting robustness that some people described—not without admiration—as a "peasant" quality. This stolidity was not always a blessing: His composure was such that he sometimes had to simulate the strong feelings called for in certain situations. But I believe that on the day of this meeting he did not have to feign indignation. It seeped from every pore, making him unusually pugnacious.

"I am obliged to note," he said, "that the leaders of the republics, at this serious and even dangerous juncture, are engaging in political intrigue and are changing their positions. Under these circumstances, they should have told me frankly that they no longer wanted a union. Personally, I think that by acting in such a way as to cause the ruin of the state, you are taking on an extremely heavy burden of responsibility."

Gorbachev did his best: He called on the "boyars" of the republics to exercise their common sense and fulfill their responsibility; he summoned up as allies his foreign partners and domestic public opinion ("I am sure that the people would support us"), trotted out legal arguments, and even tried to shame the members who had made an about-face.

Sensing that all of his efforts were running into a staunch opposition that had been formulated and possibly even coordinated in advance, he said wearily, "Well, as representatives of the republics, you may find some value in talking among yourselves. I see that you no longer need a president."

This was no capitulation but a last-ditch effort to shake up the mutineers, to scare some sense into them. Nor was it a bluff or blackmail, as had been the case during some Central Committee plenums. That day, Gorbachev really was prepared to resign, but he felt that if he had to, he should fight to the end and not give up easily.

"I feel a profound sadness and disappointment," he said in summing up the discussion. "I don't understand how you can go on. You know that by creating a kind of poorhouse instead of a unified state, you're going to make society suffer tremendously. We're already drowning in shit!"

This expression was more or less blurted out, and was a measure of how upset he was. Actually, Gorbachev was one of the few Russian political leaders who did not resort to the obscenities and expletives that are so common, even routine, in everyday conversation. He tended to use coarse language only when he had lost patience, or when he was trying to imitate someone or bring himself down to his level.

"You'll see," he went on, "that you will soon be replaced by forces whose program can be summed up in a single phrase: to repeal all the laws and rewrite the Constitution. So think it over, but bear in mind that if you reject the concept of a confederal state, you'll be going on without me."

He rose abruptly and headed for the door. While walking, to keep his exit from turning into a departure, he announced, "A break!" His staff, the experts, Revenko, the head of the apparat, and Union ministers Shaposhnikov and Shevardnadze got up and left the room with him.

The procession wended its way down to the first floor and set up camp in what was known as the "fireplace room." The presidents of the republics remained upstairs. With Gorbachev out of the way, they could have taken the opportunity to set up their community of independent states without having to hole up in Belovezhskaya Forest.

Downstairs, Gorbachev, still exercised from the battle that had just taken place, vented his anger: "They just can't seem to throw off that populist influence!" He spoke in the plural, but he was obviously referring to only one of the leaders: Boris Yeltsin.

Nevertheless, Gorbachev could not stand by passively and wait for events to take their course. With his aides, he began formulating his version of the State Council resolution regarding the first item on the agenda. He proposed that rather than sign the treaty themselves, all the members of the council should make a collective appeal to the parliaments of the republics, asking them to study the draft and to appoint delegations empowered to sign it. The President's wording was taken upstairs. A short time later, a top-level delegation arrived: Yeltsin and Shushkevich had been given the task of transmitting the republics' version of the compromise to the President. The two drafts were essentially in agreement.

On coming into the room, Yeltsin said in a challenging tone, "Well, here we are. We have been delegated to kowtow before the czar, the great khan." It was obvious that this parliamentary mission was very hard on his ego. Gorbachev saw how much it was costing him to make the effort and said in a conciliatory tone, "Fine, fine, Czar Boris."

It didn't take long to work out the joint wording. The final version noted that in submitting the joint draft of the treaty to the parliaments for review, the members of the State Council expected that the treaty would be signed and ratified before the end of the year.

The meeting then resumed, and the members returned to the text of the treaty. At this stage, Yeltsin agreed to withdraw his demand that the phrase "unified confederal state" be deleted. It was decided that this amendment and all the others would be discussed by the parliaments, which would in effect make the draft treaty hostage to the elites of the republics.

Yet the powers of the State Council were strengthened by common agreement: Henceforth its decisions would be binding for the executive branch, that is, for the same leaders who, a few hours earlier, had been fighting desperately to strip "the center" of any power over them. But these obvious contradictions did not bother anyone. It was clear that the end of the game had been postponed and that the signing of the treaty, for which Gorbachev had been waiting so impatiently, had moved off again like the ever-receding line of the horizon. The "confederal" and democratic state had barely had time to materialize before it began to dissolve like a mirage in the desert.

This was further confirmed by an argument that took place between Yeltsin and Shevardnadze concerning the duties of the Union foreign minister. This was Shevardnadze's first council meeting after resuming office as chief of diplomacy. He had had a long talk with Yeltsin when he was first appointed, and during the coup he had spent the crucial night inside the besieged White House with Yeltsin. All of this led him to believe that he was entitled to more favorable treatment from the Russian government than his predecessor, Boris Pankin. However, Shevardnadze's attempt to broaden the mandate of the foreign minister as set forth in the treaty met with an icy reception from Yeltsin, who even went back on his recent vow not to establish Russian embassies.

When all the members of the State Council had signed the joint communiqué, which was more an epitaph for the Union than the proclamation of a brave new world, Gorbachev tried to organize another group press conference like the one that had raised everyone's hopes after the previous meeting. However, neither Yeltsin nor the other "republicans" would allow themselves to be trapped a second time. Gorbachev had to face the eager journalists alone. He made no attempt to conceal his disappointment, confirming that the republics had taken a step backward. In the final analysis, the only potential ally he had left was public opinion. The USSR had ceased to be a state, but at least it was still a single country, in which one could hope for a consensus.

The second part of the session was devoted to preparations for economic reform in Russia. Gorbachev asked Yeltsin to describe the Russian leaders' plans. Yeltsin announced their intention to deregulate prices on consumer products (except energy), some food products, and vodka as of December 16. The floor was opened for debate.

The rise in prices, combined with the obvious consequences of the restructuring of the economy, such as massive unemployment, would make for a drop of one-third in the standard of living. This estimate, as it turned out, was about ten times too low. At least, such were the conclusions drawn from the calculations performed by the specialists on the team led by Yegor Gaidar, the prime mover of the Russian plan for economic reform. For a society whose economy was half destroyed, and much of whose population was already precariously balanced at the subsistence level, this could mean not only economic distress but social catastrophe.

"We are convinced that there is no other solution," Yeltsin said firmly. "The important thing is to keep people off the streets, although we are not sure that we can do that everywhere."

The leaders of the republics realized that the locomotive of Russian reform could no longer be stopped. At the same time, for most of them, especially the representatives of the Central Asian republics, the deregulation of prices in Russia was a threat to their countries' very existence because of their dependence on Russian oil and the ruble. Without disputing the overall intentions of the Russians, the presidents of these republics, caught unprepared, merely asked that the beginning of the reform program be postponed so that they could have more time to work out social protection measures.

Gorbachev was gratified to see Yeltsin confronted with the complexities and contradictions of the vast USSR, but he refrained from siding with the other republics. "Security measures must be taken, of course," he said, "but we shouldn't drag our heels, either. Do whatever you can, but for heaven's sake, do something!"

Grigory Yavlinsky was asked to take the floor and give an assessment of the potential effects of the Russian government's program. A team of young economists who favored Yeltsin's "shock therapy" was now about to implement basically the same ideas that Yavlinsky had incorporated into his 500-Day Plan—but this time, these concepts were to be applied under straitened economic circumstances and with no pity for the suffering population.

Drawing on all the experience in political diplomacy that he had acquired in his dealings with the apparat, Yavlinsky painted a devastating picture of an economy falling into ruins, with production plummeting and social unrest on the rise.

"Is it still possible to open the parachute?" Gorbachev asked. "To do that, you would have to catch up with the person who is falling, give him the parachute and help him put it on," Yavlinsky replied. Yavlinsky didn't actually use the words "reckless adventurism," but the phrase was implicit in what he said.

In this situation, Gorbachev willingly resumed his role as the great compromiser. He backed Yeltsin's decision to speed up reform. "If we don't do it, we'll go bankrupt anyway," he said. Nevertheless, he requested that the timing and the sequence of the stages be carefully reconsidered, and he warned the other leaders against gloating if Yeltsin should fail. "If reform breaks down in Russia, it will die everywhere in the Soviet Union. That is why those who say in private, 'let Yeltsin solve his own problems' are wrong."

At the end of the meeting, he received a telegram from the leader of Azerbaidzhan. He read it aloud. Mutalibov was asking the State Council to take emergency measures in order to defend his republic against Armenian "aggression." Duly mandated by the other members of the council, Gorbachev made emergency calls to both the Armenian and the Azerbaidzhani leaders and invited them to come to Moscow two days later to discuss the deteriorating situation.

The urgent crisis in Nagorno-Karabakh unexpectedly provided further support for the existence of the State Council, and thus of a union. The impasse in

Karabakh after four years of unresolved conflict between Armenia and Azerbaidzhan confirmed the need, if not for a repressive "center," at least for a peacemaking supranational mediator, an arbitrator, or in Russian parlance, a "justice of the peace." Gorbachev could not disregard this additional opportunity to legitimize the Union, even as the result of a negative experience, since he knew that he had virtually no other hope of reconciling the parties.

The session ended with another attempt—perhaps the last one—by the republics to defend their rights against their Russian "big brother," by appealing to the president of the Union for mediation: During the frenzy of wholesale nationalization, when all enterprises and organizations located on Russian soil were being placed under Russian jurisdiction, the mint, Gosznak, had been "Russified." This, understandably, caused some consternation in the other republics.

Yeltsin defended himself against the accusation that he was trying to appropriate a strategic instrument necessary to the Union (which had not yet been liquidated) by explaining that Russia was taking control of only the "physical plant" and employee benefits and that it would continue to honor all orders from the State Bank, Gosbank. These arguments convinced no one. Yeltsin backed down, agreeing to "leave coin production" temporarily under the control of the center and subsequently to turn it over to the interbank union provided for in the economic accord. Having carved out this little island of common space where the red flag of the USSR could continue to fly—as the waters rose around it—the members of the State Council left Novo-Ogarevo late that night, never to return.

After their departure, everyone on the President's team, including Yavlinsky, assembled for a light meal—the last time they would eat together at Novo-Ogarevo. The tone was that of a dinner among friends. No one bothered with presidential protocol—not out of negligence but because everybody, including the President, was very tired.

Fight to the Finish

The next day, during the interval between two sessions of the State Council, Gorbachev met with his aides. He outlined his trip around the country and the main impressions it had made on him: He felt that people wanted change and were willing to accept a lower standard of living in order to achieve it but that they expected the "center" to implement real measures. And there was something else that he had found very inspiring: Everywhere, from Irkutsk to Bishkek, the fate of the Union was a prime concern. According to Gorbachev, people felt that failure to preserve a unified state would mean disaster.

Gorbachev had been pleasantly surprised by the warm welcome he had received. He was certain that a large percentage of the population in the provinces sympathized with him and was willing to support him. And that meant that he had every reason to be optimistic about the outcome of a presidential election.

As usual, to "let off steam" from the day before, he described the last session of the State Council in detail, emphasizing the results that left some hope for a rational course, or at least did not preclude that possibility. "It's hard to work with people whose position changes every time the wind shifts," he complained. "Even the media apparently give more thought to the fate of the Union than some allegedly responsible politicians do."

In his opinion, at that session Yeltsin had contracted an obligation to start coordinating his decrees on price deregulation and the subsequent phases of reform with the republics. "If he doesn't do that, reform will become reckless adventurism," he said, using the phrase Yavlinsky had avoided. "We are in a situation where the train is already moving and everybody is running in front of it trying to lay track."

He asked his top political advisers and a few specially invited experts to offer their political and sociological prognosis as to how society would react to the changes the reform package was designed to introduce. This assessment was to be in the nature of a political timetable. "Because in the spring," he said, "the Right will be getting ready not to seize power but to pick it up where it has been dropped."

With the current economic problems beginning to weigh more and more heavily on the governments of the republics, Gorbachev's aides advised him to concentrate on the more general aspects of his office: He should be a symbol of the unity of the country, its strategic role internationally, its position in global politics, and its potential as a cultural and ethical force.

Theoretically, this was perfectly sound reasoning, bolstered by parallels with presidential governments and even parliamentary monarchies in other countries. Once liberated from the constraints of executive duties, the head of state should assume a more exalted position. But these recommendations by Gorbachev's inner circle were too lofty, and the President was left alone to face the contradictory and often irrational reality of his country—a reality that could hardly be said to fit any abstract pattern.

❀   ❀   ·   ❀

The next session of the State Council was held at the Kremlin on November 27. This session was actually a continuation of the session of the 25th and was devoted entirely to the conflict in Karabakh. It was attended by the leaders of Azerbaidzhan and Armenia. The heads of the army, the Ministry of the Interior, and security had also been called in.

Gorbachev opened the meeting with a brief address in which he proposed that the council seek a mutually acceptable solution to the conflict and asserted that it would be dishonorable to stray from this path, as some people were advising. "How can we ignore Karabakh if we are making every effort to help Yugoslavia?" he said.

After Gorbachev's remarks, Mutalibov and Ter-Petrossian presented their views of the situation and the course it was likely to take. They both spoke reasonably and with restraint, noting that they were in favor of political solutions and acknowledging that the problem of Karabakh could not be solved by force.

Their respective peoples had already paid a high price for the fact that this reasonableness on the part of their leaders was so late in coming. At last count, there were more than 1,000 dead and 8,000 wounded. After four years of conflict, both parties were virtually back to square one from a military standpoint, but the relations between the two peoples had been exacerbated by the recent bloodletting and the militant decisions made by their respective parliaments and governments. All that seemed to lie ahead was another impasse and more bloody fighting. Gorbachev proposed that the council take another look at the possible directions the situation might take.

Scenario 1: The Soviet army would leave the zone of conflict, naturally taking its weapons with it. Armed or perhaps unarmed people, even women and children, would try to block its path. It would have no choice but to fight its way out of the encirclement. The border would have to be opened up, and there would be a flood of refugees. In addition, problems would arise between Azerbaidzhanis and Iranians and between Armenians and Turks. Result: another international conflict, and a big headache, not just for us but for the world at large.

Scenario 2: Foreign governments would actively intervene in the conflict, with a buildup of foreign troops. However, the Russian government did not have authorization to deploy the army outside its own national boundaries. So what was the solution? And besides, military methods had to be allied with a political solution.

The defense minister supported Gorbachev's conclusion: Troops could not replace the organs of civil power, which must function on their own. The takeoff point for any solution would have to be political. The most important thing was to subdue the partisans in both camps who had developed a taste for bloodshed.

Shevardnadze took the floor and immediately elevated the discussion to a higher plane. "We are facing the threat of a global conflict" was the essence of his message. He considered it obvious that this conflict, as it evolved, would not remain confined within our borders. No one could tell what Iran and Turkey might do. The conclusion to be drawn from his dramatic speech was clear: We could choose either community and cooperation or civil war—perhaps even world war.

After this passionate warning, which was strongly reminiscent of Shevardnadze's prophecy about the right-wing coup d'état, the meeting was temporarily adjourned. Gorbachev took advantage of the break to draft a resolution. Its main points were as follows: repeal of the illegal actions taken by the supreme soviets of the two republics altering the legal status of the autonomous region of Nagorno-Karabakh; resumption of bilateral negotiations in the spirit of the resolutions made at the Zheleznovodsk meeting (this was a bow to Yeltsin and Nazarbaev); a cease-fire and withdrawal of the illegal armed troops from the zone of conflict; lifting of the blockade on Armenia.

This resolution was actually designed to reestablish the authority of the Constitution of the USSR in Nagorno-Karabakh, since it had been attacked by the extremists and even by political leaders of both parties. Remarkably, Gorbachev's language was acceptable to both presidents. One would have been hard pressed to come up with a more convincing illustration of the usefulness of a unified state.

The heads of the two independent Caucasian states left the council session together. The television cameras had time to record their quiet, almost friendly conversation; but the fatalistic expressions on their faces also came through. Although this council meeting might have confirmed that the leaders of the Union republics could still come to a mutual understanding, the hope that their agreements would actually be complied with grew fainter with each passing day.

The crisis in Karabakh had escalated from the exacerbation of a chronic but minor ethnic conflict to a maelstrom that was pulling in the entire Caucasus, including Georgia, as well as Turkey, Iran, and, ultimately, Russia. Only Russia had the means to prevent those involved directly in the conflicts—including itself—from sliding into "the devil's alternative." But Russia proved unable to do so, either as a member of the Union or after it had acquired its own unlimited sovereignty.

❀   ❀   ❀

Meanwhile, Gorbachev's aides had gone on to implement their own recommendations on the creation of a new, more "monumental" image for the President, one that would help to raise him above routine problems. As chance would have it, the first member of the intelligentsia to meet with Gorbachev was the sculptor Ernst Neizvestny, a specialist in "monumental propaganda." Neizvestny had become embroiled in a conflict with Khrushchev that had forced him to emigrate to the West; a few years later, however, he had created the monument for Khrushchev's tomb in Novodevichy Cemetery.

It would have been hard to find a better partner for a metaphysical discussion. It turned out that Neizvestny had been a philosophy student at Moscow State University while Gorbachev was going to law school there. He arrived in the company of two of his best friends from that era: Anatoly Chernyaev, who had become one of Gorbachev's close advisers, and Yuri Kariakin, an author and essayist who had served as a deputy in the Union Parliament during the perestroika years.

Initially, the two men took some time to size each other up. The conversation ran in two parallel but separate veins. Neizvestny began with the idea that mythology was inevitably at the root of all totalitarianism. He said that the monument to the victims of Stalinism that he had created, which was going to be erected simultaneously in three cities in the Soviet Union, would actually be a monument to the utopian consciousness, "to the ogre that devoured itself."

Gorbachev countered that the whole country had been living in a world of inverted values for many years. Responding to a remark by Kariakin, he commented that Dostoevsky's *The Possessed* had been his bedside reading for years. This was the book that had changed him into a "dissident."

Moving on to the present, he said that it worried him to see history repeat itself: "It's crazy to go around shouting that we have to banish socialism from our soil. Socialism has been the work of whole generations and millions of people. Each of us in his own way is a product of this utopian and ultraradical idea."

His humiliation before the Russian parliament in August suddenly came to mind.[45] "In principle, on political and moral grounds, I should not have tolerated that. But I saw their eyes: These people had no pity for me or for themselves. Behind that hatred there is nothing but darkness."

"How is it you've lasted this long?" Neizvestny wondered. "It's like slaloming through a minefield. You know, you're at a turning point in history, and things seldom work out for people like you."

"It's probably a combination of a lot of things," Gorbachev answered with a shrug. "Good health inherited from my parents and my peasant ancestors, a strong spirit, thanks to Raisa Maximovna, and, especially, faith."

Neizvestny nodded, with a look of compassion and understanding. "People need faith," he said, "even if it is false. Do you remember the plaque Luther nailed to the door of his church? 'I believe, and cannot do otherwise.'"[46]

"We are unique subjects for students of transitional periods," Gorbachev said. "You know why we have such a hard time leaving the past behind: We're leaving ourselves." He recalled a meeting with Leonid Leonov, a dean of Soviet literature. "He told me, 'Your tragedy is that the changes you have envisioned will not bring quick results; but people want a better life right away, and they've earned it.'"

"I am feeling very sad," sighed Neizvestny. "There is a struggle going on inside me. In one part of my soul, I am a staunch democrat, and even an anarchist: I would give my life for freedom. Not because it is an 'acknowledged necessity,' as Engels taught, but the ability to go your own way. Still, I am in favor of order, the state. Given their profession, sculptors are often believers in the state."

"This may be the most difficult period of all for me," Gorbachev confessed in turn. "I feel that democracy cannot be defended without a certain authoritarianism. Although people have always blamed me for demanding extraordinary powers, nobody has ever wondered why I never used them."

"I wonder if you didn't have more latitude with the old, tame Central Committee than you do with the aggressive new leadership," said Neizvestny.

"It doesn't matter. We've beaten them on the most important issues," Gorbachev replied. "Unfortunately, those who have replaced the Communists are in many ways worse, not better, than they were. This is an indication that our society is very ill. Those who denounced the Communists have set up a system of privileges for themselves that the Communists never dreamed of. They jostle each other like hogs at a trough. Crassness, greed, and venality are flourishing. I would like to believe that this is a crisis from which society will emerge cured."

The meeting lasted almost two hours—further evidence of the President's new freedom. He was not interrupted by phone calls, and no one asked him to drop what he was doing and settle a border dispute or organize deliveries of food supplies. He belonged less and less to his official duties and increasingly to himself—and to the ages.

❀   ❀   ❀

December 1, the date of the referendum and the Ukrainian presidential election, was approaching. There was nervous anticipation in Kiev, in Moscow, and in Washington.

On the day before the vote, when domestic policy regulations dictated that all election propaganda had to stop, a rather unsettling signal emerged from Washington. A press leak indicated that if Ukraine voted for independence, the United States would establish diplomatic relations with it.

This could only be taken as encouragement for the states with separatist leanings and as a direct attempt to influence the result of the elections. Chernyaev and I reported the news to Gorbachev, who immediately called Eduard Shevardnadze. Shevardnadze obviously did not want to sour relations with the Americans and advised Gorbachev "not to take these unofficial rumors seriously."

Gorbachev, indignant, nevertheless dictated a brief communiqué from the presidential press service, expressing the Kremlin's "astonishment" at the news. The Americans felt that they had acted hastily and had exceeded the bounds of propriety. Bush called Gorbachev on November 30 and assured him that Washington was in no way seeking to "create any difficulties whatsoever for Gorbachev or for Yeltsin, even inadvertently."

Bush explained that after the referendum, the outcome of which was easy to predict, the issue of recognizing the independence of Ukraine would arise in one way or another, and he supported Gorbachev's argument that all of this should not prevent—and even might contribute to—Ukraine's return to the process of signing the Union Treaty.

Gorbachev's reply was curt, clearly suggesting that the United States had touched on a very sensitive subject that he still considered within the province of the domestic affairs of the Union over which he presided. "The leaks from the White House," said Gorbachev, "have been seen in a negative light here. Many people feel that the United States not only wants to influence events in the Soviet Union—which it is already doing—but also to actually interfere in our affairs."

Gorbachev warned Bush not to be hasty or "become agitated" over the issue of an independent Ukraine. He cited the situation in Yugoslavia, where it was the Americans who were holding back the more impatient Europeans. He spoke again of the problems that would arise in the Crimea, the Donbass, and other regions of Ukraine if the results of the referendum led to a break with the new union. "That would turn twelve million Russians and people of other ethnic origins who live in Ukraine into 'citizens of another country.'" He asked Bush to take these considerations into account so that the situation could "evolve naturally, which is why we have to give it time." Gorbachev also let Bush know that he had discussed the situation with Yeltsin and that after the referendum, they were probably going to approach Kravchuk and propose a meeting between the presidents of the Union, Russia, and Ukraine.

Bush told Gorbachev in a conciliatory tone that the United States wanted to obstruct any radical elements, in Russia as well as in Ukraine, and would make any action that might lead to diplomatic recognition of Ukraine contingent on settlement of the nuclear weapons issue, compliance with human and minority rights, application of the disarmament treaties, and the fulfillment of obligations relating to the USSR's foreign debt.

With the approach of the Ukrainian referendum, it was becoming increasingly clear to Gorbachev that the nightmare of a divided union might soon become a reality. He tried to keep that thought at bay while striving to convince domestic and foreign public opinion of the harm that would be caused by disintegration.

"Our country is a unique human community," he explained to Mortimer Zuckerman, editor in chief of *U.S. News and World Report.* "It has been evolving for a thousand years, and everything in it is bound together tightly by history, culture, shared traditions, family and interpersonal ties, the fact of living together, the division of labor, cooperation in industry and science. If we split apart, that process would be so painful that under the present conditions it would be a catastrophe." At the time, these words were taken as an appeal; they now sound like a prophecy.

"If Ukraine leaves the union," said Gorbachev in November, "the Crimea will insist that its 1954 annexation to Ukraine be repealed and will demand to be given back to Russia. But if Ukraine remains in the new Union of Sovereign States, the Crimea will have no objection to belonging to Ukraine."

He addressed the same subject in an interview with the Belorussian newspaper *Narodnaya gazeta.* "We must not rend a fabric that has been woven over the course of centuries. . . . Seventy-five million people live outside the boundaries of their ethnic homelands. Will they all have to become second-class citizens? And we don't want to hear the old assurance that everything will be guaranteed by bilateral treaties concluded between the republics. I do not believe that that can solve the problem if we don't preserve the state, which provides for the legal defense of each individual. . . . In abandoning one extreme, that of the overcentralized unitary state, we must not allow ourselves to be dragged into chaos and the dismantling of the unified state. That would mean an irreparable loss for us all."

No one was listening to Gorbachev at this point. Instead, the reverse logic was gaining credence: The structures of the USSR should be tossed out once and for all in order to get rid of the President, who was putting up such obstinate resistance.

It was during these last few days of November that the Russian and Ukrainian presidential advisers grew dissatisfied with mere long-distance entente and established direct official contact with each other. Gennady Burbulis, Yeltsin's éminence grise, made a discreet trip to Kiev to assure Kravchuk of support: Immediately after his victory in the referendum, Russia would back his interpretation of the results as a vote in favor of leaving the proposed union and would in turn use this Ukrainian position to block the treaty negotiations in Novo-Ogarevo once and for all.

This tacit agreement was a real gift for Kravchuk: He had Russia's go-ahead to establish Ukraine immediately as a sovereign nation within boundaries undreamed of by even the most extremist Rukh elements. For the Russian leadership, however, the most important stakes in the game were the head (and the office in the Kremlin) of the president of the Union, and it was willing to see every raise, no matter how high. As the philosopher Alexander Tsipko would subsequently write, the "Crimea for the Kremlin" swap had been arranged. Gorbachev's fate and that of a country of more than 300 million inhabitants were thrown into the pot in absentia.

❀   ❀   ❀

Two days before zero hour, November 29, Gorbachev met with his team of political advisers: Bakatin, Velikhov, Petrakov, Popov, Ryzhov, Sobchak, Shevardnadze, Yavlinsky, Yegor Yakovlev, and Alexander Yakovlev.[47] The meeting lasted from three in the afternoon until nine in the evening; in the words of the press release, those present "stated that they were unanimously in favor of immediate signing of the Union Treaty."

Naturally, these advisers did not have to spend six hours together to convince each other of that. Most of their time had actually been spent working out joint reactions to the decisions that the Russian government was constantly firing off without consulting the Kremlin, and that were so many loops in the noose tightening around the Union's neck.

On this particular occasion, the Russian leadership had suspended the extension of credit to the USSR's Gosbank, which automatically stopped payments to everyone who depended on the Union budget, including the army. This news reached me in the midst of the meeting between the President and his political advisers, and I placed the dispatch in front of him without a word. After an exchange of excited exclamations and a few telephone conversations with the president of Gosbank, Viktor Gerashchenko, it was decided that Yeltsin should be asked to come over and explain the situation. Gorbachev agreed to see him the next day.

The meeting between the two presidents took place on November 30 and was devoted "to examining the situation relating to the implementation of the state budget during the last quarter of 1991." By placing a financial gun to Gorbachev's head, Yeltsin extorted from him a promise "to substantially reduce the operating expenses of the Union." In exchange, Russia said that it was willing to "assume responsibility for the credit guarantees granted to Gosbank in order to cover the minimum necessary expenses agreed upon for the last quarter of 1991."

Yeltsin had every reason to be satisfied with the results of the meeting. He had managed to hamstring the monster of the Union *nomenklatura* and at the same time to show everyone that the balance of presidential power in the Union was now in his favor.

Sunday, December 1, was spent waiting for the first results of the Ukrainian referendum. Since early evening, zealous, obliging informants, offering scraps of information from polling places in the Donbass, Nikolaev, Odessa, and the Crimea, kept alive Gorbachev's vain hope that "his" Ukraine would not buy into the nationalists' promises and, although voting for Kravchuk, would refuse to take the bait of independence, or at least would be divided on the issue.

Before the final results were announced, the President signed an urgent appeal to members of Parliament and had it sent to the parliaments of the various republics. He revealed the contents of this message during a television appearance on December 3.

It was a race against time. As Kravchuk's victory in Ukraine turned into a landslide, Gorbachev used this appeal in an attempt to reinitiate the process of approval of the Union Treaty, like a driver tinkering with the engine of his stalled car. "I have decided to appeal to you," he explained to the members of Parliament, "because of my growing concern regarding the preservation of our homeland. The historical logic of the existence of this vast, united country has been broken, and the disintegration has exceeded the bounds of rationality; it has gone so far that it has taken on a destructive character. The draft Union Treaty has been submitted to you for approval. Either your decision will draw all of society closer to new ways of life, or each of our peoples will be condemned to long and hopeless attempts to manage on its own. Clearly, the latter situation would have severe consequences. The collapse of our multiethnic community will bring millions of our fellow citizens such unhappiness as to far outweigh all the possible temporary advantages of separation—a collapse fraught with national and interrepublic confrontations, and even wars. . . .

"This would be a catastrophe for the entire international community, the end of all the achievements made possible by the new political thinking, the inevitable loss of our international influence, at a high cost to all our peoples. Over the past few years our state has become one of the pillars of the new world order that is being established. If it crumbles, a chain reaction will follow whose consequences for all of humanity are difficult to foresee. . . .

"My position is clear: I am in favor of the new Union of Sovereign States, a confederal democratic state. I want my opinion to be known to everyone as you make your decision. We cannot delay any longer. Any loss of time could have disastrous consequences."

A presidential election was also held in Kazakhstan that Sunday, and Nursultan Nazarbaev was reelected by a majority worthy of the preperestroika years: more than 98 percent of the vote. This gave Gorbachev the chance to play down the devastating effect of Kravchuk's triumph. As soon as the first reliable estimates had been released, Gorbachev called Nazarbaev and Kravchuk to congratulate them "on a provisional basis," since the official tallies were not in yet.

Gorbachev summed up the results of the elections as follows: "The will of the peoples of the two republics to consolidate their independence and their sovereignty, as expressed in the two elections, gives them a new freedom to make an informed choice and to decide whether to join the new Union of Sovereign States. Independence is not an obstacle on the road to a new Union Treaty. On the contrary, the complete sovereignty of the republics is precisely what enables them to make considered and voluntary decisions concerning their membership in the future union."

This reasoning was a little forced, since Kravchuk's impressive victory (61.6 percent of the vote for him and 90.3 percent for independence) obviously had elevated him to the position of a national leader who could withstand a test of strength with Gorbachev, based on this popular mandate that the President of the Union so painfully lacked.

Russia would be the key player in this situation. Theoretically, there should have been no radical changes in the Russian position, since even though the results of the Ukrainian elections had not been known ahead of time, they were certainly easy to foresee. Nevertheless, the Russian leadership preferred to view the results of the referendum as a completely new development. It decided not to miss this opportunity to break with the proposed union and the obligations it had contracted during the Novo-Ogarevo process. And it had an almost perfect excuse to do so, in the form of Ukraine's obstinacy in the treaty negotiations.

Actually, the scenario for the breakup of the new union had already been worked out down to the smallest detail and the legal phraseology established. Everyone was just waiting for the director to call "Action!"

It was advisable not to injure Gorbachev ahead of time, of course, in order to avoid any surprises on his part. A strategy of appeasement was therefore adopted. Yeltsin informed Gorbachev of his intention to go to Minsk to discuss bilateral problems with Shushkevich. He said that at the same time it would be a good idea to hear what Kravchuk had to say so that they could find out his intentions regarding the new union. In addition, Yeltsin said that he would like to coordinate with Gorbachev the tactics that he should use to persuade the Ukrainian president not to break away from the union.

After this meeting between Yeltsin and Gorbachev, the two presidents told the press separately that they "could not conceive of the union without Ukraine." Yeltsin added that "every effort must be made to convince the Ukrainians to sign the Union Treaty." He also tacked on a remark that failed to attract any particular attention at the time: "If that doesn't work, we'll have to consider other options."

Gorbachev later described this meeting in his book *December 1991*:[48] "I spoke with Yeltsin before he left for Minsk. I presented my arguments, both old and new. But he just kept saying, what about Ukraine though? Can you guarantee that it will be part of the union? I began to sense that he had a hidden agenda. And when I found out that Burbulis and Shakhrai[49] were going to Minsk, it all became clear. Burbulis at one time had written a memo that was shown around in various offices even though it was marked 'strictly confidential.' What did this memo say? That Russia had already lost half of what it had gained after the August putsch. That cunning Gorbachev was setting a trap to revitalize the old 'center,' and the other republics would support him.

"All of this is contrary to Russia's interests and must be stopped. With this in mind, I tried to convince Yeltsin that Ukraine could be drawn into the process of approving the treaty and that the most important step was to get the Russian Federation to sign it first. But he rejected my arguments, and I could already sense why. The Russian leadership was tired of having any 'center' at all. These are the roots of what happened in Belovezhskaya Forest."

Gorbachev spoke of his phone conversation with Kravchuk to the mayor of Berlin, Eberhard Diepgen, whom he received at the Kremlin on December 2. "I asked Kravchuk: You've heard what I've said about independence for the republics. Why have you decided to interpret it as meaning that you have to leave the union? Other republics proclaimed their independence before you did and are still taking part in the building of the new union.

"There is nothing strange about the fact that the majority of the Ukrainian population voted for independence. Who would have wanted to vote against it? Last March, however, roughly as many people said they were in favor of preserving the union with Ukraine's participation. That means that if the question had been worded differently, 'independence outside of or within the union,' the results would have been different."

On December 3, Helmut Kohl phoned Gorbachev to ask him a direct question: "Tell me, Mikhail, what is really going on in your country?" Gorbachev answered that the main issue, for him, was the future structure of the state. If too much time was allowed to go by, there would be a tremendous risk of disintegration that would affect not just the economy but society as a whole. He said that if matters dragged on for another month or two, several aspects of the reform process might be called into question.

"And how do you see the situation in Ukraine?" Kohl asked.

"You see," Gorbachev replied, "what they're trying to do is present the referendum as a vote for separation from the union. Independence and sovereignty are automatically considered to be in the nature of a separation. But that isn't true. If

Ukraine leaves, if it suddenly breaks away from the union, we will be facing some very dangerous events." Gorbachev was asked the same questions by Lech Walesa and Jozsef Antall over the next few days.

Although Poland's position, dictated by considerations of realpolitik, was that it would be the first to recognize Ukraine, President Walesa was careful to express his support for Gorbachev: His phone call was very cordial, and a few days later, in an appearance on Soviet television, he launched an emotional appeal to "support Gorbachev" and the path he advocated, that of gradual democratic reform. The Polish ambassador to Moscow, Stanislaw Ciosek, confirmed to me that Walesa was willing to pay a visit to Gorbachev and sign a treaty with the new union if that would help him to preserve it.

Gorbachev met with Hungarian prime minister Jozsef Antall on December 6. "The crucial thing," Gorbachev explained to him, "is not to allow the process of reformulating the Union to become a process of decomposition. That would be our common tragedy, and the international community's as well."

By way of reply, Antall shared some insights from Hungary's history. "The tragedy is not the crumbling of an empire, as the example of Austria-Hungary shows. Tragedy begins only where boundaries divide people artificially. After World War I, Hungary lost two-thirds of its historical national territory and almost half its population. This should be kept in mind, and sovereignty for the republics must be achieved within a stable, civilized framework."

Antall also offered some "friendly advice," as he himself called it: "In any event, it is impossible to lead a country such as yours from a single center. The republics must feel that they are sovereign and must establish forms of self-government. This is the only foundation on which a natural union can grow." Unfortunately, in place of this universally acclaimed, logical, rational, "natural union," another prospect was becoming increasingly apparent to Gorbachev: the "Lebanization" of the country—or, to choose an example closer to home, its "Balkanization."

Antall, of course, could not refrain from mentioning the events of 1956 in his conversation with Gorbachev. Paradoxically, although the invasion of Czechoslovakia by the Warsaw Pact troops in August of 1968 had been assigned a suitable political "classification" and filed away in the historical archives, there was still some ambiguity in the official attitude toward the action in Hungary, which had been much bloodier and more violent. Neither the president of the USSR nor the Soviet Parliament had issued any official statement of regret or condemnation of this act of armed intervention in the domestic affairs of a friendly neighboring state and a "fraternal" people.

During the press briefing that preceded Antall's arrival, I had mentioned the Budapest action as unacceptable interference in Hungarian affairs and had expressed rejection of the political thinking that had inspired it, which had subsequently been termed the "limited sovereignty," or Brezhnev, doctrine. Naturally, I was the only person bound by these statements, even if they were understood as an unofficial expression of the President's thinking. Whenever I was about to hold a press conference, Gorbachev liked to go over current events and the "hot" issues with me beforehand. With the head of the Hungarian government about to pay a visit, we both knew quite well what points would be addressed and were therefore prepared.

The fact that Gorbachev did not confirm the statement I made during the briefing indicated that it could be considered as having been made on my own personal initiative. Nevertheless, the Hungarians referred to it as an official statement of Gorbachev's position.

Antall, in addressing the still unsettled dispute, said that the Hungarian Party felt there was no reason to treat the Hungarian intervention any differently from the invasion of Czechoslovakia. He repeated what he had said to Soviet ambassador Boris Stukalin in 1989, when he still belonged to a semilegal political opposition party: "If you take the handcuffs off our wrists, we will become your truest friends."

Antall said that he had been both a witness to and a participant in the events of November 1956 and had even been condemned to death. He told Gorbachev that the secret police, and not the insurgents, had been the first to open fire on the Soviet troops. "At that time, there was no danger of fascism in Hungary," he explained. "Mr. President, you can speak your mind on the past with a clear conscience, without betraying the memory of the Soviet citizens who died in Budapest." He handed Gorbachev a commemorative medal stamped with the image of two hands clasped in friendship.

Gorbachev, visibly moved by this speech, reassured Antall, stating that he firmly intended to bring the matter to resolution. He promised to take the earliest opportunity to publicly confirm the Soviet leadership's assessment of this "tragic page" in the history of the two peoples. He found this opportunity just a few minutes later, during the joint press conference held with Antall after their talk.

Gorbachev's condemnation of the 1956 intervention brought the history of Soviet-Hungarian relations to a dignified close. A half-hour later, again in the Catherine Room of the Kremlin, Antall met with Yeltsin and joined him in starting a fresh page in Russo-Hungarian relations. While some members of the Magyar delegation were still bidding farewell to Gorbachev's staff as they left the room, Antall was already extending his hand to Yeltsin, who had come in through another door.

❁   ❁   ❁

The mysterious meeting of the three Slavic leaders would be held shortly in Minsk, and Gorbachev kept wondering whether he had done everything in his power to influence the situation or had missed some opportunity. On December 6 he called Kravchuk and Nazarbaev to propose that they meet with him in his office on Monday the 9th, noting that Yeltsin and Shushkevich had already agreed to come. The two newly elected presidents gave their consent.

On December 7, Gorbachev received a group of U.S. businessmen who were working to provide children with access to education and had come to the Soviet Union on a humanitarian mission. "I am going to use every means at my disposal to get through to the people. I am sure to obtain support," Gorbachev told them at the end of the meeting.

Actually, Gorbachev's actions at this point were like those of a professional tennis player who is about to lose a match but still struggles for every ball because he knows that until that last point is lost, regardless of his opponent's advantage, anything is possible, including victory. There was a joke going around Moscow that the acronym for the Union of Sovereign States meant "the Union to Save Gorbachev," since the initial letters are the same in Russian. But the appeals Gorbachev was making to the country and the world were intended to save the unity of the state and his plan for reform.

While the leaders of Russia, Belorussia, and Ukraine held their discussions behind tightly closed doors in Minsk and, later, in a secluded corner of Belovezhskaya Forest near Brest, Gorbachev gave two important interviews: He kept an old promise he had made two years earlier to appear on the French television program *Sept sur sept,* with Anne Sinclair, and he engaged in a nearly two-hour discussion with a political commentator on Ukrainian television. The first program was to be shown in France and throughout Europe, where the national leaders were preparing to announce political union at Maastricht. The second was destined for Ukraine and the rest of the Soviet Union, which was on the verge of irreversible disintegration.

Gorbachev considered these television appearances very important. Before meeting with the French news team, Gorbachev spent an hour with Chernyaev and me, going over the main topics that would be addressed during the program.

His last important interview on France's Channel 1 (TF1) had taken place on October 1, 1985, on the eve of his first visit to France. For the occasion, he had allowed the TF1 cameras to be brought into the Kremlin and had agreed to answer questions from three journalists: Alain Denvers, editor in chief for political affairs, anchorman Yves Mourousi, and Dominique Bromberger, a specialist in international affairs. This was a major event at the time: It was very unusual for a general secretary of the powerful CPSU to bow to the demands of media professionals. For the French television audience, this broadcast was the pilot episode for the long-running series on Gorbachevian perestroika, which combined all the elements of the most fascinating programs: passion, intrigue, suspense, drama—in fact, more of this last ingredient than was needed for a mere thriller, since the drama was being played out by a people, a country, and its leader and demanded very real suffering on the part of the lead actors.

This first broadcast on TF1 was also Gorbachev's first interview with a foreign television station. He wasn't quite himself yet: His answers to the journalists' questions were preceded by a long, prerecorded speech aimed at the French television audience. And the journalists had a very skeptical attitude toward the new general secretary.

On that occasion, Dominique Bromberger had arrived in Moscow a day ahead of time and had reluctantly agreed to a preliminary meeting with Leonid Zamiatin, head of the Central Committee's international information department. At that meeting Bromberger insisted on his right to ask "any question" during the interview. This right was exercised by his colleague, Yves Mourousi, who began the interview by asking Gorbachev, "Are you a modern man?"—not realizing that he was addressing a man from the future.

Six years later, in December 1991, Gorbachev was about to fade into the past. The more I think back on that interview, the more convinced I am that the political world of the future, which was already clearly evolving at that time, a world without the USSR, will sorely miss his experience, his passionate commitment, and his warmth.

Talking with French journalist Anne Sinclair, Gorbachev was relaxed and charming. Always the southerner, he became more animated with women, especially pretty ones, and showed his best side. "In politics, you have to keep up with what's happening," he explained to Sinclair. "And another important lesson, in international relations as well as domestic politics, is that it's useless to rely on force. Nothing can be settled by violence. Look what it's doing in Yugoslavia: cities destroyed, an economy ruined, millions of dollars lost, so many lives swept away, so many people wounded, so much unhappiness. . . . You have to rely on political dialogue, on democratic methods, on mutual understanding, on cooperation and compromise. I have been convinced of that for a long time. It is the credo of my domestic and foreign policy."

He also told Anne Sinclair and Ulysse Gosset, TF1's permanent Moscow correspondent who was present for the interview, how Leonid Kravchuk had promised to sell the Foros dacha "to whoever wanted it" just to keep him, Gorbachev, from

be preserved as it is now. I want it very much. But I am convinced that if Ukraine chooses the path of separation, changes will be set in motion that you will be dealing with for generations to come.

"I hope that the Ukrainians hear me, not just with their ears but also with their hearts, and that they understand that I want to share my deep concern with them. Don't shake your head, don't shake your head. You know that I am from Ukraine; I have the right to speak this way, to appeal to all the peoples of Ukraine to consider carefully. I'm proceeding on the assumption that there are still normal people, sane people, aside from all these crafty politicians. And they will understand this conversation. It is time for me to say good-bye to the television audience. I hope that it will not be forever, and I beg you once again not to make a mistake at this very important stage in the development of our common destiny and history."

With these words he bade farewell not just to the Ukrainians but also to the entire television audience of the USSR and its former republics. At the very moment when his interview was being rebroadcast by the television station of the Union, that state, by a decision of the three republic leaders assembled in Belovezhskaya Forest, ceased to exist.

tional affairs. This was a major event at the time: It was very unusual for a general secretary of the powerful CPSU to bow to the demands of media professionals. For the French television audience, this broadcast was the pilot episode for the long-running series on Gorbachevian perestroika, which combined all the elements of the most fascinating programs: passion, intrigue, suspense, drama—in fact, more of this last ingredient than was needed for a mere thriller, since the drama was being played out by a people, a country, and its leader and demanded very real suffering on the part of the lead actors.

This first broadcast on TF1 was also Gorbachev's first interview with a foreign television station. He wasn't quite himself yet: His answers to the journalists' questions were preceded by a long, prerecorded speech aimed at the French television audience. And the journalists had a very skeptical attitude toward the new general secretary.

On that occasion, Dominique Bromberger had arrived in Moscow a day ahead of time and had reluctantly agreed to a preliminary meeting with Leonid Zamiatin, head of the Central Committee's international information department. At that meeting Bromberger insisted on his right to ask "any question" during the interview. This right was exercised by his colleague, Yves Mourousi, who began the interview by asking Gorbachev, "Are you a modern man?"—not realizing that he was addressing a man from the future.

Six years later, in December 1991, Gorbachev was about to fade into the past. The more I think back on that interview, the more convinced I am that the political world of the future, which was already clearly evolving at that time, a world without the USSR, will sorely miss his experience, his passionate commitment, and his warmth.

Talking with French journalist Anne Sinclair, Gorbachev was relaxed and charming. Always the southerner, he became more animated with women, especially pretty ones, and showed his best side. "In politics, you have to keep up with what's happening," he explained to Sinclair. "And another important lesson, in international relations as well as domestic politics, is that it's useless to rely on force. Nothing can be settled by violence. Look what it's doing in Yugoslavia: cities destroyed, an economy ruined, millions of dollars lost, so many lives swept away, so many people wounded, so much unhappiness. . . . You have to rely on political dialogue, on democratic methods, on mutual understanding, on cooperation and compromise. I have been convinced of that for a long time. It is the credo of my domestic and foreign policy."

He also told Anne Sinclair and Ulysse Gosset, TF1's permanent Moscow correspondent who was present for the interview, how Leonid Kravchuk had promised to sell the Foros dacha "to whoever wanted it" just to keep him, Gorbachev, from going there any more. He threw up his hands in astonishment at this, as if he himself were surprised by what he had just heard.

It was in the interview with the Ukrainian television commentator, however, that Gorbachev really spoke his mind. He addressed the Ukrainians as if they had not voted for Kravchuk and independence yet, as if it were really possible to turn back the hands of time—in short, as if he were still their president. It was at once impressive, moving, and sad.

"I consider this to be a conversation with the people of Ukraine," he said. "I do not agree with those who say that the vote for independence is a vote to break with the union. I have no doubt that the people of Ukraine are in favor of cooperating with all the sovereign republics, that they are in favor of the new union and new diplomatic relations. They want to build, not destroy. I receive a great deal of information on this subject. A month ago, a poll was taken in Kiev, Moscow, Leningrad, Krasnoyarsk, Alma-Ata, and Novosibirsk, I believe. The results have been released: In Moscow, 80 percent said they were in favor of preserving the Union—a renewed union, of course. In Kiev, it was 64 percent; in Alma-Ata, 72 percent.

"There is another kind of information: living, human. The driver of my official car took a few days off recently because of a death in the family: His uncle had passed away in Lugansk.[50] He went there for a few days to attend the funeral. He told me that people there do not have the slightest intention of separating from the union; they say they have lived together and will keep on doing so. . . . Anything else is out of the question.

"Why would Ukraine or Russia, Belorussia or Kazakhstan, or Kirghizia lose their sovereignty if they make their choice themselves, totally independently? Why not take part in the creation, the building of a new union, a union that would meet their needs, fit their current stage of development, their current role, their capabilities. . . . Those who have been thrust to the fore by the wave of democracy should not act like oracles who know everything in advance, willing to casually write off something that has been ten centuries in the making. Generations have spent all this time building the state; other generations will come after us; and some people want to cut this vast population to pieces, wreck the destinies of millions. The union must be preserved; otherwise, there will be a catastrophe. And in that catastrophe, everything will be lost.

"People must listen to us, they must. I want to tell you everything so that people will realize, in Ukraine, that I love this country, this republic—that I more than love it. You know that. I have no ulterior political motive in this. The Ukrainians must know my mind. I want all of you to understand me: the Ukrainians, the Russians, and everyone who lives in Ukraine. I want Ukraine to

Final Hours

On the evening of Sunday, December 8, my wife and I were returning from our dacha in Uspenskoye, west of Moscow. The previous week had been especially stressful from both a political and an emotional standpoint—as had every day since I had agreed to join Gorbachev's staff. So I was looking forward to spending the rest of the evening at the Pushkin Museum, where Svyatoslav Richter was giving a concert.

The cellular phone rang in the car. I knew it would be the President and asked the driver to stop so I could talk undisturbed. Gorbachev, who was clearly on edge, wanted to know when central television would be running his interview for viewers in Ukraine. I told him that it was to be broadcast that same evening, after *Vremya*, the main news program. This answer did not satisfy him: He wanted to know if the program was definitely going to be run, whether the tape would be shown uncut, and what the exact time would be. His voice bristled with impatience.

I called the television news editor's desk from the car. The interview had, in fact, been scheduled and was going to be run at eleven o'clock that night. I called Gorbachev back. "That's too late," he said through clenched teeth. "Tomorrow is a workday, people will be going to bed early, and it's important that they be able to see the interview before they find out the results of the meeting in Minsk."

It was obvious that he already knew what these results were, and that on that frigid Sunday evening, far from his office, his bank of telephones and his phalanx of aides, with whom he could have evaluated the situation and worked out a modus operandi, he was pacing like a bear in a cage. He wanted to respond to his rivals immediately with the only weapon he had to hand, his interview, and he believed that if it were broadcast one hour earlier, it would still not be too late.

He told me later that Shushkevich had called his dacha and had told him that the three leaders meeting in Belovezhskaya Forest "had reached an agreement," which he offered to read to him over the phone. He had also informed Gorbachev that the minister of defense, Shaposhnikov, was aware of the situation, and that Yeltsin had already spoken to Bush.

Gorbachev had exploded, "You talk to the president of the United States of America and your own president doesn't even know what's going on! That's a disgrace!" He asked for Yeltsin to come to the phone and summoned him to the Kremlin the next day to explain himself. Yeltsin said that he would be there and that he would speak for the "troika"—himself, Kravchuk, and Shushkevich.

145

Later on, it was rumored that the other two *pushchisty*[51] had not come to Moscow because they feared for their personal safety. In point of fact, a plan had obviously been worked out in advance, according to which Yeltsin would be sent as the bearer of a "sealed message" that he could no longer alter. This would eliminate the possibility that Gorbachev's charisma, his experience, and the pressure he would bring to bear might be able to destroy the plans laid in Belorussia, as they had once before. Thus Gorbachev, like Gulliver, would be unable to break the bonds by which he had been tied to the ground during the night.

It is probable that on a purely personal level, Kravchuk and Shushkevich preferred not to confront a vanquished leader to whom, in the final analysis, they owed their own rise to power. In a phone conversation with Revenko the next day, a confused and flustered Shushkevich explained that he couldn't come to Moscow because he had to "think everything over and get some sleep. . . . Everything has been so unexpected, the way it's worked out." Obviously, if Gorbachev and Yeltsin decided to expand the meeting once they had gotten together, he would certainly come. To my knowledge, Kravchuk and Shushkevich have not seen Gorbachev again since their December 1991 coup d'état.

❀   ❀   ❀

The Richter concert was as wonderful as one might have anticipated. With no desire to cut the evening short, we went on to a late supper with the Italian and Dutch ambassadors, whom I knew quite well. The conversation carefully skirted the subject of the hour. Minsk was not mentioned; one doesn't speak of rope in the house of a hanged man. We talked about Georgia and the astonishing metamorphosis of the former dissident and professional democrat Zviad Gamsakhurdia into a sort of Georgian duce. "He's translated a lot of Shakespeare, but he hasn't retained much of it," the Italian ambassador, Ferdinando Saleo, commented sarcastically.

The true story of President Lear was unfolding at that very moment. At home, the phone was ringing off the hook: Muscovite friends who had heard the first news out of Minsk, Bernard Guetta of Paris. In talking to him, I said, "It's a democratic Foros."

I called Vitaly Ignatenko and Yevgeny Primakov, and we scheduled a meeting to exchange views on the new situation. "Mikhail Sergeevich has called me," Primakov announced. "They've decided everything: They're going to create a Commonwealth of Independent States with Minsk as the capital. They've cleared it with Bush." This coup, in contrast to the one that took place in August, left no hope that the USSR and its president would be "resurrected."

The next day I went into Gorbachev's office just after his arrival at the Kremlin. He was composed, well rested, and ready for action. He tried to make up for his brusqueness of the evening before with regard to the timing of the Ukrainian interview by telling me that he felt everything had gone off well.

Gorbachev was waiting to meet with Yeltsin. The appointment was scheduled for noon, and Nazarbaev was to be present—in fact, he had already arrived in Moscow. The President and I exchanged our impressions of the events that had taken place in Belovezhskaya Forest. Gorbachev was in a combative mood and said, "They're going to have to explain all this to the country, to the world, and to me."

He said that he had already spoken to Nazarbaev, who was equally indignant, and was waiting for an explanation from Yeltsin. "And Yeltsin?" I asked. "He promised to come, and then he called me back to tell me that he feared for his personal safety," Gorbachev explained to me. "He was afraid of being arrested. I said, 'Are you crazy?' And he said, 'I'm not, but somebody else might be.' To make a long story short, I managed to convince him. He'll come."

Later on, rumors circulated in Moscow that the antiterrorist arm of the former KGB, the famous Alpha Group, was getting ready to arrest the Belovezhskaya "troika" when at the last minute they received an order to pull back. There was even a report that concrete blocks had been transported to the Kremlin in preparation for a siege. No evidence was ever brought forward to confirm these rumors.

When I left Gorbachev's office Nazarbaev was already waiting in the anteroom, and he went straight in to see the President. A minute later Yeltsin arrived, accompanied by a bodyguard.

The three met for an hour and a half. Afterward, Nazarbaev, looking somber, left directly for the airport. He explained to the press, without attempting to soften his remarks, that he was offended on both a political and a personal level. Not only had the three Slavic leaders broken the Novo-Ogarevo accords behind the President's back, their fait accompli was an insult to the national dignity of the Asiatic republics.

Yeltsin made no comment on the meeting. He merely indicated that he had expected a one-on-one conversation with Gorbachev and had not welcomed the idea of a third person being present. Later, he complained that Gorbachev and Nazarbaev had put him through a regular interrogation.

I went into the President's office immediately after Yeltsin came out and found Gorbachev in a state of bafflement. "What can we tell the press, Mikhail Sergeevich?"

This question, which had become routine for us, tended to have an instantaneous effect on the President. It opened the doors of his office to me at almost any hour of the day and during any meeting (as long as I observed certain proprieties, of course). It served as a constant reminder to him that there was an authority that outranked his own: public opinion—the opinion of the people, who had the right to expect from him not only information but also reports on the actions and intentions of the authorities on whom their fate depended.

Gorbachev never shirked this responsibility at any time. Rather the opposite, in fact: On several occasions, he criticized me for waiting to be invited to meetings or interviews, or because the press corps or the journalists themselves were not present where events were taking place and news was being generated. "The press secretary should know everything I have to say and everything about me," he decreed at one point.

He was intensely interested in the weekly press conferences and the main questions asked at them. Despite the important matters with which he was preoccupied on the days of these briefings, I knew that he expected to find out what had gone on at them and would not go to bed (nor would I) until he had been briefed, even if he had to call me very late from his dacha or his car.

"What should I say, Mikhail Sergeevich? There's a crowd of journalists waiting." Generally, Gorbachev drew a clear distinction, even in terms of linguistic style, between official information intended for the media and his unofficial recountings of events. That day, he began carefully dictating to me, weighing every word, the statement that I was to read to the press. "Tell them that during the meeting of the president of the USSR with Yeltsin and Nazarbaev, a summary from the president of Russia on the meeting in Brest was heard and discussed. Many questions were asked in order to shed light on various aspects of the accords concluded there. It was agreed that the president of the USSR would circulate the *initiative* [he emphasized this word] of the leaders of the three republics, as their own *proposal* [also emphasized], to the parliaments of the other republics, to be reviewed in tandem with the review of the draft Union Treaty that has already begun."

That was all he said. Based on these three sentences, I had to prepare my statement for the improvised press conference and the answers to countless questions, not to mention two or three interviews for the Russian television news show *Vremya,* the American CNN, and the traditional briefing at the media center of the Ministry of Foreign Affairs the next day.

Realizing that I would get nothing else for the official version, I moved on to the President's impressions of the interview and his thoughts on what actions the situation might demand from him. He gave me a (brief) glimpse of his emotional response to the Belovezhskaya meeting and smiled at a few forced pleasantries that I essayed in order to improve his mood, such as "without Mishka in the forest," an allusion to a popular brand of chocolates, "Mishki [teddy bears] in the forest."[52] He also told me that he would make an official statement sometime that day. He asked Shakhnazarov to write a draft and discussed its contents in an informal meeting with Shakhnazarov, Alexander Yakovlev, Revenko, and Shevardnadze. The statement was polished and was released the next day, December 10.

"On December 8, 1991, in Minsk, the leaders of Belorussia, the RSFSR,[53] and Ukraine concluded an accord regarding the creation of the Commonwealth of Independent States.

"For myself, as the president of the country, the chief criterion by which this document must be judged is the extent to which it makes it possible to preserve the safety of the citizens, to pursue the policies aimed at surmounting the present crisis, to guarantee that the state structures will continue to function, and to ensure the continuation of democratic reform.

"This accord has some positive aspects.

"It has the participation of the Ukrainian leadership, which has not recently been active in the Union Treaty process.

"The document emphasizes the need to create a single economic space, operating in a coordinated manner, with a single currency and a common banking and financial system. It expresses a willingness to cooperate in the fields of science, education, and culture, and in other spheres. It proposes a certain level of interaction in the military-strategic area.

"This text is so important and so profoundly linked to the interests of the peoples of our country and the international community that it must be evaluated fully from a political and a legal standpoint.

"Here, at any rate, is what is obvious to me. The accord states directly that the USSR shall cease to exist. There is no question but that any republic has the right to leave the Union; however, the fate of a multinational state cannot be sealed by the will of the leaders of three republics. This can be decided only by constitutional means, with the participation of all the sovereign states and allowance for the will of their peoples.

"The proclamation of the end of Soviet law is both illegal and dangerous, since it can only intensify chaos and anarchy in society.

"The speed with which this document has appeared is very surprising. It has been discussed neither by the people nor by the supreme soviets of the republics in whose names it has been signed. This is all the more surprising because it was drafted at a time when the parliaments of the republics were negotiating the draft Treaty of the Union of Sovereign States prepared by the State Council of the USSR.

"It is my profound conviction that in the present situation, all the supreme soviets of the republics and the Supreme Soviet of the USSR should debate both the draft Treaty of the Union of Sovereign States and the Minsk accord. Since the latter proposes another configuration for the state structures, a matter subject to the authority of the Congress of People's Deputies of the USSR, this congress must be convened. In addition, I would not rule out the need to hold a popular referendum on this issue."

These last few sentences triggered a barrage of questions at the press conference the next day. The journalists wanted to know if Gorbachev had decided to use Parliament to repudiate the Belovezhskaya accords; when and where a referendum might be held; and by what methods—political, governmental, or even coercive—he intended to protect the unified state, the Novo-Ogarevo process, and himself.

In stating Gorbachev's position, I had enough information to be able to say, "He is not going to defend his position and his power if the price that has to be paid is another rift in society and the risk of causing additional political—or perhaps even armed—conflicts." At the same time, it seemed obvious to me that the President was counting on some kind of signal from this country into which he had breathed new life. He hoped for—he expected—a reaction to what had just happened in Belorussia. He thought that the society, now that it had been roused to greater freedom, would rise up, perhaps in a different way than it had the previous August, to defend its right to decide its own fate or at least to participate in such decisions.

He was counting on the members of Parliament who had not been consulted about the decisions that had been made in their behalf; on the media, which had experienced glasnost and should not be singing the praises of a new, more decisive power so obediently and with such relief; on the intellectuals and the politicians whom he had led into perestroika by promising them that from now on, power would be accountable to and controlled by the people.

That is why he did not discuss his own decisions in his statement and commentary but instead, keeping to a tried and true formula, invited society to demand that he take action, to give him a mandate. But there was no response. People's faith in Gorbachev had given way to disappointment in both the reform program and the man. As in Pushkin's tragedy *Boris Godunov,* the people remained silent.

Gorbachev's statement made clear reference to the absence of the proper legal formalities in the Minsk accord. He felt that such initiatives exceeded the constitutional authority of leaders in the executive branch and even farther exceeded the mandate that had been given them by the last Congress of People's Deputies. Only Congress had the authority to ratify or disavow the initiative by the three Slavic presidents.

There were three ways that Congress could be convened: on a motion by at least one-fifth of the deputies (450 out of 2,250), on a motion by one of the two councils of the Supreme Soviet, or by a decision on the part of the president of the

USSR. However, Gorbachev did not want to take the initiative and convene Congress unless he could be sure of support. For the entire week after the meeting in Brest, he had desperately been waiting for the people to give him some kind of signal. What he failed to realize was that the best way to be certain of having this support would be for him to make a decision himself, regardless of the political risks.

Nevertheless, this waiting game may well have been the proper way for Gorbachev to proceed, in view of his hopes of bringing the country under the rule of law. Above all, he wanted to remind society as a whole, including the legislators themselves, that it would be better to amend constitutional law than to let it be broken. At the same time, his main concern, as he himself said, was to maintain stability and to guarantee the safety of the citizens of the USSR and of the world.

Other issues were raised during the press conference. The fate of the "nuclear button," which according to Kravchuk was already "divided three ways," was a source of concern. It was not easy to imagine a system in which three different fingers in three separate capitals would be poised on the same button. Despite the tension at the conference, the atmosphere relaxed momentarily when I told one of the journalists, who was unable to get the hand-held mike that had just been passed to him to work, that he should press the on button "with one finger only."

Another question inevitably came up: To what extent could the decisions of the Belovezhskaya "troika" be compared to last August's attempted coup? If Gorbachev had felt that the two actions were comparable, he would have sent the Alpha Group to Minsk or laid an ambush for Yeltsin in his office. Before he could take that kind of action, however, he would have had to perform a coup d'état in his own mind. A few possible parallels notwithstanding, he considered the events of December to be fundamentally different from those of August. The prior situation was a direct confrontation between partisans and opponents of democratic transformations in the USSR. This time, however, it was a matter of differences— although differences of principle—regarding the methods and means to be used in implementing changes and the speed with which these should be accomplished. Both sides seemed to be moving in the same direction: toward continuing and deepening democratic reforms, developing free market relationships within the economy, and maintaining civilized relations with the outside world.

Another question that was raised was whether the President would resign—a natural concern, under the circumstances. The new leaders of Russia, sensing power almost within their grasp, had been making public statements about Gorbachev's possible ouster now that he had been stripped of his power and had no more weapons with which to fight back.

The Russian minister of foreign affairs, Andrei Kozyrev, gave this assessment in an interview with the German newspaper *Das Bild*: "Gorbachev is not a leper, and we will find plenty of work for him to do." His colleague, Minister of Information Mikhail Poltoranin, who already looked on Gorbachev as an ex-president, took it upon himself to invent honorary positions for him along the lines of honorary president or director of the new commonwealth's Coordinating Council for Foreign Policy Issues. "He should have no fear that he will suffer the same fate as Erich Honecker,"[54] he said reassuringly while Gorbachev was still in office.

Other members of Yeltsin's entourage, such as Sergei Stankevich and Galina Starovoitova, also tried to find some symbolic role for Gorbachev during the transition period. Having been "hatched" during the perestroika years, they may have been somewhat embarrassed by the cavalier (to say the least) manner in which he was being pushed to resign. Or perhaps they felt that their thoughts on the subject might act as an anesthetic during the painful but inevitable surgery that was going to be attempted on this stubborn patient.

Gorbachev, who had mustered all of his self-control, listened to the various hypotheses and merely commented laconically to me, "Maybe they should ask me whether I agree to participate, first."

For this reason, when I was asked at the press conference about the possibility of his resigning, I could answer in good faith, "The President is not thinking about resigning at present. He has much more to do."

We had not yet grasped the meaning, and the irreversibility, of the changes that had taken place since the previous Sunday. "I do not feel that the Gorbachev era is coming to a close, although it is conceivable that after a while, we and the world will no longer be dealing with Mikhail Sergeevich Gorbachev as government leader, with all the powers that that position implies.

"At the same time, though, we are talking about a man who has linked himself to historical processes rather than to a specific post and functions, and these processes will undoubtedly continue independently of the manner of his own participation in them. I think that we will be talking about the era that he inaugurated for a long time to come.

"You ask whether the current situation should be viewed as positive or negative, and I would answer along the same lines as a weather forecaster (which is how I think politicians ought to relate to current reality): It can be seen as more or less favorable. In any case, there is no sense complaining about it. One can and should analyze it, base one's conclusions on it, and, naturally, adapt to it. Sighs and complaints and other emotional reactions can be left to the memoirists—and I do not have the impression that Mikhail Gorbachev has reached that stage quite yet."

With these words, I ended the last of the ten press conferences that I gave as spokesperson for the president of the USSR.

Checking the Pulse

During the second ten days of December, Gorbachev worked feverishly to express his views to the country before it made the fatal move of putting the decisions of the "troika" into effect. He poured all his energy into this effort, using every avenue open to him, especially television and the press; unfortunately, his options were becoming fewer every day.

Various media organs and journalists who had been trying to get Gorbachev's attention for months, and who had obediently lined up to interview him, suddenly found that he was available. As Gorbachev divorced himself from the power and privileges of office, he unconsciously and instinctively demonstrated qualities that revealed what a remarkable politician he was, as he had done during the early years of perestroika. He tried to neutralize his opponents; he sought allies and found them among the people who made up his most reliable and natural base of support, whom he had previously neglected for that very reason.

During this period, he spoke for several hours with the editor in chief of *Moscow News,* Len Karpinsky, an old college friend. He also gave incisive interviews to *Komsomolskaya pravda* and to Vitaly Tretyakov of *Nezavisimaya gazeta,* who represented the new generation of postglasnost journalists.

He seemed to be discovering, with astonishment, the community of skilled, astute young journalists that had come together during the perestroika years. He came to the pleasant realization that for some time, he had not been as alone as he had thought. But he also realized that in their view, he was not—as he still believed himself to be—the irreplaceable leader and guardian of this flowering of democratic talent. And that was less pleasant.

The journalists, too, obviously benefited from these meetings: With Gorbachev's help, they could obtain the answers to many questions that millions of people throughout the dying empire were asking themselves and that they would have put to Gorbachev if they had had the chance. Sometimes, in fact, the journalists' questions were more interesting than the President's answers. But on some occasions, in making his reply, Gorbachev himself posed questions that only time and history could answer.

"Don't you feel, today," Tretyakov asked him, "that your policy goal of getting the Union Treaty signed and your pursuit of the Novo-Ogarevo process toward that end have proven to be mistaken?"

"No, I am convinced that the Union Treaty is an indispensable basis for reforming the unitary multinational state. . . . I am interested in realities, in the world that surrounds us, in its interweaving of human, economic, and strategic elements. That concerns all of us, all the republics, even the Baltic states. They will all have to agree, since if one part of the structure is destroyed, everything is destroyed. . . .

"People say that Gorbachev provokes people with the ideas he expresses. No, all I do is draw their attention to the facts and their consequences so they'll think of them when the time comes to make final decisions. I don't want anyone to suspect me of double-dealing. Maybe the time has come to say that I do not aspire to any leadership role in the new structures. I am not running for office. I want to respect the choice made by the representative bodies, or by the people themselves. But this choice must be made in a constitutional manner. . . . Let the people decide. They must be given the chance to do so."

But the people remained silent. They were so used to seeing the authorities act in their name without their participation that they no longer believed them—especially after they had realized that once in power, even their elected leaders behaved in exactly the same way as their predecessors who had been overthrown.

Gorbachev received no response to his many appeals to the parliaments, the people, the country. They were tired and were no longer willing to follow him—or anyone else, for that matter. It was the end of perestroika. Gorbachev realized this himself during the week after the meeting in Minsk and, as a consequence, had made his decision to resign.

During their conversation, Tretyakov asked him, "Are you happy, Mikhail Sergeevich?"

"I don't know any happy reformers," Gorbachev replied with a wan smile. "But I'm contented with my lot. Not only did I have the good fortune to take part in the monumental process of transforming my country, I led that process. That's what keeps me going."

But he still had to travel each of the "four fourths of the way," as Vysotsky sang,[55] and climb his Golgotha bearing his cross on his own shoulder. Moreover, the time that remained to him had to be used not to put his thoughts, emotions, and papers in order but to get across to the people ideas that they might not actually hear until later, after he was gone. Apparently he had to leave in order to be heard.

On December 12, Gorbachev met with a large contingent of television journalists and commentators and newspaper editors at the Kremlin. I had originally intended to hold this meeting at the new press center built especially for the presidential apparat. The President's staff had always had to use the impractical rooms at the Kremlin or the foreign minister's press center for interviews with the media, and the new building would have made this job easier for us. But after Minsk it was clear that it would be used by others.

Gorbachev made his entrance into the hall of the State Council, where about forty journalists were assembled, and headed for his usual seat as presiding officer. I intercepted him and guided him gently but firmly to the center of the table. He nodded, agreeing to the rules of the game. "I'm used to sitting over there," he told the journalists apologetically. "This is where the Politburo met, and also the State Council.

"You know, when we first started planning this meeting, I said, let's invite a lot of journalists and speak freely. I feel that we should concentrate today on the issues that are the focus of general attention: What is the future of reform? How can the country be pulled out of this crisis? What measures should be instituted?"

One of the first questions addressed him concerned the possibility of another military coup d'état. It was clear to all present that the person who asked it was implying that the President, as commander in chief of the armed forces, could order such an action himself, especially since by saving the President the army could save the new union, and thus itself, from partitioning and humiliation.

Gorbachev answered emphatically that he would use his position as commander in chief to take care of the army and to hold it together, although that was very difficult in a country that was being reshaped. This important government institution must perform its duties to the letter. Any politician who tried to use the armed forces for personal ends would be unworthy of support and should be condemned. Any policy that relied on the use of tanks would fail to achieve its ends. It would lead to an impasse.

"Over the past few days," he said, "I have spoken and met with the leaders of the armed forces. Yeltsin has, too, by the way. The army is a special government institution. It is society's guarantor of safety and stability. One doesn't provoke an armed man. If people start drawing it into disputes about whose borders are where, who should live where, and whose army it is, that will cut off all progress in reform, it will bury reform. There will be no democratic way out of the chaos that will result."

The issue of Gorbachev's possible resignation was raised again. "Everybody is claiming that this question has already been settled and that a position has already been found for you elsewhere. What can you tell us?"

"What's done is done," said Gorbachev with a shrug. "I am not going to go into what I have already said concerning my political and legal assessment of the Belorussian accords. If they are complied with, the Union will cease to exist and the laws will no longer be valid. That means that we will no longer have a state, or national boundaries, or anything whatsoever: Everything will be outside the law.

"I spoke to Boris Nikolaevich the day before his trip to Minsk and ran through all the arguments in favor of the new union. And his answer was, can you guarantee us that Ukraine will sign this treaty? I said to him, do you want to know how to draw Ukraine into this process? Russia has to be the first to sign. Then Ukraine will try to fit into the framework. It has to, there's no other way for it to go. And the eight republics will sign. But no! And I already sensed why not: because the Russian leadership is tired of the 'center.' That's just the way things are."

Someone asked another legitimate question: "All the leaders of the sovereign republics are not merely members, but officials, of the CPSU, of which you were the head. Some have become rabid nationalists, others recommend partitioning the country, and a third group are anti-Communists. Let's look at this through the eyes of an ordinary citizen. How can he believe these politicians who were all swearing by the same faith yesterday and today have become rivals, each one taking off in his own direction?"

"I think that they are the only ones who can answer that question. We see what is happening with them now, and we will certainly see what will become of them."

The "nuclear button" was also discussed. "We know where it is right now," Gorbachev said shortly. "In the future, they'll have to work it out. Without me."

And the last exchange, at the end of the conference: "What does the future hold for you? You have talked about resigning . . . "

"Yes, I'm going to resign."

"A man of your stature, a politician of your experience, at your age?"

"I'll survive, never fear."

"Pardon us for not believing that you're going to retire."

"I will resign; if everything turns out that way, I will resign. There is no doubt on that score."

"If you resign in anticipation of what is going to happen, aren't you going to regret it for the rest of your life?"

"I have done everything that was in my power. I think other people, in my place, would have given up long ago. They tried to break me down, to crack me. The Party, the military-industrial complex, my friends and colleagues in the new union, everybody has worked me over. Nevertheless, I feel that I have put across the main ideas of perestroika, including the economic and political reforms and the renewal of the international state, even if I have made mistakes, made hasty decisions in some cases, or let opportunities slip away due to errors in judgment. . . .

"I set a great task for myself, and now it has been accomplished. Other people will come along. Perhaps they will do better. I want these efforts to end in success, not failure."

In conclusion, Gorbachev took his statement, with several handwritten comments, out of his briefcase: "Do you want to know what the partitioning of Russia will signify for the world? This is what the Russian thinker Ivan Ilin wrote at the turn of the century: 'The separation of an organism into several parts never leads to greater health, or creative equilibrium, or peace. Quite the opposite: It will always be a morbid disintegration, a process of putrefaction, of general contamination. And the entire world will be dragged into this process in our time. Incessant disputes, confrontations, and civil wars will erupt within the territory of Russia and will constantly expand into global conflicts. And this expansion will be absolutely inevitable, since the major powers of the world, both European and Asian, will invest their money, their commercial interests and their strategic planning in the newly created small states. They will compete with each other and try to dominate in the key areas. Moreover, imperialistic neighbors will claim direct or concealed supremacy over the unorganized and unprotected new structures, and we must be prepared to see the dissectors of Russia try to conduct their hostile and unseemly experiment, even in the post-Bolshevist chaos, by fraudulently presenting it as the supreme triumph of freedom, democracy, and federalism.'" Gorbachev paused for a moment and commented, "I'm not the one who's saying this, in case you're thinking that these are my words."

Then he continued: "'Two possibilities will take shape: Either a Russian national dictatorship will emerge, take the reins of government, and lead Russia toward unity by halting all the separatist movements in the country; or it will not emerge, and inconceivable chaos will set in, with displacements of people, revenge, pogroms, a complete breakdown in transportation, unemployment, famine, cold, and anarchy.' This is totally unacceptable. I am sure that we are making a mistake. That is why I am so concerned. Dangerous time bombs lie concealed in the history of our state."

As Gorbachev took his leave of the journalists, he probably regretted not having held this kind of press conference sooner. That same evening, the Russian television news show ran a brief but eloquent report on the meeting. There were no long quotations from the President: just images of his face, his gestures, and a cup of tea he was holding in his hand. The camera, the cameraman, and millions of viewers lingered for a long time on that cup of tea, as if from a desire to preserve the image of the emblem of the Soviet Union painted on its side.

The next day, *Komsomolskaya pravda* concluded its report of the interview with these words: "He did everything he could. And what he did could have been done by no one else."

Thus the young Russian press bade farewell to the knight of glasnost who had set it free.

Last Rites

The countdown began. Gorbachev and Yeltsin had originally agreed that the transition period, during which the Union would be laid to rest, would last for one month. But every time Yeltsin and his aides made a public statement they shortened the time frame.

The parliaments of the three republics ratified the Belovezhskaya accord with a unanimity worthy of the Brezhnev era. De facto, the Union was no more. It was decided to dispense with the funeral rites that would ordinarily be considered appropriate to the age and status of the deceased. The new tenants were anxious to move in and were pressing the relatives of the departed to vacate the premises.

The representatives to the USSR Supreme Soviet, who had come through the trial by fire of the first free elections in Soviet—if not Russian—history, received word that the Supreme Soviet was being dissolved, as the majority of the representatives of republics had been recalled to their respective parliaments.

Gorbachev was exasperated by the manner in which the parliament that he had worked so hard to create had been so quick to wave the white flag again, just as it had after the putsch. In commenting on the situation during a December 13 interview with *Time* magazine correspondents Strobe Talbott and John Kohan, he could not conceal his bitterness: "I urged Yeltsin not to break up the Union Parliament because this would be a sin that would weigh on him, as it did the Bolsheviks who dissolved the Constituent Assembly in 1918. Give them the chance to hold one last meeting. They understand everything and will make the necessary resolutions themselves, since the representatives of the republics are in the majority. Think of our reputation in the world."

Talbott began the meeting by asking bluntly, "Will you still be president next Monday? You've already talked about resigning so many times." This was a reference to Gorbachev's meeting with the Soviet journalists. At that point, however, Gorbachev still considered the possibility of his resignation a purely internal matter, a domestic problem that should be settled *en famille.* He felt that he should remain the president of the USSR in the eyes of the outside world to the very end. And he played the role that had fallen to him, that of the host welcoming his guests on the front steps while his house burns down behind him, with confidence and ease.

He even chided the members of the American administration (he probably had James Baker in mind) who were already saying "the Union no longer exists" and expressed hope that the United States would adopt a more balanced attitude toward processes "whose outcome is important to us all." He repeated his assertion that he would accept any arrangement that would settle the country's crucial problems by legal and constitutional means, and not "on public squares and in the woods." He said that he hoped he was "wrong three times over" in expressing fears that the path the republic leaders had chosen would stall the development of the market economy, democracy, pluralism, and reform "because that has been my life's work."

He was asked what complaints he might have against Bush, who had spoken with Yeltsin by phone during the Belovezhskaya meeting. He answered impassively, "Those are Yeltsin's ethics, not Bush's. I know that Bush wanted to avoid choosing between us until the very end. It's too bad people don't realize that over here. Here we are at a critical stage in the development of the country, and inexperienced politicians are back in power. What can you do? As for myself, I feel that since the main purpose of my existence has been achieved, my life is a success."

The American journalists, like their many predecessors, came away from this meeting infused with some of Gorbachev's conviction and energy, as well as his faith in his political future. "You have reassured us," they told him. "We came here thinking that this would be our last interview with the man *Time* has distinguished twice, first as its Man of the Year, and just recently as Man of the Decade."

The most important thing to Gorbachev was that the Americans had treated him as a president in office rather than as one who was resigning. This was especially important to him on the eve of what he felt to be a crucial meeting with Secretary of State James Baker, who was coming to Moscow for talks with both him and Yeltsin.

The signal was picked up in Washington. Bush called Gorbachev personally. That evening, Gorbachev recounted their conversation to me over the phone. "I told him everything: about the unconstitutional nature of the Minsk accords, our mutual relations, Baker. He listened to me very attentively and felt that we should keep in touch on a regular basis. Overall, it was an intense conversation."

Another "intense" conversation that was much more gratifying to Gorbachev's self-esteem took place the next day, December 15, with François Mitterrand. When the call came through, Gorbachev was getting ready to leave for a concert. Claudio Abbado was in Moscow with his orchestra and would be performing the Mahler symphony whose great impact on him Gorbachev described in his book *The August Coup.*

At that point he had already read the portions of Mitterrand's interview on *Sept sur sept* that related to him. "I salute you, not just as a politician, but as a friend," Gorbachev said in opening the conversation. Then, picking up where they had left off in Latche six weeks earlier, he reported to Mitterrand on the commitments he had made at that time. "I informed my inner circle and the country of your position and our agreements. Unfortunately, domestic processes have gotten off track. Things were done behind the president's back, and even without the knowledge of the parliaments, and the country was taken by surprise. I believe that my job, at the very least, is to make sure that the decisionmaking process concerning the future destiny of the state takes place within a constitutional framework."

Gorbachev was also troubled by the deteriorating relations between the Slavic and non-Slavic peoples. The leaders who had signed the Belovezhskaya accords had shown an extreme lack of delicacy in dealing with the Muslim republics, holding them at arm's length and presenting them, like the rest of the country, with a fait accompli. The leaders of these republics, who represented more than half the population of the country, were predictably indignant. They held a meeting in Ashkhabad, chaired by Nazarbaev, and responded to the decisions of the Belovezhskaya "troika" by drafting their own platform intended to restore parity within the future commonwealth.

Nazarbaev announced to Gorbachev over the phone that the leaders present at the Ashkhabad meeting had not only proposed some amendments to the accords but were also calling for a meeting of the State Council. This would automatically mean that Gorbachev would be restored to the office of president. As a result, their proposal would clearly be unacceptable to anybody who saw the commonwealth as a doughnut-shaped structure, including the hole at the center.

Gorbachev told Mitterrand about his conversation with Nazarbaev, as well as his telephone "conference" with Yeltsin and Kravchuk the day before. Ukraine was trying to bring the units of the Soviet army stationed on its soil under its own command as soon as possible. Gorbachev had taken the initiative by calling Kravchuk and attempting to reason with him, explaining that hasty unilateral decisions were going to "scare everyone, since Ukraine would suddenly be in possession of the third-largest European army." Kravchuk backed down.

Gorbachev recounted his conversation with Yeltsin to Mitterrand, awkwardly tossing in a few profanities to better express his indignation. Gorbachev had gotten Yeltsin to agree to issue a mollifying statement to the press, explaining that everything would be done "in stages."

Knowing how thin-skinned the French were on nuclear defense issues, Gorbachev confirmed to Mitterrand that he would maintain rigid control of strategic weapons "to the very end."

Mitterrand asked what he felt the prospects were for the commonwealth. Gorbachev reiterated his appraisal of the Belorussian accords, explaining that he had no intention of participating in the dismemberment of a unified country. "You might well ask what sort of partners we have in people who fail to see the obvious and who reject previously reached agreements. I see two reasons for their behavior. The first is the difficulty of making a break with totalitarianism. The second is the pernicious influence of the separatism whose detrimental effects you and I have discussed."

When asked about his own fate, Gorbachev said, "I don't know what the governing bodies of this commonwealth will be, and thus whether I will be able to participate in them. I'll decide that later on. That's not the most important thing. What bothers me is that now, while our country is in such a difficult situation, Westerners are racing to be the first to announce that the Union no longer exists." Baker's unfortunate phrase was always echoing in his mind.

"It's sad," he confided to Mitterrand, "to see sensible politicians running to jump on the bandwagon. As the French put it, *'C'est la vie.'*" As he said this phrase in French, he winked at Chernyaev, myself, and Alexander Yakovlev, who had just come into the office with his characteristic limp, the result of a leg wound received during the war. "That, in a few words, is our situation," he concluded. "Thank you for hearing me out."

Mitterrand's response to Gorbachev's account of the situation was just what Gorbachev needed most at that point: not advice, which would have been of no use to him, or compassion, which he would not have accepted, but confirmation of France's attitude toward his country and its peoples and an expression of high esteem for his personal efforts. Mitterrand characterized these actions as "an important positive element that ensures the necessary and stable development of democratic processes within the USSR, as well as in its relations with the outside world."

"As before," Mitterrand continued, "I feel that you are still the guarantor of stability for your country. I would like you to know that now, in the face of these grave difficulties, France is closely watching each of your actions and initiatives with sympathy and understanding."

Gorbachev was an atheist and was not in the habit of making confession. Nor, as a resigning president, did he expect any last rites. But had he felt such a need, he would surely have turned to Mitterrand.

❀   ❀   ❀

After Sunday's brief respite, Monday signaled the "second round"—the beginning of the second week after the Minsk accords. It opened with Gorbachev's meeting with Baker, who had arrived in Moscow the day before. After a brief conversation with Kozyrev, Baker had spent Sunday evening with his old colleague Eduard Shevardnadze. They had had dinner together, chatting like old friends.

I went to see the President before his interview with Baker, in order to gauge his state of mind as he began his week. A pretext for my visit was afforded by Yeltsin, who had already seen Baker that morning. During the press conference that followed their meeting, he had said that Gorbachev would have to "define" his future destiny "himself." Gorbachev listened unflinchingly to this news, and then, seeing my mortified expression, exclaimed, "All of this is just small stuff, Andrei. The important events are still ahead of us."

I still don't know whether he was trying to boost my morale or build himself up for the meeting with Baker, which would be taking place soon in the Catherine Room of the Kremlin. Only his most trusted allies—Alexander Yakovlev, Chernyaev, and Shevardnadze—were invited to that meeting. I would like to think that it was not merely because of our professional obligations that his personal interpreter, Pavel Palazhchenko, and I were included in this small circle.

Gorbachev had some difficulty beginning the conversation with Baker. He was evidently struggling to overcome some physical malaise. His face was very flushed, suggesting either a fever or an attack of high blood pressure. Baker noticed this and casually extended a tablet to him. Apparently this member of the jet set had some experience in getting through stressful situations.

Gorbachev said he was pleased that the president of the United States had sent his secretary of state to the USSR, where he was to perform a delicate mission (Baker was also scheduled to go to Kiev and Alma-Ata), "since we are interested in pursuing everything that we have undertaken in the relations between our two countries."

He briefly reviewed the situation as it stood before Minsk and said that he did not feel that the Novo-Ogarevo process had come to a dead end yet. "I have spoken personally with the leaders of the six republics who were willing to sign the treaty." The problem, he said, could be summed up in one word: Ukraine. "It is a simple question of whether the others will follow Ukraine down the same blind alley, or pull Ukraine out."

Even if the Minsk meeting had "ruined everything," Gorbachev said that he accepted it as a reality despite the fact that the only thing it had produced so far was a plan "that would be difficult to live by."

"I want them to succeed. I don't think it can work, but I hope I'm wrong. If they fail, everything that we have accomplished so far will be threatened." This "we" clearly referred to the comrades in arms seated next to him.

Baker began cautiously, trying to determine the lay of the land. "For a long time," he said, "you have been our partners and our friends, and you will remain our friends. We would like you to remain our partners as well, but we realize that

that depends on your domestic problems. In addition, we feel ill at ease when we begin to suspect that you are being treated dishonorably." The ambiguity of this phrase left room to interpret it both as an excuse for his recent negligence in referring to the "former Union" and as a condemnation of the unceremoniousness with which the legitimate president was being pushed to resign.

Baker candidly expressed his doubts regarding the concept of the Commonwealth of Independent States, which was still an empty envelope with no contents. The chief "riddle," he felt, was how ten different states could hope to have independent foreign policies and a common defense policy. "Who will give orders to the commander in chief of the armed forces?"

Gorbachev, for his part, expressed regret at having prophesied too well. Ever since the day after the Minsk accords were signed, Ukraine had been trying to change them. Gorbachev felt that it was just as likely to abandon them completely later on. Kravchuk was already refusing to go to Alma-Ata, where the Slavic and non-Slavic republics were to negotiate the foundations of the CIS. (The day before, the president of Ukraine had declared that he could see no advantage in discussing anything with the Asiatic republics: "Let them join the accords that we signed at Minsk!" he had exclaimed.)

"If the Russian people react with indignation to such an attitude," Gorbachev continued, "the government will soon cease to be democratic. Proponents of authoritarianism are already starting to make themselves heard." To soften this transparent reference to certain absent individuals, he turned to Yakovlev and said, "Alexander Nikolaevich, admit that in your heart of hearts, you are a dictator."

"Oh no, not that guy!" said Baker when the phrase had been translated.

"The worst of all, though," Gorbachev resumed, "is that this tormented society might well submit to a dictatorship. That is why my role as president is to create the right conditions so that all the changes can take place within a lawful context. I've told Yeltsin: This is necessary if you want to look like democrats and reformers, rather than desperadoes." The interpreter stumbled over this last word, and his American colleague helped him out by giving him the translation in an undertone.

The problem was that in deciding to dissolve the Union, no one was thinking of the country's international obligations, its seat on the United Nations Security Council, the leadership of the armed forces, border protection. All of this, in Gorbachev's eyes, was representative of "the improvisation and amateurism to which our culture is giving way." Nevertheless, if this transformation had to take place, then it must at least do so in a constitutional manner. The West, for its part, should respond by granting emergency aid, especially food aid. "Otherwise, the general dissatisfaction will reach critical mass and sweep the system away completely."

He explained to Baker why he insisted on calling a final meeting of the Supreme Soviet: "It's important for the future." And he added, "A real process is under way, and we must involve ourselves in it in order to overcome the present state of uncertainty as rapidly as possible. Because this uncertainty is the most dangerous thing."

Baker showed him his notebook with satisfaction. "I've noted down your advice: Use the issue of recognition by the West to achieve progress toward forming a viable commonwealth."

"Yes," Gorbachev confirmed, nodding. "Otherwise we will have a disaster." The two men said their good-byes and left the Catherine Room by separate doors. No one brought up the usual question of whether they should give a joint press conference.

❀   ❀   ❀

Gorbachev continued with his meetings the next day. The first was a Kremlin reception for the participants in the conference "The Anatomy of Hatred" that was taking place in Moscow. They included Nobel Peace Prize recipient Elie Wiesel, Jack Matlock (the former U.S. ambassador to Moscow), Bronislaw Geremek and Adam Michnik of Poland, and François Léotard of France.

Gorbachev had sent a written message to the conference in which he touched on a subject that was very important to him, the relationship between ethics and politics. "I reject amoral means in politics," he wrote. "I do not accept the use of force in order to achieve a goal, even if someone accidentally or deliberately prevents me from reaching that goal. All violence engenders hatred, and hatred is always destructive. And violence can transform the noblest idea into evil against humankind and society.

"I am proud that the new thinking, our new political ethics, has helped to eliminate hatred from international relations, and to make trust in and respect for human rights the most important elements in world politics.

"My country is going through the difficult, dramatic process of choosing its destiny. I hope that hatred will not enter into this painful process. I believe in the ultimate victory of justice and peace in my homeland and throughout the world."

Since they happened to be in Moscow during these historic days of the end of the Soviet empire, the conferees naturally were not satisfied with this written message from Gorbachev and managed to obtain a meeting with the man himself. The President received them with the free and open manner of someone who has made important decisions and feels a burden lifted.

He was even magnanimous toward his successors. "It's good that new generations of politicians are coming along. Maybe they will appreciate that we had the courage to begin—which means that we have some worth." In so saying, however, he was probably not thinking of the men who had just wrested power away from him.

Religious terms were also beginning to crop up in his vocabulary, as he perhaps began to think increasingly in terms of eternity. "We all have to learn to rid ourselves of hatred, and the best way to do this is to keep in mind that we are all creatures of God—although, as an atheist, I interpret this phrase in my own way."

Elie Wiesel asked him whether he believed that history repeats itself and whether another Gulag might occur in one or another of the republics. Gorbachev replied firmly, "I do not believe that our society will backslide. It has learned too much about itself in recent times." Nevertheless, he did not rule out the danger that people might take to the streets because of the crushing burden of economic change. "This would be a democratic form of social protest, even if there is a risk that it might sweep away the existing democratic structures."

He also mentioned the meeting of the republic leaders that was scheduled to take place in Alma-Ata at the end of the week and for the first time announced his intention to send the participants a message in which he would bring "some important ideas" to their attention. He repeated this plan to the director of the German television station ARD, Friedrich Nowottny, whom he saw immediately afterward. Nowottny had not come for an interview this time: He was a member of a German delegation that had brought a large fund of humanitarian aid to the USSR for delivery to a special commission headed by Svyatoslav Fyodorov, a well-known Russian ophthalmologist and businessman.

Nowottny took advantage of this meeting to ask Gorbachev three precisely worded questions that sounded German even in Russian translation. "How long will you remain master of this house? Do you still have control over the nuclear button? How should we interpret Yeltsin's conduct toward you?" In answering this last question, Gorbachev preferred not to accentuate the problem. "If a list were to be drawn up of the points on which we agree and those on which our opinions diverge, it would be obvious that our positions match eighty percent of the time. Our main differences of opinion relate to tactics, timetables, and methods."

To close the interview, he quoted a line of poetry by Alexander Blok to Nowottny and the Germans who had accompanied him: "Peace comes to us only in our dreams." But he immediately amended, "Actually, we no longer have peace even in our dreams."

As on every Tuesday, I gave a press conference, but it was far from peaceful. I had asked the journalists to table any questions about Gorbachev's possible resignation, if only for the day. But Yeltsin, by citing a "one-month deadline" for the President's resignation, had destroyed the moratorium and subjected me to a barrage of questions to which I was unable to provide any definite answers. I was also asked if Gorbachev was going to Alma-Ata, and whether he considered himself a transitional figure, with his country moving on to a new era and his own receding into the past.

One year earlier, the Nobel Peace Prize had been presented to Gorbachev (or rather, his representative) in Oslo. Few politicians have been awarded this prize while they were still in power. Now Gorbachev would have to replace his laurel wreath with a crown of thorns.

Burying a Time Capsule

When I look back on the days of that last fateful week, each of them seems to stretch into infinity. Like everyone else who was observing (and taking part in) the denouement of the political drama that was unfolding, I saw only what was happening on the surface—just the crater left by the submerged eruption of political and individual passions.

I believe that as of Wednesday, December 18, Gorbachev still had not made a final decision to resign: He was waiting for the news from his last line of defense, Alma-Ata. He was not yet aware that only eight days remained to him in his office at the Kremlin.

That morning he received the editors of *Komsomolskaya pravda,* the largest-circulation young people's newspaper in the country. The journalists were in luck: Gorbachev clearly wanted to tell them everything that was on his mind. And they proved to be excellent partners for him in this conversation—because of their professionalism, of course, but also because in Gorbachev's view they personified the new generation that he wanted to address. This interview was, for him, like burying a time capsule.

He began by explaining to the journalists that he felt it was important to convene the Union Parliament for a final session, even if it were only symbolic. This would ensure a smooth transition from one government to the next. Yeltsin was hesitating, he said, for the simple reason that "there's no telling how they're going to vote." I couldn't help recalling the many strenuous past debates before the Congress of Deputies, the Supreme Soviet, or the Party plenums, where Gorbachev had mounted the dais even though he could not be sure of the outcome of the voting.

The journalists asked him if he intended to go to Alma-Ata and whether he felt that he might play any kind of role in the institutions that would be created there. It was obviously unpleasant for him to have to reiterate that the leaders of the republics had not invited him. "I can tell what my role will be until Alma-Ata. Afterward, we'll just have to see," he said, without elaborating.

However, when asked to discuss the various "betrayals" that he had suffered during his long political career, he used the opportunity to describe—undoubtedly for the first time—his view of the "obstacle course" that he had had to conquer as he progressed along the path of his reforms. "What our plan would have to accomplish was to bring the country out of a systemwide crisis. True, we did not understand this at the beginning. We realized that the implementation of reform would affect the vital interests of strong bases of power; but at the beginning, during the first two years of perestroika, we failed to see why we couldn't bring about fundamental changes by inventing grand slogans and just moving forward.

"It turned out that the monolithic structures in place would not yield to action exerted from the outside. Moreover, as soon as the interests of the governing strata were threatened, reform skidded to a halt.

"It became obvious that without pressure 'from below' and without an alternative political process, it would be impossible to achieve any practical transformations. The nineteenth conference of the CPSU, which legalized the pluralism of opinions within the Party, was the first step on the road to political pluralism. As this movement advanced, resistance by the conservatives increased. With the formation of the Russian Communist Party,[56] the fight against reform and against the general secretary who was spearheading it became a battle to the death." (Some time before, in an interview with Bernard Guetta for *Le Monde*, I had referred to the election of Ivan Polozkov to the leadership of the Russian Party as a "coup d'état" within Party ranks. This was one year before the 1991 putsch.)

Gorbachev went on: "At that point, it would have seemed natural to conclude an alliance with the democratic forces inside and outside the Party and to wage a final battle against the reactionaries. And this would, in fact, have been reasonable from a strategic standpoint; but not from a tactical one. It was too soon. The balance of forces in the Politburo and the Central Committee was not good. The military-industrial complex was still too strong."

Hearing this logical pattern imposed on the past, one could fall into the illusion that perestroika emerged fully formed, Minerva-like, from the head of this Stavropol Jove. The main advantage of Gorbachev's line of reasoning was that it was impossible to refute. And he himself sincerely believed it at the time.

"It was a dangerous mission into the enemy camp, and the conservatives were in no hurry. At the beginning, they were calmly waiting for the people's dissatisfaction to come to a head. It was the draft Union Treaty that pushed them into taking drastic action: They could not tolerate its being signed."

"Didn't you wait too long to form an alliance with the democrats?" asked Vladislav Fronin, the editor in chief of *Komsomolskaya pravda*, in an attempt to question Gorbachev's logic. "That is true," Gorbachev acknowledged. "That alliance was concluded at the time of the Novo-Ogarevo process. I reached a decision in that regard after the tragic clash between the Moscow demonstrators and the forces of order.[57] But you're right, it should have been done sooner, in the fall of last year. We paid a high price for that wasted time."

The previous fall, however, had been spent in the throes of a battle between the radical democrats, on the one side, and the alliance between Ryzhkov's government and the Union Parliament, on the other, over the 500-Day Plan developed by Shatalin and Yavlinsky. So the apparent logic of Gorbachev's interpretation does not stand up to the contradictory evidence of reality.

Gorbachev was also asked how he felt about a "Commonwealth of Independent States." He replied frankly that he did not believe in that structure but preferred not to cause a rift in public opinion on the subject. "You are going to say that that's not logical. Perhaps. But it's certainly in keeping with the absurdity of the situation. . . ." Gorbachev did not evade any of the questions he was asked about his private life. The journalists wanted to know why Raisa Maximovna had decided to burn all their correspondence after the putsch. "It was August 27," he recalled. "Raisa Maximovna had accumulated a great many letters, especially from our youth. I used to write to her on a regular basis when I was away on various trips and missions, expressing myself openly and passionately, like the radical that I still am. Those were personal letters, and they were very frank.

"You know, Raisa Maximovna has very deep feelings about the world that has bound us together for so many years. And she doesn't want our family, herself or the children, to be exposed unnecessarily to scrutiny by the outside world. For her, our home is an island. When I went home that day, I found her in tears. She told me, 'I just burned all our letters. I can't imagine someone reading them if another Foros were to happen.'"

A great deal has been said around the world—most of it negative—about how Raisa Maximovna presented herself during her trips abroad. In my personal opinion, there are two factors that should be kept in mind. The first is purely psychological and is her inability to behave naturally in front of the camera. She undoubtedly felt ill at ease at finding the whole world watching her, and this made her tense up and seem cold.

The second factor is a matter of circumstance. Before Gorbachev, the wives of Soviet leaders were ignored completely. People hardly knew whether the leaders were married or not. During their trips out of the country, they seemed to be asexual beings; the only evidence that they had a libido at all came in the form of lurid and usually not very credible rumors. By helping her husband give a familial aspect to the office of supreme leader of the USSR, Raisa Maximovna undeniably had a positive effect in breaking a kind of reactionary taboo.

In so doing, however, she became a focus of public attention. It was so unusual for the media and the people to see the Soviet First Lady at close range that undue importance was ascribed to mannerisms and attitudes that had gone unnoticed in the wives of Western leaders. This phenomenon was undoubtedly intensified by the closeness and deep understanding between Gorbachev and his wife.

I cannot mention the bond between the two of them without recalling the "tea parties" that Gorbachev used to hold after he took office as a way of gathering his principal aides and coworkers around him. The idea was to review the problems of the day in a generally relaxed and informal atmosphere. Gorbachev encouraged us to speak freely, and the discussions sometimes lasted into the small hours. Raisa Maximovna used to appear when she felt that it was getting late, take up a position near her husband, and, whatever the importance of the subject under discussion, give him to understand that it was time to quit for the night. Many men (and I may be foremost among them) would have responded with some irritation to a similar attitude on the part of their wives. But not Gorbachev.

After Gorbachev had answered the question about his wife's correspondence, the journalists from *Komsomolskaya pravda* chose to change the subject. "You have many contacts in other countries now. How does the rest of the world view the future of our country?"

"With sympathy. At such a difficult moment in our country's history, it is our good fortune—hard earned—that the world has a different attitude toward us than it did in the past, that it empathizes with us and helps us. That means that we have somewhere to turn for support."

The President ended with a remark directed at the future: "My principal hope rests with the new, young politicians." With that, this message for future generations was sealed into its capsule and left for posterity.

It was time to get back to the harsh realities of daily life. With Shakhnazarov, his domestic affairs adviser, Gorbachev had to finish writing his address to the leaders who would be attending the meeting in Alma-Ata.

Circumstances being what they were, this was the only way Gorbachev would be represented at Alma-Ata. The letter was sent the next day, December 19. In it, Gorbachev wrote that he felt he had the moral and political right to share certain thoughts with "the comrades." He warned them that the process of partitioning and dividing up the country, which ran counter to the long-term historical process of its formation, would not be an easy one. It would be a "tremendous turning point" that would shake the lives of the peoples and citizens of the country to their very foundations. The situation was made even more dramatic by the atmosphere in which this transformation was taking place: a profound crisis in every area—economic, political, interethnic—accompanied by a substantial drop in the standard of living.

The core of the President's message was a list of the minimum conditions without which the future commonwealth would not be viable. He cited seven.

To begin with, the commonwealth must be interpreted as a multinational structure composed of completely equal states and nations. He even proposed a name for it: the Commonwealth of European and Asiatic States. This was similar to the names that had already been put forward by two such disparate figures in Russian history as Sakharov and Lenin.

The second building block of his plan was to keep the borders open and to offer the option of citizenship in the commonwealth as a whole. Otherwise, he warned, the people might reject the idea of the commonwealth altogether.

The economic basis of the future interstate union would be "a socially oriented market economy," which, in order to function, would require the appropriate "structures for economic interaction." This neutral phrase was open to a wide variety of interpretations, ranging from a mere monetary and fiscal union to a highly structured central government.

In the area of national security, the President warned, any attempt to break up the military and strategic system could trigger a disaster of global proportions. "Collective command is an absurdity," he wrote. Unified oversight and command structures for the strategic forces, including all of the basic components, both military-technical and defensive, would have to be outlined immediately.

In addition, he said, steps should be taken to maintain joint political representation in the international community. "I cannot imagine how a common strategic defense system can be preserved without a common foreign policy." According to Gorbachev, the most reasonable solution would be to have a single structure responsible for conducting foreign relations, adapted to the needs and principles of the commonwealth, including the question of its membership in the United Nations Security Council.

The sixth point was political coordination in the areas of science and culture, language, the preservation of monuments, museums, archives, and the like.

The seventh and last point was the procedure for legal succession. "This new age in the history of the country must be ushered in with dignity, in compliance with the norms of legitimacy." The President felt that the misfortunes that had befallen the peoples of the former USSR had been caused primarily by "abrupt breaks, destructive reversals, and forcible seizures in the course of their social development." He did not mention the October Revolution, but the context becomes clear enough if one recalls the famous phrase by Raymond Aron—of which Gorbachev probably was not aware—to the effect that "revolutions rend the social fabric that has been tirelessly and continuously woven by history."

Gorbachev added a businesslike ending to this political last will and testament, which was addressed not so much to the leaders of the republics as to his political and spiritual heirs: "These are my general views, dictated by my sense of responsibility for the ultimate success of the great task begun in 1985."

Departure

O*n December 17*, representatives from the ABC television network came to Moscow intending to persuade Gorbachev to take part in the "historic taping" of the last days of the Soviet Union.

At first, the project seemed unrealistic. Gorbachev still was not convinced that there was no way to return to the past of the Union. Moreover, the very spirit of the program, this "view from the Kremlin," the indiscretion of a camera poking into the secret corners of the palace, which was traditionally off limits even to Soviets—all this was so out of the ordinary that Gorbachev was instinctively wary. And yet, armed with patience and tact, fortified by support from the presidential press service and from Soviet television under the direction of Yegor Yakovlev, the Americans got what they wanted. They blended into the walls of the Kremlin so completely that even the guards stopped paying attention to them.

In putting the program together, ABC newscaster Ted Koppel acted as a kind of John Reed in reverse. Seventy-four years earlier, Reed, a journalist sympathetic to the Communist cause, had witnessed the "ten days that shook the world," the birth of Soviet Russia, from the inside. Koppel had come to witness the final hours of that revolution, which had taken place so many years before.

Koppel came into my office on the third floor of the government building at the Kremlin on Friday, December 20, after a 5,000-mile flight. He undoubtedly was not expecting to hear what I had to tell him. We were unable to promise him an exclusive interview with the President because Gorbachev was too busy. Besides, the idea of Koppel reporting on the last days of the USSR was highly problematic, and we would never be able to explain to anyone in the country why the Americans were covering this story. And finally, the main sticking point: "You have to understand that the meeting of the republic leaders in Alma-Ata starts tomorrow, and nobody knows how it's going to turn out."

Koppel was dumbfounded. He had come to Moscow for two or three days, intending just to tape an informal conversation in a relaxed setting, preferably by the fireside at the dacha, with the remarkable president of a great country as he prepared to leave the political scene and pass into history. Koppel had expected to be back in the United States in time to celebrate Christmas with his family. But here he was, and everything was still up in the air. His first reaction was annoyance. "Can you guarantee me that I'll get what I'm after if I spend Christmas here?"

"No," I answered honestly. "The only thing I can promise you is that you'll be able to come to the Kremlin every day and observe whatever is going on there. You may also be able to film some of what you see." He decided to stay.

Later, when he was saying good-bye to Gorbachev after the long series of talks they had together, he thanked the President for granting him so much time. Gorbachev did not thank Koppel, but I think he was grateful because the journalist had been among those who did not leave him facing the prospect of resignation alone. Koppel's interest and compassion confirmed to Gorbachev that the world realized the loss to the country's political life and general well-being that would accompany Gorbachev's departure from the Kremlin.

The Americans worked as a team with Soviet television personnel, taping everything: the visitors arriving at Gorbachev's office, his final telephone conversations with foreign leaders, his last walk to the Kremlin, and his departure from the empty palace. They knew they were recording history.

❀   ❀   ❀

On December 20, the day before the meeting in Alma-Ata, a sudden calm descended on Moscow: Yeltsin and his followers had left for Kazakhstan. The day before, there had been intense jockeying among the Union ministers for the privilege of joining Yeltsin on the plane.

Gorbachev stayed on at the Kremlin in what was, for him, an unfamiliar role: For the first time in six years of perestroika, he was no longer a leader, or even a participant in major political events. Instead he had become their object, the defendant waiting for the eleven jurors deliberating in Central Asia to pronounce their verdict on the fate of his country, his political agenda, and himself. He had done everything that he felt was necessary, and everything that he could do. All that remained for him was to spend the day going through the usual motions as president of the Union, if only to keep his mind off what was going on.

He tried to respond to an anxious letter from the president of the Moscow City Council, Yury Luzhkov, informing him that 350 stores in the capital had run out of meat. He sent telegrams to the leaders of the republics and the regions, now independent of the center, asking them to speed up deliveries. He stated his intention to ask Kohl and Havel for emergency aid. He also clung hopefully to the promises of humanitarian aid proffered by an American, Jim Harrison, who had come to see him.

Nothing could make him forget about Alma-Ata, however. "Let's hope that tomorrow *they* will agree on some form of coordination," he said to Harrison.

And Alma-Ata, not meat, was the topic of conversation when Gorbachev received a telephone call later that day from Germany's Chancellor Kohl. The friendly relations that had developed between the two leaders in recent years and the style of Kohl's approach moved Gorbachev to extreme frankness: "I am in the most difficult situation," he said, and then amended, "Not me personally, but my country. Yesterday I sent a message to Alma-Ata."

He explained his ambivalent attitude toward the commonwealth: "I don't believe that they will succeed, but I would like them to."

Responding to a direct question from the chancellor, he announced for the first time, "If a commonwealth is constituted in Alma-Ata and if the participants ratify the agreement, I will resign. And I will not put off that decision for long." His tone clearly indicated that he had just made an official statement. I looked at my watch. The president of the USSR had made the first official announcement of his coming resignation at 10:45 A.M. Moscow time, December 20.

"As I've said before, I will not participate further in the dismantling of the state. I am going to retire and devote my time to public service. Yeltsin is worried that I might head the opposition forces. I have told him, 'As long as you continue to move forward with democratic reforms, I will support you.'"

He clearly felt a need to explain the nuances of his position to Kohl. "You may wonder why I don't resign right away. It's because this is my affair—I started it. I don't want the process to leave the bounds of constitutionality, or the commonwealth itself to be stillborn. Everything that we, including you and I, have done all these years in the world and in Europe is too important to me."

Kohl wished him endurance and promised to call him again later. Gorbachev thanked him for the call, and for the Christmas present he had received the day before. "As we lift our glasses on New Year's Eve—as we will most assuredly do—we will remember your good wishes," he promised.

❁   ❁   ❁

Saturday, December 21, finally arrived. Because of the time difference with respect to Alma-Ata, by the time I arrived at work the meeting of the leaders of the eleven republics[58] was nearing its culmination. The meeting was adjourned at noon. The news agency Interfax distributed the following historic communiqué: "The USSR has ceased to exist. On December 21, at Alma-Ata, during a closed-door meeting, the leaders of the eleven sovereign states agreed to terminate the existence of the USSR.

"It was also announced that eight republics of the former Union, including Moldavia, have joined as founding members the agreement regarding the formation of the Commonwealth of Independent States, which has been signed by

Russia, Ukraine, and Belorussia. All of the Union republics except for Georgia and the Baltic states have entered the commonwealth.

"Interfax has also learned that there has been no decision yet on Georgia's membership in the commonwealth, since the Georgian representatives at Alma-Ata do not have the necessary plenary powers.

"The protocol of the agreement by the leaders of the independent states and the Alma-Ata declaration of the leaders of the eleven states are to be signed during the next two hours.

"Concerning the armed forces of the CIS, a proposal has been made to set up an interim command and leave it in place until December 30. A long-term, permanent structure will be created at that time."

Express item number 5 followed:

"The leaders of the eleven sovereign republics that have formed the Commonwealth of Independent States have issued a proclamation to the president of the USSR, Mikhail Gorbachev, informing him that the USSR and the institution of the presidency of the USSR have ceased to exist. In this proclamation, the heads of the independent states thank Mikhail Gorbachev for his great and constructive contribution."

In Moscow, it was already one o'clock in the afternoon. I learned that François Mitterrand was calling Gorbachev from Paris and went into the President's office. Three of his closest friends were there with him: Yakovlev, Shevardnadze, and Chernyaev. They had just finished discussing a new version of the President's resignation statement.

Gorbachev picked up the phone. Yakovlev and Shevardnadze went out, taking the statement and the President's comments with them. Chernyaev and I took our usual seats, opposite Gorbachev.

The connection was poor; Mitterrand's voice faded in and out at first. Then the problem was corrected.

Mitterrand was the first person to call Gorbachev after the Alma-Ata decision, and during those first few minutes, Gorbachev urgently needed such an understanding and sympathetic listener. He told Mitterrand that he was waiting for official communications from Alma-Ata and that he hoped the differences of opinion among the participants would be resolved and everyone would sign the final accord. He repeated his fear that the treaty might be weakened by further reservations on the part of the Ukrainian parliament, and then he announced to Mitterrand, as he had to Kohl, that he would be making a decision about resigning during the next few days.

"Thank you for your friendship, Mr. President," he said to Mitterrand. "I want to assure you that in my country, as well as in the sphere of foreign affairs, I will continue to act in the interest of the momentous and noble cause that we have undertaken together. And I will do so in whatever capacity I may assume."

To reassure Mitterrand, who was uncharacteristically emotional, he added, "I am calm. I'm doing what I can to make what is happening here as painless as possible." The conversation lasted for twenty minutes.

An hour later, the President—short of resigning but already deposed—entered the "television room," where he was to tape an interview for CBS television. One of the first questions he was asked related to his attitude toward Yeltsin. "We recognize and have valued his role in the opposition, including that of defender of democracy. In terms of his role as a statesman, he has yet to prove himself in a position of power and responsibility."

What would he wish for Yeltsin? "I think it wouldn't hurt him to take a more democratic approach," Gorbachev answered after a moment's thought.

What were the commonwealth's chances of survival? "It had better not turn out to be a soap bubble."

This was followed by the unpleasant but inevitable question, "Don't you feel that Yeltsin and the other republic leaders are humiliating you?" Gorbachev answered with a studied detachment obviously intended to shield his wounded pride. "I leave that to their consciences. I must rise above emotions."

The CBS taping was followed by an interview for the newspaper *Moskovskaya pravda.* It was as if Gorbachev wanted to make use of every last minute that remained to him as the official leader of a country that was sinking into the abyss of history. Or perhaps he was just afraid of being alone.

The readers of *Moskovskaya pravda,* formerly published by the conservative Moscow City Party Committee (*gorkom*), were nonsupporters of perestroika, people who either did not believe in reform or who vacillated on the subject. Gorbachev laid out his position for them. "The market is not an end in itself. It must work to the benefit of people. To accomplish this, an entire system of measures is needed, the most important one being stimulation of the producers. If producers are not interested in their work, the goods will not be produced. Imagine what would happen if price deregulation were accompanied by a steep drop in production volume! Prices would go sky-high. . . .

"The government must develop a precise system of protective mechanisms in anticipation of a future rise in prices. People who work in the production sector, for example, must be given the chance to earn enough to live on under the new conditions. For those who depend on the state budget—teachers, doctors, students, retirees, and other groups of citizens—measures must be instituted in advance that will enable them to face changing price levels with equanimity. Otherwise, people will be defenseless."

Yet another question was asked about his resignation. "After Alma-Ata, it will become a reality."

The workday was drawing to a close, but Gorbachev taped one more television interview, this time with Ted Koppel and Yegor Yakovlev. This was not the exclusive interview with the President for which Koppel had rushed to Moscow, but an evening conversation with a mysterious man who was bowed, but not broken.

Koppel asked him whether there was still some way he could hold on to power if he wanted to. Gorbachev nodded as if he considered the question a good one. "You know, there are people who change their opinions and their positions in order to stay on top and, still worse, hold on to power. For me this is unacceptable. If what is happening didn't matter to me and if I wanted to remain in government more than anything else, then that would not be too difficult to achieve. But I have always wanted much more than that. It isn't just about power but about the essence of what is happening here in our country."

This politic answer was too pat for Koppel, and he made another attempt to probe his subject. "Do you recall the fate of Winston Churchill, to whom his country owed so much, especially for his leadership during the war against the Nazis, but who was forced out in the first postwar parliamentary elections in 1945? We couldn't look him in the eye at the time. Today, I am looking you straight in the eye. What is going on in your mind?"

Gorbachev smiled. He finally understood what Koppel wanted of him. "All right; I will answer you with the parable of a king who wanted to learn the basic wisdom of life. He charged his sages to write it down for him. They worked for many years, filling forty volumes. Then, when the king at last lay dying, they summed everything up in one sentence: 'Man is born, suffers, and dies.'"

"That is exactly what I would have expected from you, Mr. President," said Koppel feelingly.

Before going home, Koppel came to the offices of the press service to thank me for facilitating matters. "To me, the President's departure is a remarkable example of dignity," he said as we were saying good-bye.

The final meeting between Gorbachev and Yeltsin prior to the transfer of power was scheduled to take place on Monday the 23rd at noon. At the Alma-Ata meeting, the leaders of the republics were initially supposed to have discussed and approved all the practical details arising from their intention to eliminate the presidency of the USSR: establishing the amount of the President's pension, his material circumstances, the number of bodyguards he would be assigned, and so forth. However, they subsequently decided to let Yeltsin handle this problem by himself: "spoils of war," if you will.

Gorbachev, with input from Revenko and Shakhnazarov, wrote several draft joint decrees in preparation for his talk with Yeltsin. These related to the suspension of operations within the offices of the president of the USSR and the Interstate Economic Committee and the transfer of personnel to other positions; the creation of the Gorbachev Foundation; and, naturally, the establishment of the terms of the Soviet president's retirement. Gorbachev also planned to discuss what was to be done with the state and Party archives, which were partly intermingled and were currently being housed at the Kremlin, and, of course, the procedure for passing on the secret codes for the nuclear button.

At eleven o'clock, the time when Gorbachev usually arrived for work, the Soviet-American television crew was already jammed into the pressroom. I went into Gorbachev's office as he was leafing through the text of his upcoming statement. "I'm thinking about doing this tomorrow evening. There's no sense in dragging things out," he said.

"Mikhail Sergeevich," I replied, "wouldn't it be better to wait until Wednesday? Tomorrow is December 24, Christmas Eve. In many countries this is the biggest holiday of the year. Let's let people celebrate in peace."

"All right," he said. "But Wednesday at the latest."

I asked his permission for the television crew to tape Yeltsin's arrival for this last historic "meeting of the two presidents." Gorbachev consented with a vague wave of his hand.

Returning to the reception room, I gave the nod to the cameraman, who was waiting impatiently near the door. He dashed off to find the rest of the group. I was still a little worried, however. It seemed to me that the relations between the two presidents were tense enough already and that Yeltsin might suspect that Gorbachev was trying to put something over on him if he suddenly came upon television cameras in the anteroom. So rather than be satisfied with one president's approval, I decided to ask the other one for his as well.

I intercepted Yeltsin as he was leaving the elevator and asked him if he had any objections to a television crew taping his arrival at Gorbachev's office. He cut me off short. "Out of the question," he said. "Otherwise I'll cancel the meeting." I did my best to soothe him: Naturally his wishes would be respected. To the great disappointment of the American and Soviet journalists, I shepherded them out of the reception area. Yeltsin did not come into Gorbachev's office until he was certain that the television "ambush" had been dispersed.

Their meeting lasted almost ten hours. During the dinner that was served to them in the Walnut Room next to the president's office, they were joined by Alexander Yakovlev. Gorbachev's inner circle and the press waited nervously for the results of this first frank discussion in the history of the relationship between these two equally singular Russian leaders.

The only source of information on the progress of the meeting was Zhenya, the Kremlin waiter who was shuttling back and forth between the Walnut Room and the kitchen carrying bottles and plates of food. In response to the impatient questions put to him by the representatives of the various departments who intercepted him in transit, he announced, "The mood seems to be good."

That same evening at six o'clock, Gorbachev was scheduled to have a telephone conversation with John Major. It was obvious that his meeting with Yeltsin would not be over by then. Chernyaev, Yegor Yakovlev—who had come to the Kremlin expressly for the purpose—and I waited for the call in the president's anteroom, certain that the conversation would not take place. At six o'clock on the dot, however, Gorbachev came out of the Walnut Room looking flushed, leaving Yeltsin alone with Alexander Yakovlev.

Major's call came through right on time. Gorbachev was a little dazed and at first was unable to manage the tone he usually assumed in conversation with other leaders with whom he was on familiar terms. But it took him only a minute or two to recover. "Today, dear John, I'm trying to accomplish what is most important: to keep what is happening here from resulting in losses. You know, I still feel that the best solution would be a unified state, but there are the republics' positions to consider. For the time being, I do not see any dangers comparable to the situation in Yugoslavia. That's what matters the most to me. To you, too, I imagine.

"Boris Yeltsin and I have been talking for six hours now. I can tell you that we have a common understanding of our responsibility to the country and the world. I want to help Yeltsin, because his is not an easy task. I just told him that as long as democratic reform continues, I intend to support and even protect him. As far as nuclear weapons are concerned, you should have no fears on that count: Everything is solidly protected and the firmest control has been established. I ask you to help the commonwealth, and Russia in particular. Russia specifically. I hope you understand me."

Operating under the twofold constraints of diplomacy and an open telephone conversation, and knowing that he would not have a chance to communicate with Major on a more confidential basis in the foreseeable future, Gorbachev was probably emphasizing Russia and the democratic processes taking place there because he considered it to be his trump card and his best hope for the future—a future in which he, too, might still play a part.

"Sometime during the next two days (he looked in my direction as if confirming our agreement for Wednesday) I will make my decision public, but I don't want to say my farewells yet because any turn of events is still possible, even a reversal."

Major, at the other end of the line, thanked Gorbachev feelingly for "his clarity and his comprehensive analysis." He confirmed that the West had the will and the desire to aid Gorbachev and the leaders of the commonwealth. One of the reasons for this was "gratitude for everything that [he had] accomplished over the past few years."

"Whatever decision you may make during the next two days, you will unquestionably occupy a special place in the history of your country and the world. . . ." Gorbachev was visibly moved. "Thank you for everything. Raisa and I have grown very fond of you, both you and Norma. I allow myself the weakness of saying so now because in two days I will be in a different situation. And that gives me the right to speak freely."

As he hung up, he commented that everything had been worked out with Yeltsin. "I'm going back in to wind things up."

He returned to the Walnut Room. Yegor Yakovlev and I asked Zhenya, who was rushing back and forth through the hall with redoubled energy, to bring us something to eat, since neither of us had had any dinner. He served us bread and jam and coffee. We sat down at the kitchen table, next to a TV set tuned to the "Dance of the Cygnets" from Tchaikovsky's *Swan Lake*—which I recalled had also been broadcast the day of the August putsch. On the other side of the wall, the indefatigable Americans were waiting in the television room, "just in case." They had threaded their antenna for the satellite hookup through one of the windows of the Kremlin. One of the Americans was talking to somebody in New York, and not about professional matters, as I could tell when I listened in.

The president's office, a little farther down the hall, was empty; but the red flag in one corner, an eyeglass case, and the mysterious briefcase, still poised at the end of the table, confirmed that Gorbachev was still master there. In the Walnut Room, which adjoined the office, a conversation that probably had ceased to be official several hours before continued among three men who had been acquainted with each other for many years but who had never really known one another. And farther along the same corridor was the office-apartment of Vladimir Ilyich Lenin, closed up and sealed owing to the lateness of the hour.

That is the surrealistic tableau that would have presented itself to anyone who could have taken a cross section through the building and looked into the rooms on the third floor. Atop the dome, the red flag of the Soviet Union was still flying.

❀   ❀   ❀

On December 24, Gorbachev said farewell to the members of his staff. About fifty associates, aides, advisers, and department heads had gathered in the hall of the State Council at the Kremlin. The President and his chief of staff, Grigory Revenko, arrived together as usual. Gorbachev tried to be reassuring as he appeared before this gathering; these were people with whom he had worked for many years, and some of them had been with him since the first shaky steps of perestroika. He began by describing the outcome of the Alma-Ata conference, of which everyone was well aware, since it had been front-page news for the past three days, and he confirmed that the era of the USSR was drawing to a close. "Tomorrow I intend to announce my resignation."

Given the results of his meeting with Yeltsin the day before, he was able to somewhat allay the fears of his associates, who were already imagining Yeltsin's thugs descending on the Kremlin to "liberate" the seat of power from everything reminiscent of Soviet history—including, first and foremost, the members of the old team. Gorbachev announced that everything would take place in a civilized manner and that a reasonable interval would be allotted for "changing the guard" and for dismantling the Union apparatus. The two presidents had also agreed that a bilateral commission led by their representatives would handle the task of finding jobs for all personnel. "That means all of us," he noted wryly.

He added that he planned to continue working in the public arena, but henceforth through the Gorbachev Foundation, which he was in the process of setting up. He then gravely wished everyone all the best and withdrew. His loyal band, not completely reassured, watched him go with emotion.

❀   ❀   ❀

He gave a more detailed account of his meeting with Yeltsin to an intimate group consisting of Alexander Yakovlev, Shakhnazarov, Revenko, and myself, whom he called together in his office shortly afterward to discuss the launching of the foundation.

Yeltsin had behaved appropriately. He had listened attentively, Gorbachev told us, to what "Alexander Nikolaevich [Yakovlev] and I were trying to warn him about." He had also asked Gorbachev to lend him his support because of the difficulties of the present situation, or "at least not to criticize him for the next six months."

However, he had refused to meet Gorbachev's requests concerning his office and his staff and had drastically reduced both his pension and the number of his bodyguards. "That doesn't really matter, though. The main thing is that we agreed about the foundation. Yeltsin is afraid that I'll turn it into a breeding ground for the opposition, but I assured him that I had no such intention."

The rest of the day was spent in intense consultation on the legal aspects of registering the foundation. Shevardnadze and Stanislav Shatalin agreed to be founding members. Each of them had broken with the President at one time but had come back to him in his hour of need.

The Italian ambassador, Ferdinando Saleo, brought Gorbachev a message from President Francesco Cossiga and a friendly letter from Giulio Andreotti. Gorbachev asked the ambassador to relay his thanks to them for their support and for their invitation to visit Italy. He took the opportunity to reiterate that his purpose in setting up the Gorbachev Foundation was not to place himself once more at the head of the opposition but simply "to aid the cause."

"My main concern is that the reforms should take place. And the only way the problems can be solved is to avoid bickering. You see, it's not easy to wipe out totalitarianism by a frontal assault because it lurks inside every one of us. It's not an object, with an exact shape that can be determined. Its seeds are scattered throughout the social organism and are firmly rooted in the collective consciousness. That is why changes and transformations are so difficult to bring about."

The last person he spoke with that day was Canadian prime minister Brian Mulroney, who telephoned Gorbachev. "I am not leaving politics and public life," he told Mulroney at the end of the call. "I have great plans. . . ."

He ended the day by arranging his personal papers and rereading his final statement, which had been prepared with the input of several of his closest aides. The major contributor, of course, was Chernyaev, his most faithful and trusted collaborator (whom Gorbachev had once introduced to Felipe González as his "alter ego"). Alexander Yakovlev also participated in the editing process, as did a number of volunteers, presidential advisers, and outside contributors. Each of them suggested better word choices or ways to improve the tone of the address, but the last word, in every sense, was Gorbachev's.

On December 25,[59] the President arrived at the Kremlin later than usual and closeted himself in his office. His anteroom was strangely empty; not a single visitor was present. All the receptionists had come in at the same time (they normally alternated twenty-four-hour shifts) to sort out the books Gorbachev was taking with him and discard papers that were no longer needed.

For a long time, Gorbachev had preferred his office in Staraya Ploshchad at the Party Central Committee headquarters. This building had been the real seat of power for decades. Moreover, it housed all the files, records, and documents that were essential to his work. He considered the Kremlin offices rather impractical and uncomfortable, better suited for diplomatic meetings and official ceremonies than for serious business.

The creation of the office of president had reversed his perspective. As time went on, he had gotten used to his new office and had managed to make it one of the symbols of the presidency. The historic Kremlin thus became the renewed seat of a power that was, finally, democratic.

Chernyaev and I had several pending matters to discuss with Gorbachev. Chernyaev needed him to sign some farewell letters that Gorbachev had decided to send to his foreign colleagues, and I was to brief him for the taping of his statement and the CNN interview that would follow.

When we went into his office at about three o'clock in the afternoon, the President wasn't there. We waited for a few minutes; then Chernyaev, anxious to send off the letters, knocked on the door of the resting room that was situated at the back of the office, behind the worktable. Gorbachev did not answer right away. Then, without opening the door, he asked what the problem was. "Just a minute; I'll be right out."

He appeared after about five minutes, fresh and looking fit despite a slight redness of the eyes caused by lack of sleep or the tension of the past few days. He began to sign the letters, first reading them over carefully, as he always did: to Andreotti, to Baker, and so on.

I showed him the front page of *Moskovsky Komsomolets,* whose headline was a quotation from Pushkin: "No, I shall not die completely!"

"My soul, by the lyre, will survive me and will escape corruption," Gorbachev completed with emphasis, smiling.

Once the letters had been signed, Chernyaev left. The President and I stayed on alone. He took up the final version of his speech and, arming himself with a pen, began to read it aloud, asking me for my opinion wherever he had any doubts. He stopped at the phrase "addressing you for the last time in the capacity of president of the USSR."

"Chernyaev proposes that we delete 'USSR,'" he said.

"No," I objected firmly. "That in particular should stay in. First of all, until you are done reading this statement you will still be president of the USSR. And second, even when you have ceased to be president, you will still be President Gorbachev to the world; after that, we'll see."

He made a few more changes. In the paragraph citing the democratic victories of recent years, he added, "We must not relinquish them, no matter what the circumstances."

The telephone rang. A very agitated Raisa Maximovna was calling from the dacha. Some of the new security men had come out to order her to "remove her personal belongings from the premises of the governmental representative." (This was Special Services jargon for the President's official residence.)

Gorbachev shoved the pages that he was annotating out of the way and immediately called the chief of security, Vladimir Redkoborody, who had been his own head of security a few days earlier. "You're really out of line, and you'd better straighten up!" he exclaimed angrily. "You're talking about somebody's home, here. Do I have to report all this to the press?" Redkoborody made excuses, citing orders from on high and excessive zeal from below, but in the end he promised to call off his people.

It took the President awhile to calm down. He said a few vehement words to me about "those jerks."

"You know, Andrei, the fact that they're acting this way makes me certain that I'm right," he said suddenly, and with that thought, was able to regain his equanimity. He would need it that evening.

Around four o'clock, Yeltsin, in response to an inquiry from CNN, announced that he would come by Gorbachev's office at about 7:20 P.M. to take possession of the nuclear button. It had already been announced that Gorbachev would give his resignation speech at seven o'clock.

The press corps was now faced with the arduous task of coordinating appropriate time intervals between Gorbachev's speech for central television, the CNN interview that was to follow, and the taping of the final hours of the presidency "for posterity."

One of the historic events of these final hours was a telephone conversation with George Bush, scheduled for five o'clock. At the appointed time, I had Koppel and Yegor Yakovlev's joint crew come into the president's office. We were unable to locate Bush right away; he was spending Christmas at Camp David. Finally he came on the line. Gorbachev wished him and Barbara happy holidays and told him that he would be resigning in two hours. He then moved on to the problems that were on his mind: He asked Bush, with special emphasis, to give his support to the consolidated formation of the commonwealth as a whole and to recognize the sovereignty of the individual states. "We must stimulate collaboration, not disintegration."

He also asked Bush to support Russia, which was carrying most of the burden of reform. Anticipating a question from Bush, he said that before he left office he would issue a decree transferring the right to use nuclear weapons to the president of Russia. "There will be no discontinuity in this area. You can celebrate Christmas in peace."

Before concluding, Gorbachev explained that in leaving he had no intention of "hiding out in the taiga." He wanted to play an active part in political and public life, to aid perestroika domestically, and to consolidate the new thinking in world politics. "Our roles may change, but the friendship that has arisen between us will always remain. Good-bye!" The last word was in English.

Bush spoke at greater length than Gorbachev, and the American journalists gathered around the President's desk tried to use their microphones to pick up the flow of English that could be heard through the receiver.

"What you have accomplished will go down in history," Bush said in closing. "I hope that our paths will cross again. We will be happy to have you visit us when everything has calmed down—perhaps here at Camp David. I salute you and thank you for everything you have done for peace. Thank you for your friendship."

The last person to call Gorbachev before zero hour was Hans-Dietrich Genscher. Their friendly conversation melted the thin layer of ice that, despite their best efforts, had begun to form in their relationship, and Gorbachev was happy about that.

When he finally got off the phone, the President had the journalists leave his office and suggested to Yegor Yakovlev and me that we have coffee together. His resignation was only one hour away, and he obviously did not want to be left alone with his much-read statement, the menacing button, an uncertain future, and, especially, his own thoughts.

Nor did we want to leave him alone. We sat down at the oval table at which Gorbachev had customarily received his guests and began talking about everything and nothing. One question that arose spontaneously was, wasn't he afraid that somebody would try to get revenge on him by ferreting around in his past? "I'm not worried," he replied. "My conscience is clear. Do you really think there could have been any very extraordinary privileges available in Stavropol? There were no special apartments, nor even a special store. We bought our food at the canteen run by the *obkom*.[60] Until recently, Raisa Maximovna was keeping all of our receipts.[61]

"And what about Krasnodar?" I asked. "Krasnodar is right next door to you, and some incredible things went on there at Medunov's."[62]

"Medunov, that's something else again," said Gorbachev. "Andropov and I tried to do something about him. Yury Vladimirovich told me, 'We have to take him in hand, we can't ignore the warning signs.' I read complaints against him myself, especially from the local Jewish population: bribes, extortion. And what orgies in the official dachas! He wasn't afraid of anything. And for good reason: He had direct access to Brezhnev."

Gorbachev spoke of the period when he had first joined the apparatus of the Party Central Committee and the Politburo in Moscow, after 1978. "So," he continued, "when I started digging, Shchelokov[63] came out against me. One of his aides, who was dying, called me to his deathbed to tell me that Shchelokov had given the order to 'destroy' me."

Before we knew it, an hour had gone by. At ten minutes to seven, Gorbachev came back to the subject of the moment. "Where are they going to be filming? Why not in my office?" He undoubtedly saw a certain incongruity in making his final statement on the set of the Kremlin television studio rather than where he had actually worked. But it was too late to make any changes. In ten minutes he would be appearing live before the country and the world.

"CNN broadcasts to a hundred and fifty-three countries," Yakovlev said. "And the eleven countries of the CIS as well," added Gorbachev, without missing a beat. "Well, let's not take the risk of changing the location," he decided. And as if sloughing off the relaxed mood of the past hour of reminiscence, he rose abruptly and, opening the door of the resting room that led into the hallway, left the office. He would never return there as president again.

❀   ❀   ❀

The studio, which was known in the Kremlin as "room number 4," was bustling with technicians, photographers, and journalists from three television networks. Gorbachev entered the room at five minutes to seven and, greeting people he knew as he passed, made his way with some difficulty to the brightly lit table, where a microphone awaited him. He was carrying a briefcase containing his speech and the decree enacting his resignation from the post of commander in chief of the armed forces.

Gorbachev placed the decree in front of him and then asked suddenly, "When should I sign it, before or after my statement?" He was speaking to Yakovlev and me, who were trying to manage all this chaos. Our opinions differed, and we each had our own set of reasons for one or the other approach. While we argued, Gorbachev asked me for a pen and tested it on a sheet of paper. "I prefer a smoother-writing one," he said. The head of the CNN crew, who was present at the taping, reached over my shoulder to offer his own pen. Gorbachev, satisfied with the instrument and paying no further attention to our discussion, placed the decree in front of him, signed it with a flourish, and set it aside. His abdication of nuclear power thus took place unnoticed by outside observers.

He gave the remaining three minutes to the photographers and reached for the text of his speech at seven o'clock on the dot. "Dear compatriots, fellow citizens . . ." His voice sounded unnatural and hollow. It seemed on the verge of trembling, as did his chin. But as he continued to read one could see him gaining control of his emotions, aware that his words resonated with conviction and dignity.

"I leave office with anxiety," he said at the end of the address. "But also with hope and with faith in you, in your wisdom and your strength of mind. We are heirs to a great civilization, and it is now up to each and every one of us to ensure that this civilization is reborn to a modern, dignified new life." He thanked all those who had struggled with him in "a just and good cause" over the years and acknowledged that mistakes could have been avoided if better choices had been made.

I consider this one of his best speeches. When he deviated from his notes to add, "I wish all of you the very best," I think many people must have felt that an unpardonable and irreparable error was being made as the country and the world looked on.

After a five-minute break, the CNN crew set up their equipment in front of the President. Every country in the world—except for the former Soviet Union—saw and heard Gorbachev's answers to questions about his resignation, his reaction and that of his family, his relationship with Yeltsin. Central television rebroadcast the interview two hours later.

At one point, Gorbachev showed the television audience the final decree of the president of the USSR concerning the transfer of nuclear authority. All that remained now was for him to implement it.

Gorbachev left the journalists in room number 4 and went back to his office, where Marshal Shaposhnikov was already waiting for him. Yeltsin, as promised, would arrive soon to pick up the nuclear codes. The ceremony of turning over control of the button was to be filmed by ABC, this time with Yeltsin's consent. But some bizarre news awaited Gorbachev and the film crew: Yeltsin, displeased with Gorbachev's speech, which he considered a political attack on the Russian leadership, had declared that he refused to enter the office of the former president of the Union. He proposed a meeting on neutral ground, in the Catherine Room.

Personally, I am certain that this preposterous idea was suggested to Yeltsin by one of his close advisers during the broadcasting of Gorbachev's final statement, when it became clear that he was leaving office with dignity and with his head held high, not like a vanquished foe but like someone compelled to yield to a force that he cannot, or will not, overcome.

This time it was Gorbachev's turn to be brusque: He rejected Yeltsin's proposal and announced that he would send everything that was necessary through Shaposhnikov. Two very ordinary-looking men in civilian clothes were sitting in the president's anteroom with an instrument that looked like a cellular phone. These two colonels, who accompanied the President wherever he went, were in fact the "button," or rather one of the elements in a complex network equipped with redundant security devices. They disappeared into the corridors in search of their new boss.

A half-hour after Gorbachev's resignation speech, I left the Kremlin by the Spasskaya Gate to go to the Moscow studios of the French television network

Antenne 2. The Russian tricolor was already flying over the dome of the government building. A number of foreign journalists who had come on the scene too late to film the historic lowering of the red flag were forced to appeal to some very enterprising Muscovites who had taped the event on a Camcorder. The asking price was quite reasonable: 200 French francs for a VHS cassette.

During my appearance on the French television news show, I was asked if Gorbachev had left office of his own accord or whether he had been forced out or removed. I explained that he had been overthrown by processes that he himself had initiated and that his feelings were probably divided between the satisfaction of having accomplished tremendous reforms in his country and fears as to what its fate would be.

After I had left the studio my car phone rang. I was told that the President—no longer "of the USSR"—wanted to see me. I went back to the Kremlin. In the Walnut Room, sitting at the table, were Gorbachev and the last of the faithful: Yegor and Alexander Yakovlev and Chernyaev. There were not thirteen of us at the table that evening, and even if Judas had been in Gorbachev's entourage, his betrayal would have already taken place.

Gorbachev probably never imagined that his farewell supper at the Kremlin would be an informal meeting with a few friends held in an empty, half-lit room of the palace. Some friends may have been missing at that table; but at least no one there was de trop.

In his book *December 1991,* Gorbachev describes his feelings about this gathering: "The president of the USSR was not given a farewell ceremony, as is the custom in civilized countries. None of the presidents of the sovereign republics, the former Soviet republics, felt that they could come to Moscow or even call me, despite the fact that I had had ties of friendship with most of them for many years.

"And Boris Nikolaevich Yeltsin seemed to be in particular haste. . . . He informed the journalists of our meeting on December 23 in an improper, inaccurate, and rather crude manner. Other actions that followed left both me and the general public with an unpleasant impression.

"During those last few days spent at the Kremlin, until the evening when I resigned, my closest collaborators and friends, who had shared with me all the enormous tension of the drama of the last months of my presidency, were at my side. There were also journalists, from our own country and others. All of these people demonstrated a real understanding of what was taking place. Many of them remained at the Kremlin for several days and nights. And they were moved not only by professional interest but also by sincere feeling. I felt this acutely . . . especially since I had had conflicts with some of them in the past."

The party broke up at about eleven o'clock. Yegor Yakovlev went to the television studios to help edit the last footage to be included in the Soviet-American film on the President's resignation. It was broadcast the next day.

Gorbachev and I arranged to meet the following day. He promised to grant his first interviews as former president of the USSR to Italian journalists from *La Repubblica* and *La Stampa*.

❀   ❀   ❀

Gorbachev arrived at the Kremlin on December 26 looking somber. The day had begun with problems caused by the behavior of the security people and other staff, who were now under other orders and were rudely and deliberately making Gorbachev aware of the change in his status. "They're throwing me out of the dacha, and they've taken the car away," he angrily complained.

The conversation with the Italian journalists gave him an opportunity to forget about this disagreeable development. The Italians asked him how he felt in his new role. "I am in good spirits," he answered. "Generally, once a decision is made, no matter how difficult it is, you feel better. The change in my living conditions doesn't scare me: My family and I are not spoiled people. And retirement may be the very thing I need."

As far as I can recall, this was the first time I heard him try to summarize the mistakes he had made during his seven years in government. First, he explained, the previous stability of the economy should have been used to get the country moving sooner, and faster, in the direction of a market economy. The Novo-Ogarevo process should have been started earlier, and efforts should have been made to consolidate the democrats. The need for this kind of action became apparent in February 1991. "But I did not make any progress in that direction until after a confrontation with the democrats in Moscow in March."

Finally, it was not enough just to dismantle the old leadership structures; new ones should have been set up quickly. "None of this cancels out the most important thing: my conviction that the right choice was made in 1985. I feel that from a historical perspective, I have been proven right.

"It's as if I've lived several lives over the past seven years. I myself changed as the country did, but I also changed the country. After all, it's a rare opportunity to help restore one's homeland to the world community, to universal values. That's why I feel that whatever happens, my destiny has been fulfilled."

The Italians asked him if he believed that it would still be possible to modernize Russia within the bounds of the democratic process.

Gorbachev said he was convinced of the universal value of the principles of democracy and human rights. They were important everywhere, and obviously in Russia as well. However, it was essential to avoid imposing foreign models on a unique situation. "We have our own reality, inspired by tradition, history, a unified country that has formed by a natural process.

"Yes, like many of my compatriots, I have spiritual ties to Europe, but I am no less bound to the East. The main thing is that I am a very down-to-earth person. I keep my feet on the ground. I don't believe those who claim that life in Russia can be like life in Sweden or Italy—any more than I believe people who feel that Russia has a unique mission.

"These disparate trends have always been present and at odds in Russia's spiritual and political culture. Russia must recognize that it is a bridge between the two cultures, that of Asia and that of Europe, and, simultaneously, a part of human civilization. As for myself, I feel that I am part of the shared process of humanity's search for liberty and justice. Each person has the right to strive for these things, and perhaps our experience will provide new stimulus toward the globalization of the world."

"What were your feelings last night when the red flag was lowered from the Kremlin?"

"For me, the Soviet flag is our history and our life. The change of symbols should not have been accentuated in that way. One has to have some tact in dealing with people: We're talking about whole generations."

"How does your family feel about your resignation? Are they relieved?" Gorbachev was clearly grateful to the journalists for this question. Without it he would not have been able to say everything that was on his mind. His answer was brief, however: "I am grateful to my family for having endured all this."

❀   ❀   ❀

The journalists arranged a real farewell ceremony for the President. We called it the "final briefing by the presidential press service." The meeting took place in the Hotel October, formerly owned by the Party, which, by an ironic twist of fate, had been rechristened the President with the arrival of new management.

When Gorbachev, weary and pensive, entered the hall of the hotel with his staff and began to climb the stairs, the assembled journalists greeted him with an ovation. Their applause reflected sympathy and compassion toward a deposed leader—natural, under the circumstances—but above all, respect for the courage, perseverance, and hard work of a man who had done his best to keep the promises he had made to himself.

The journalists' welcome, their comments, and their questions brought back the President we had always known. One of the guests commented to me, "You've saved him from a heart attack."

After more than two hours of answering questions, submitting to mini-interviews, signing autographs, and receiving good wishes, Gorbachev said good-bye to the press and his former coworkers and headed for home.

The next day, on arriving at the Kremlin, where he was to meet with some Japanese journalists, he was told that his office was occupied. We had to prepare for the meeting in Revenko's office, one floor down. We learned that someone had called the head of Gorbachev's secretariat at dawn with the information that Boris Nikolaevich intended to occupy *his* office in the Kremlin at eight-thirty that morning. The plate bearing the inscription "The President of the USSR, M.S. Gorbachev" had been taken down during the night.

After December I never went back to that hallway, or, of course, into the anteroom of Gorbachev's former office. The last time I stopped in to see the President, I asked him to autograph a copy of his book *The August Coup* for me. He turned it over in his hands, thinking, and then wrote something rapidly. I thanked him. I didn't open the book to the flyleaf until I was on my way out of the office.

"Dear Andrei Serafimovich," he had written. "I give you this book as a souvenir. I thank you for your collaboration, which, I hope, will continue. The most important events are still before us. It is noon on the clock of history."

I looked up automatically and was astonished to see that the hands of the clock in the anteroom actually stood at noon. Only later did I find out that the clock had stopped.

Afterword:
A Mythical Kingdom
Vanishes—Again

Now that the dramatic chain of events leading to the collapse of the USSR is over and the states and peoples of that vast totalitarian empire have embarked on a new phase, it might seem appropriate to make a final assessment of the "Gorbachev era." To some, this seems all the more fitting because the main element in the almost utopian agenda that became linked with Gorbachev's name, the effort to secure revolutionary changes through reformist compromises, seems to have receded irretrievably into the past.

But it would be unfair and inaccurate to say so. First, if we are indeed witnessing the end of an era, it cannot be said to be Gorbachev's era alone. This has been the collapse of an entire civilization (or at least of the attempt to build a new one), the sinking of yet another Atlantis, another utopian apparition, into the depths of history.

The lowering of the red flag from the roof of the Kremlin signified more than the departure of the first and last president of the USSR: It was the end of an era in Soviet and world history—the era that began in 1917 and that was linked throughout with the name Lenin. In a sense, this event might even be said to mark the end of the political history of the twentieth century, dominated as it has been by the efforts of communism and fascism to build and disseminate their totalitarian models for society and the world order—models based on the domination of the individual by the state and on the monopoly of a single ideology and social system that brooked no alternatives.

Today, almost fifty years after the overthrow of fascism in Western Europe, socialism in Central and Eastern Europe is crumbling before our eyes. There is no guarantee, however, that one or the other will not rise again in another form, in other parts of the world.

But this is only one way of looking at this turning point in history. The second viewpoint, in some ways, refutes the first, since it is concerned not with the end of an era but with its continuation into the future. It may be that we are witnessing only the initial phase of a profound change whose progress must be measured in historical rather than political terms.

Whatever Mikhail Gorbachev's ultimate fate may be, his name will forever be linked to the initiation of this process of reunification of world history, which had proceeded along separate paths since 1917. Despite such flattering—and wholly justified—assessments of Gorbachev's historical role, however, his career as president is now over and his political agenda has failed. During this final phase, he was unable to repeat the political miracles he had been able to accomplish earlier.

The Commonwealth of Independent States, created behind Gorbachev's back and founded solely on the common desire to abolish the center that he symbolized, confirms that his plan for the democratic reconfiguration of the Soviet empire within the framework of a unified state was only a romantic dream, twice interrupted by reality. This plan was dealt a mortal blow by the revolt of reactionary bureaucratic elements and received the coup de grâce from the "democratic putsch" carried out by the leaders of the republics.

Today, as we stand poised between two epochs, about to pass from the history of the USSR and the Gorbachev era into an uncertain future that may or may not prove to be the "history of the CIS," it is fitting to look back at the past—though not with the intention of rewriting history, of course. Rethinking past decisions and furnishing advice after the fact may be a seductive occupation, but there is little to be gained from it.

Yet, now that the page of perestroika has been turned, we might well ask ourselves whether this movement and its initiator might have come to a happier end. Before he can finally pass into history, Gorbachev must still be called to account for the results of his actions vis-à-vis the current political situation and his contemporaries.

Gorbachevian perestroika was a source of tremendous hope in its early days. It promised prosperity for the peoples of the USSR and unprecedented security and stability for humankind. But instead, it plunged the country into a crisis even more profound than the one it was intended to alleviate. Who is responsible for this? No one but Gorbachev's predecessors, as his supporters claim? Or primarily Gorbachev himself—for having tampered with what was better left alone, as one school of thought would have it; or, according to another, because of inexcusable faintheartedness, indecision, and procrastination?

I think one has to begin by separating the human factor from the objective ("extrahuman") factors and by trying to determine what, precisely, could have been avoided by no one—even by as remarkable a politician as Gorbachev.

Obviously, there was no way to ward off a severe crisis during the transition from one social system to another, or to avoid paying a high political and social price for this change. Gorbachev himself began to realize this after the first two years of perestroika's euphoria: He often said that it was impossible to transform a multinational country as complex and as traumatized by its own history as the USSR without causing pain.

Nevertheless, he undoubtedly never imagined the extent to which seven decades of totalitarianism had destroyed the country's internal structures—the natural economic, social, and moral ties that bind society together. The devastation was such that when Gorbachev, with the magnanimous gesture of a liberator, threw off the carapace of political constraint and ideological falsification that was stifling society and proposed that these artificial props be replaced with the natural underpinnings of law, pluralistic democracy, and a market economy, the outwardly powerful state collapsed under its own weight.

The glinting, terrible armor of this superpower proved to be nothing more than an exoskeleton—and not that of a living organism yearning for freedom but of a gelatinous mass incapable of assuming the shape of a modern society.

"Without slaves there can be no dictator," according to a famous adage. Stalin's worst crime, after the extermination and mutilation of tens of thousands of lives, was to impose a slave mentality and fear of freedom on his people. This is the powerful resource on which both the conservatives and the radicals of the pseudoleft hope to draw—all those who, borne along on the wave of disorder, offer the masses the illusion of fast, simple solutions.

The situation is worsened by the difficulties and crises of the current phase of reform, where the problems of the past and those of the still murky future entwine to form one huge, intricate knot. Our society has matured enough to firmly reject its unacceptable, authoritarian past but is afraid to advance into the unknown territory of a market economy and free enterprise, for it sees in them the threat of enslavement by the capitalist system with its social injustice, egotism, and indifference to the fate of the human race. The only way out of this situation is to cut this Gordian knot—not with a sword but with a new burst of democratic momentum.

Gorbachev's decision to undertake perestroika required great personal courage. What he had to do was announce that the emperor was not wearing any clothes. The masses followed him willingly and enthusiastically, not only because they agreed with his analysis of the past but because at that point he was neither an anonymous child in the crowd nor a dissident, but the "emperor" himself.

Today, society must break through to a higher level of freedom and responsibility. But although it has lost its faith in the infallibility of kings and emperors, it still does not have any faith in itself. Our society has not yet learned to resolve its own contradictions with tolerance and the politics of compromise, and to make constructive use of pluralism, which many still see as an oddity rather than a public good.

One of the paradoxes of perestroika is that this society, availing itself (thanks to Gorbachev) of the democratic means of self-expression, is displaying, in a rough and sometimes aggressive manner, its own conservatism and pervasive totalitarian mentality.

To free itself from this mentality, society will undeniably need more than the "500 days" once approved by the Russian parliament. This is certainly enough time in which to pass the necessary laws, but they will bring results only when the people become convinced from their own experience that a market economy means respect for human rights and the sanctity of the individual, for the law and private ownership; that financial well-being comes not from an ideal system of centralized government distribution but from one's own labor; and that equality is not the result, but the starting point, the underlying principle, of democracy.

It will obviously take many years, perhaps even many generations, before realization dawns. All the same, the path that our society must follow is the one it has embarked upon—there is no other path. Though we may not yet be aware of it, we have already passed the point of no return. One doesn't return to a place that everyone else has abandoned.

❀   ❀   ❀

Gorbachev's foreign policy was also one of the reasons for the breakup of the monolith that was the Soviet Union. Many strategists in the past, Bismarck being foremost among them, warned that it was impossible to conquer Russia by threatening it or by attacking it from the outside. Both Napoleon and Hitler tried and failed. Soviet Russia was broken neither by the intervention of Japan and the Western powers during the first few months after the October Revolution nor by the blockade that followed World War II.

Russian, followed by Soviet, leaders (especially Stalin) learned to use this foreign threat effectively, even to the point of inventing it when necessary, cultivating a "siege mentality" in order to consolidate the country from within and to strengthen the state's totalitarian control over its citizens and the central power's control over the national republics.

As Bismarck had predicted, what outside pressure failed to do was accomplished by an internal explosion. All that was needed to trigger this explosion was to loosen the vise of the external threat that held the Soviet Union together. This was the result of Gorbachev's foreign policy, his new thinking, his plans to build an open and interdependent world whose stability would be based not on violence and the fear of nuclear war but on justice, respect for mutual interests, and a shared response to the global challenges facing humanity as it stood on the threshold of the twenty-first century.

Liberated from the fear of the enemy that had traditionally united them around Russia, the republics—or more precisely, their ambitious leaders—used the opportunity to lodge claims against Russia and their neighbors that had been building up for centuries. The empire, held together by internal violence and external pressure, exploded like a balloon that has drifted into the rarefied air of the upper atmosphere. The natural magnetism between republics and peoples united by a common history, economy, and culture, on which Gorbachev had relied, was not strong enough to counteract the combined forces of prejudice against the imperial-bureaucratic power of the center and of the aspirations of the local "barons," who did not hesitate to fan the flames of nationalist passions.

These obvious truths are, of course, apparent only in hindsight. Neither Gorbachev nor anyone else could have foreseen the effects of the explosion that would be triggered by the implementation of a civilized, modern, democratic policy in a country left at an archaic level by decades of Stalinism. It was even more difficult to guide and restrain the chain reaction unleashed by this bold plan while adhering to democratic means, that is, without betraying its principal goal. Even Enrico Fermi, who conducted the first nuclear fission experiment, would not have been equal to this task.

And finally, it was almost impossible to keep the political process within the bounds of rationality and common sense when the weapons used against Gorbachev's reformist agenda were arbitrary action and force (during the August coup), pandering to nationalistic instincts and separatist tendencies, and open flouting of constitutional norms and the still shaky concept of justice, as was the case during the meeting in Belovezhskaya Forest.

Gorbachev's critics, however, protest that he was guilty of these same sins as he followed his own twisting path, replete with compromises and contradictions. Wasn't he responsible, they ask, for causing pernicious developments in some cases and failing to prevent them in others?

As the prime mover and the permanent, sovereign leader of the hazardous process initiated in April 1985, Gorbachev naturally cannot escape responsibility for what happened in his country, or for the outcome of his actions as the head of a once powerful and unified state. In addition to the forces he unleashed that subsequently escaped his control, errors of judgment and political mistakes on his part probably could have been avoided and were crucial.

For instance, it is now clear that the events at Vilnius in January 1991 were a dress rehearsal for the August coup. They were conceived of and organized by the same forces, and perhaps by the same individuals, who would intern Gorbachev at Foros six months later. In January, however, the putschists' targets were

Gorbachev's policies, position, and democratic image—not yet his person. The fact that he remained silent for almost a week in the face of the anticonstitutional challenge by the army, the security forces, and the self-proclaimed "public welfare committees" may well have dealt a severe blow to his own political agenda.

During that fateful week, Gorbachev lost—if only temporarily—the confidence of the republic leaders, who knew that the Vilnius scenario might well occur in their own countries, and the support of his most disinterested ally, the democratic intelligentsia. In so doing, he ceded his title as the country's leading democrat to Yeltsin when there was as yet no justification for doing so—long before the barricades were erected in front of the Russian White House.

As for Yeltsin, with his unpredictability and inconsistency and his "authoritarian tendencies," viewed with such trepidation by democrats in Russia and elsewhere and yet also seen as the inevitable alternative to Gorbachev—isn't he the sum, the embodiment, of Gorbachev's missed opportunities? Isn't he also the product of Gorbachev's errors, the most unpardonable of which was his failure—or maybe lack of desire—to enlist all of the democratic elements in society, including those in the CPSU itself, in implementing and defending his reform agenda?

Finally, it is difficult not to see Gorbachev's refusal to call a general election for the presidency of the USSR as an error on his part—perhaps the fatal error. His manipulation of the Constitution, the one law that does not admit of compromise and that he should have been the first to respect, ultimately lent credence to the idea that he lusted after power and considered it an end in itself rather than a means of implementing an ambitious democratic plan. These suspicions were not dispelled until his resignation—which did not save the Union, although it did restore the honor and dignity of its president.

These are only some of Gorbachev's more obvious errors as president. I am certain that his own list would be longer and more ruthless. But we will never see it. Similarly, without his aid we are unable to draw up another list, of the errors, omissions, and compromises that he did not make despite pressure from his staff, his own resistance to practical reality, and his tragic solitude—the solitude of a man forced to do what he could rather than what he wished. That is probably what lies hidden behind his enigmatic statement, "In any event, I won't be able to tell you everything."

The paradox of Gorbachev is that he made mistakes not when he compromised for the sake of practicality (something that all politicians do), but when he betrayed himself, when he chose the bureaucratic moves of an apparatchik over democratic procedures, secrecy over glasnost, expedience over principles. No one has ever paid a higher price for his mistakes: What can be more terrible for a reformer than to see his goal fade into the distance like the receding line of the horizon? The lessons of the Gorbachev era hold true for all present and future politicians, and thus for Gorbachev himself.

Gorbachev is no longer at the tiller of our storm-tossed and leaky vessel, and as a result many people, including those who used to reproach him for losing touch with reality and for lagging behind his own country, are not as calm and optimistic as they used to be. There are obvious problems and threats emerging today, not only for the peoples of the former Soviet Union but also for Europe and the rest of the world. As it turned out, the totalitarian state could not be dismantled and put back together quickly, according to Western plans, to form a civil society and a market economy. Instead, a spontaneous process of generalized disintegration has set in—a process that can be halted perhaps only by an authoritarian regime or an overt dictatorship.

Obviously, under these circumstances it is only a matter of time before the sleeping demons of nationalism are aroused. This assumption is borne out, unfortunately, by the dramatic events taking place not only in the former USSR but also in the "westernized" countries of Eastern Europe. Apparently, the only way that societies abandoning totalitarian regimes can learn democratic truths is to repeat the mistakes made by others.

One can only hope that the strengthening of the authoritarian and conservative aspects of the post-Communist regimes will not destroy every chance of preserving the democratic gains of Gorbachev's perestroika and will merely serve as a much-needed opportunity for society to pause and catch its breath after an excessively rapid and steep ascent.

For the present, the time has apparently come for democratic politics and its supporters to make a forced halt and reflect awhile. And while the muse of democracy remains silent, it is important that the less visible elements of structural change continue to work behind the scenes, ultimately to bear fruit not in the programs and actions of the politicians now in office but in long-range social processes.

Foremost among these processes are habituation to a market economy, familiarization with the principles of justice, and the rebirth and protection of culture. The influence of these factors on society cannot fail to have a cumulative effect over the long term (in our time, one devoutly hopes) and will pave the way for a new qualitative breakthrough comparable to the historic breakthrough made by Gorbachev during his seven years as Soviet leader. It is his stellar achievement that his country was able to break the bonds that had seemed to tie it forever to the past.

January–May 1992

Appendix: Resignation Speech
of Mikhail Gorbachev
Delivered at 7:00 P.M. on December 25, 1991

Dear Compatriots, Fellow Citizens,

Due to the situation created by the formation of the Commonwealth of Independent States, I am terminating my duties as president of the USSR.

I have firmly defended the autonomy and independence of the peoples, the sovereignty of the republics. But I have also defended the preservation of the union, the integrity of the country.

Events have taken a different course. The policy of dismemberment of the country and dispersal of the state has prevailed, and that I cannot accept.

The Alma-Ata meeting has not changed my position on this matter. Moreover, I am convinced that such far-reaching decisions should have been based on an expression of the will of the people. Nevertheless, I will do everything in my power to ensure that the accords that were signed at Alma-Ata lead to a true mutual understanding in society and facilitate both our emergence from crisis and the process of reform.

In addressing you for the last time as president of the USSR, I feel that it is essential for me to offer my appraisal of the road that has been traveled since 1985, especially since there are so many contradictory, superficial, and unobjective opinions on this matter.

As fate would have it, at the time when I acceded to the highest office of the state it was already clear that something was wrong with the country. We have everything in abundance here: land, oil, gas, coal, precious metals, other natural resources—not to mention the talents and intelligence that God has liberally bestowed on us. And yet we live under much poorer circumstances than the developed countries, we are always lagging behind them.

The reason for this was already obvious: Society was being strangled by the bureaucratic-command system. Condemned to serve the ideology and bear the terrible burden of the arms race, society had reached the limits of its endurance. All attempts at partial reform (and we have had many) failed, one after the other. The country's prospects were increasingly dim. We could not live this way any longer. Everything had to be radically changed.

That is why I have never, at any time, regretted not using the office of the [Party] general secretary merely to "reign" for a few years. I would have considered that irresponsible and immoral.

I realized that to initiate far-reaching reforms in a society such as our own was an extremely difficult and even dangerous task. But there was no choice. Today I am still convinced of the historic rightness of the democratic reforms that were begun in the spring of 1985.

The process of renewing the country and transforming our relations in the world community proved to be much more arduous than one might have supposed. Nevertheless, we must give due credit for what has been accomplished.

Our society has attained freedom, has liberated itself politically and spiritually. And that is the major victory, of which we are not yet fully cognizant, undoubtedly because we have not yet learned how to use it.

Nevertheless, tasks of historic importance have been accomplished:

- The totalitarian system, which deprived our country of the opportunity for happiness and prosperity that it would otherwise have had long ago, has been liquidated.
- We have made a breakthrough toward democratic reforms. Open elections, freedom of the press, religious freedom, representative goverment, and a multiparty system have become reality. Human rights have been recognized as the paramount principle.
- The move to a diversified economy has been initiated, and the equality of all forms of ownership has been established. In the field of agrarian reform, the peasantry has seen a resurgence, private farming has appeared, millions of hectares are being distributed to the inhabitants of rural villages and towns. Economic freedom for the producer has been enacted into law, and new business ventures, the privatization of state enterprises, and the establishment of stock corporations have begun to gather strength.

In redirecting the economy toward the market system, we must keep in mind that this step is being taken for the good of the individual. During these difficult times, everything possible must be done to provide social security, especially for children and the elderly.

We live in a new world: The Cold War is over, the threat of a world war has been averted; the arms race and the insane militarization that distorted our economy, our social consciousness, and our morality have been halted.

I wish to emphasize, once again, that during the transition period I have done everything in my power to maintain control over nuclear weapons.

- We have opened up to the world, we have renounced interference in the affairs of others and the use of armed forces outside this country. In response, we have obtained trust, solidarity, and respect.
- We have become one of the mainstays of the restructuring of modern civilization on peaceful and democratic foundations.
- The peoples, the nations have gained real freedom to choose their own path to self-determination. Our efforts to democratically reconfigure the multinational state brought us very close to concluding a new union agreement.

All of these changes required a tremendous effort. They have taken place under conditions of fierce struggle, with growing opposition from the forces of the old, outmoded, reactionary past and the former Party-state structures and economic apparatus, as well as our own habits and ideological prejudices and our parasitic psychology that tries to level all differences.

They have been obstructed by our intolerance, our low level of political culture, and our fear of change.

That is why we have lost so much time. The old system crumbled away before the new one could be set in motion. And the crisis that had befallen society became still worse.

I am aware of the dissatisfaction caused by the difficulties of the present situation, and the sharp criticism being voiced against the authorities at all levels and against my own actions. But I would emphasize, once again: Fundamental changes, in such a large country, with such a heritage, cannot take place smoothly, without pain or difficulty.

The August coup pushed the general crisis to its farthest limit. The most pernicious effect of this crisis has been the collapse of statehood.

Today I am concerned about our people's loss of their citizenship in a great country, which may prove to have grave consequences for all concerned.

It is of vital importance to me to preserve the democratic victories of recent years. They are the hard-won fruits of our history, our tragic experience. They must not be relinquished under any circumstances or any pretext. To do so would be to bury all hope for a better future.

I speak of all this with honesty and directness. It is my moral duty to do so.

I want to express my gratitude to all the citizens who supported our policy for the country's renewal, and who played a part in the realization of democratic reforms.

I am grateful to the statesmen, to the leading figures in politics and society, to the millions of people in other countries who understood our plans, supported them, and came forward to meet us, offering their sincere cooperation.

I leave office with anxiety. But also with hope, and with faith in you, in your wisdom and your strength of mind. We are heirs to a great civilization, and it is now up to each and every one of us to ensure that this civilization is reborn to a modern, dignified new life.

I wish to thank from the bottom of my heart those who stood by me through all these years in a just and good cause. Certainly, some mistakes could have been avoided, and many things could have been done better.

I am certain that, sooner or later, our joint efforts will bear fruit, and that our peoples will live in a democratic and prosperous society.

I wish all of you the very best.

Notes

1. The "conservatives" were partisans of the old Communist system. The Soviet political scene during the last months of the USSR was the direct opposite of the structure that usually prevails in the West: The "right" was made up of Communists of every stripe (from neo-Bolsheviks through Brezhnevites to Stalinists) who favored a planned economy; the members of the "left" (democrats, reformers, liberals, and radicals) were generally in favor of marketization.

2. The Parliament of the USSR, instituted by the constitutional reform of 1988, consisted of two "levels": (1) The Congress of People's Deputies, composed of 2,250 members elected for a term of five years by three different methods: 750 from proportionally represented electoral districts, 750 from national electoral districts (thirty-two from each Union republic, eleven from each autonomous republic, five from each autonomous region, and one from each autonomous district), and 750 from social organizations (the CPSU, labor unions, Communist youth organizations, the Academy of Sciences, writers' and artists' unions, etc.). Gorbachev was one of the contingent of 100 deputies chosen by the Central Committee of the CPSU. (2) The Supreme Soviet, composed of two chambers (the Soviet of Nationalities and the Soviet of the Union). Each had 271 representatives elected by the Congress. One-fifth of these representatives were supposed to be replaced every year, but this rule had not been observed during the Supreme Soviet's two years of existence.

3. Pankin was the only Soviet envoy who publicly voiced his support for Gorbachev during the attempted coup. After Pankin was "promoted," a counselor at the embassy in Prague, Alexander Lebedev, took his place as ambassador.

4. A referendum on "maintaining a renewed union" was held on March 17, 1991. Six republics refused to take part: the three Baltic republics, Moldavia, Georgia, and Armenia. In the rest of the USSR there was an 80 percent turnout, and 76 percent voted in favor. Most of the yes votes were cast in rural areas and in the Central Asian republics (which averaged more than 90 percent in favor) but in no republic participating did the yes vote fall below 70 percent.

5. Rukh, the Ukrainian nationalist party, was established in 1988, a move made possible by the first liberalization measures, which allowed "popular fronts" in support of perestroika to develop in the republics. Initially an informal organization, Rukh was strengthened by its electoral successes, which demonstrated a strong following in western Ukraine (annexed by Stalin in 1939) and in Kiev. It gradually won over a majority in favor of Ukrainian independence.

6. After the October Revolution, in a move to strengthen Bolshevism in Ukraine, Soviet Russia ceded to that republic part of the industrial basin of Donbass, on the right bank of

the Donets. In 1954, in celebration of the three-hundredth anniversary of the union of Russia and Ukraine, Nikita Khrushchev made the Crimean peninsula part of Ukraine. Catherine II had won the region from the Tatars at the end of the eighteenth century, and it had belonged to Russia ever since. The populations of Donbass and the Crimea are largely Russian, and most of the Ukrainians in those areas are Russophiles.

7. Volsky acted with dignity and strength of character during the putsch. As it happened, he was the last Muscovite to receive a phone call from Gorbachev on that fateful Sunday of August 18, 1991, before the delegation of putschists paid their visit. I heard about this telephone conversation from Volsky on August 20, when I had finally managed to get back to Moscow from my dacha in Uspenskoye, making my way through roadblocks supported by armored vehicles, which the military had set up in the streets of the capital. According to Volsky, Gorbachev had been in good spirits, complaining only of an ill-timed bout of sciatica. On the strength of this telephone conversation, Volsky became a key witness who was able to give the lie to the main "legal" argument put forward by the putschists: that a serious illness had rendered the President unable to carry out his duties.

Volsky and I debated how best to present this information to the plenum of the Central Committee or a session of the Supreme Soviet in order to get all the putschists' decisions nullified. Events moved so quickly, however, that Volsky was able to discuss this subject the very next day, during a press conference called at the offices of the Industrial Union, which he directed, on Staraya Ploshchad (Old Square), in Moscow.

8. Gorbachev appointed Valentin Pavlov head of the "cabinet" (the new name for the Council of Ministers) on January 14, 1991, as a replacement for Nikolai Ryzhkov, who had developed a heart problem a few weeks earlier (after Gorbachev had made clear his intention to dismiss him). Pavlov tried to rectify the economic situation by relying on the vast sector of state-owned enterprises and the military-industrial complex at the expense of emerging private enterprise. This regressive policy took on farcical dimensions when he went so far as to denounce Western aid as a plot by capitalist banks to appropriate wealth from the USSR. In June he tried to get Parliament to grant him full powers in economic matters. Gorbachev, who was engaged in the Novo-Ogarevo process at the time, blocked this maneuver. Two months later, Pavlov was one of the members of the State Committee for the State of Emergency that attempted to assume power on August 18.

9. As a result of the putsch and the proclamations of independence issued by most of the republics, it became necessary to redefine the economic relations of these new sovereign states, which were still dependent on each other. The treaty, drafted by a committee chaired by Grigory Yavlinsky, was intended primarily to preserve the unified market.

10. Comecon, created in 1949, was the joint economic and trade organization of the socialist bloc, at first only of the countries of Eastern Europe (Yugoslavia worked with some of its agencies), later including Mongolia, Vietnam, and Cuba. It was officially dissolved on June 28, 1991.

11. In 1990, economists Stanislav Shatalin and Grigory Yavlinsky, working on behalf of the president of the USSR, developed a program for converting the economy to a market-based system in 500 days; hence the name. Gorbachev supported the plan at first and,

jointly with Yeltsin, submitted it to the Soviet Parliament, where it was rejected by Ryzhkov's government. After that, Gorbachev tried to obtain at least some formal compromise; but in the process, the plan was watered down so thoroughly as to become virtually meaningless.

12. The first summit meeting between George Bush and Mikhail Gorbachev took place in Malta in December 1989, one year after Bush's election to the presidency of the United States. It was at this meeting that real bonds of trust were established between the two heads of state. Before then, Bush had shown some reserve toward the Soviet leader.

13. The Operational Steering Committee was placed under the leadership of Ivan Silaev and his three deputies: Arkady Volsky, Yury Luzhkov, and Grigory Yavlinsky. It was a rather artificial structure meant to serve in place of the nonexistent Soviet government and charged with meeting the most urgent problems of food supply in the big cities.

14. Nazi troops massacred more than 100,000 people, most of them Jews, at Babii Yar in September 1941.

15. The White House is the name given to the building of the supreme soviet of Russia (attacked and abolished by Yeltsin in 1993), because of the color of its facade. This was where Yeltsin had his offices as president of the Russian parliament.

16. In Cyrillic alphabetical order.

17. In 1945, the USSR and Japan were at war for only one week, from August 8, 1945 (two days after the first atomic bomb was dropped on Hiroshima, on August 6), until the unconditional surrender of Emperor Hirohito on August 14. A peace treaty between the two countries was never signed, and the Japanese continue to object to the Soviet annexation of the Southern Kuril Islands (an archipelago located only a few miles from the large Japanese island of Hokkaido).

18. Armenia, Belorussia, Kazakhstan, Kirghizia, Uzbekistan, Russia, Tadzhikistan, and Turkmenistan.

19. The heads of state and the government leaders of the sixteen countries of the Atlantic Alliance met in Rome on November 7 and 8 to work out a new strategic concept and to consider the expansion of their relations with the countries of Eastern Europe.

20. Gennady Yanaev was elected vice president in December 1990, during a session of the Congress of People's Deputies of the USSR. He lost on the first ballot and owed his election to the insistence of Gorbachev, who explained to the deputies that it would be impossible to work without him. On August 18, Yanaev used his position as vice president to allow the putschists to try to maintain a semblance of legality. Actually, although this made him look like one of the ringleaders of the coup, he probably played only a minor role.

21. In Russian, the word *soyuz* (union) is masculine and is more appropriate for the name of an airplane (*samoliot*, also masculine) than the feminine *Rossiya*.

22. During the Central Committee plenum of October 1987, Boris Yeltsin, then first Party secretary for the city of Moscow and a candidate member of the Politburo, made some critical remarks against the progress of perestroika, which he felt was too slow, and attacked Yegor Ligachev, who was the Party's number two man at the time. He was de-

nounced by the Central Committee and relieved of his duties as the Moscow Party chief in November, during a plenum of the City Party Committee presided over by Gorbachev, who acted toward him with particular harshness. In his book *Against the Grain* (Summit Books, a Division of Simon & Schuster, New York, 1990), Yeltsin reports that he had fallen ill after the Central Committee meeting and that he literally had to leave his sickbed to attend that Moscow plenum.

23. These two men helped Gorbachev in varying degrees during his rise to the office of Party general secretary. Since 1983, Yegor Ligachev, as secretary of the Central Committee, had directed the Department Responsible for Party Organizational Work. On April 23, 1985, just after Gorbachev's accession to power, he assumed responsibility for ideology as well as the party organization, became a Politburo member and, de facto, the Party's number two man. Ivan Polozkov was Ligachev's deputy at the Department for Party Organizational Work. In June 1985, he was appointed Party first secretary for the province of Krasnodar. Although Polozkov was not his first choice, Gorbachev supported him over Yeltsin for the office of president of the Russian parliament. In June of the same year, he took over the leadership of the Russian Communist Party, which had just been founded.

24. González called himself a socialist, but he belonged to the Western European social democratic tradition, which had always been opposed by the Communists and which Gorbachev was now leaning toward.

25. A Cossack village.

26. A peasant cottage.

27. Colonel-General Makashov, commander of the Volga-Ural military region, was noted for the virulence of his attacks against Gorbachev, especially during the Twenty-Eighth Congress of the CPSU in July 1990. A conservative hard-liner, he ran for the Russian presidency against Yeltsin in June 1991. Supported by small groups of Communist nationalists, including the association *Pamyat,* he won 3.7 percent of the vote. He was forced into early retirement immediately after the putsch but resurfaced as commander of the extremist gangs that stormed the Ostankino television studios in October 1993.

28. *Le Putsch,* Olivier Orban, Paris, October 1991. Published in English as *The August Coup: The Truth and the Lessons,* HarperCollins, New York, 1991.

29. The feeble-minded Czar Fyodor I (1557–1598), son of Ivan IV (Ivan the Terrible), yielded the practical exercise of power to Boris Godunov (1551–1605), his brother-in-law, who succeeded him on the throne at his death. Boris is also Yeltsin's first name.

30. The Soviet army included five armed services: strategic forces (missiles), land forces, air defense, the air force, and the navy.

31. In the book of Daniel, the mysterious writing on the wall that foretold the downfall of the king of Babylon. The prophet Daniel interpreted the words for the king as meaning, in part, "You have been weighed in the balances and found wanting."

32. The USSR was founded on December 30, 1922, by the uniting of the Russian Soviet Federated Socialist Republic, the Republic of Ukraine, the Republic of Belorussia, and the Transcaucasian Soviet Federated Socialist Republic, which included Armenia, Azerbaidzhan, and Georgia.

33. November 7 and 8 were designated as national holidays commemorating the anniversary of the October Revolution. In 1991 these dates fell on a Thursday and a Friday.

34. Zdenek Mlynar, secretary of the Czechoslovakian Communist Party at the time of the Prague Spring in 1968, had gone to law school at Moscow State University with Gorbachev. They had formed a close friendship there, which was disrupted when Mlynar was expelled from the Party in the wake of the Soviet invasion of Czechoslovakia. Their ties were renewed after Gorbachev became the Soviet leader.

35. Rudolf Slansky, Sr. (1901–1952), was general secretary of the Czechoslovakian Communist Party from 1945 to 1951. Accused of heading a "ring of antistate and anti-Party conspirators," he was condemned to death during one of the Stalinist trials of the postwar era and was executed. He was rehabilitated in 1968.

36. Traditionally, all the state dachas were parceled out to party and government leaders on an equal basis. These vacation homes were controlled, protected, and administered by the security arm of the KGB (the former ninth directorate, or *devyatka*) with KGB funds. With the repeal of Article 6 of the Constitution in March 1990, which eliminated the leadership role of the CPSU, the leaders of the Communist Party reverted to the status of mere mortals and were forced to give up the state dachas, which from then on were reserved for government, rather than Party, officials. The KGB, of course, continued to administer them until the shake-up that followed the coup.

37. The leaders of Azerbaidzhan, Belorussia, Kazakhstan, Kirghizia, Tadzhikistan, and Turkmenistan.

38. Gennady Burbulis became the administration's strongman and Yeltsin's closest confidant. He has even been referred to as "Czar Boris's Rasputin." Burbulis's rise to the upper echelons of power in Russia was meteoric. With his influence he was able to gain the position of second-in-command of the Russian government after his work as Boris Yeltsin's campaign strategist resulted in a landslide presidential victory for Yeltsin. (Yeltsin's main competitor, Nikolai Ryzhkov, former primer minister of the Soviet Union, came in far behind.)

39. The August 19 coup took place on the eve of the signing of the first Union Treaty, set for August 20. One of the objectives of the plotters was to keep this event from taking place.

40. According to the legend, St. Vladimir rejected Islam because of its prohibition of alcohol consumption, for "the joy of the Russians lies in drink," and Judaism because he viewed it as the faith of a vanquished and landless people. He instead chose the Byzantine liturgy and faith.

41. Formerly Frunze (Pishpek before the Bolshevik Revolution), Bishkek is the capital of what is now Kyrgyzstan (formerly Kirghizia).

42. On August 20, 1991, the second day of the putsch, Eduard Shevardnadze made the following televised statement: "I want to believe that Mikhail Gorbachev is the victim of this plot and not its instigator, because if he were [the instigator], he would have been signing his own death warrant: a physical, moral, and political death. . . . To leave the capital and abandon his post was obviously a gross error due to a lack of judgment."

43. The title of a poem by Vladimir Mayakovsky (1893–1930), one of the seminal members of the Russian avant-garde around the time of the revolution. Like his European

counterparts, Mayakovsky rejected the vague, elevated conventions of nineteenth-century literature: "I don't believe in a blossoming Nice!" he says in the same poem. (*Russian Literature of the Twenties: An Anthology,* Ann Arbor: Ardis, 1987, p. 433.)

44. During a press conference he gave on November 21, Ukrainian president Leonid Kravchuk had stated, "The center is compromised. That is why we have to build on new foundations. When it comes to overall problems such as strategic, military, or territorial issues, I am in favor [of the union]. But there is no imperative need to keep a union with ministers, departments, and a presidential entourage—that is, to go back to the old structures."

45. On August 23, the day after his return to Moscow after his release from Foros, Gorbachev was ordered to explain his position before and during the putsch to the Russian parliament, which was highly critical of his actions. Yeltsin forced him to read the minutes of a government meeting in which nearly all of the ministers had supported the plotters. This was also the occasion when Yeltsin signed the decree suspending the activities of the Communist Party.

46. A misquotation. What Luther nailed to the door of his church was a copy of his "Ninety-Five Theses"; according to some accounts, at his hearing before the Diet of Worms he said, "Here I stand. I cannot do otherwise."

47. In Cyrillic alphabetical order.

48. The book was published in Germany by Bertelsmann in 1992. An English-language edition has yet to appear.

49. Russian state councillor Sergei Shakhrai was one of the most influential members of the team of "young Turks" (Mladoturki) gathered around Boris Yeltsin at that time.

50. A city in the Donbass region of Ukraine, formerly Voroshilovgrad.

51. An untranslatable play on words: In Russian, *pushcha* means "virgin forest." The place where the three leaders held their meeting is called Belovezhskaya pushcha; hence the association with the putsch.

52. Mishka is a Russian diminutive form of Mikhail, as well as the Russian name for teddy bears.

53. The Russian Soviet Federated Socialist Republic, the administrative name of the Russian federation. After the dismantling of the USSR, the official name of the now-independent country became "the Russian Federation," or simply "Russia."

54. At that time, Erich Honecker, the general secretary of East Germany's Unified Socialist Party (SED), who had been granted asylum in the USSR before the August putsch, had taken refuge in the Chilean embassy in Moscow. Gorbachev had decided to allow him to stay in the country for humanitarian reasons, but the Russian government made no secret of its decision to grant the extradition request filed by the German authorities.

55. Vladimir Vysotsky was a popular Russian actor and poet-singer and the symbol of an artistic counterculture until his premature death in 1980.

56. The Russian Communist Party was founded in June 1990. Before then, Russia, unlike the other republics, had not had its own branch of the Party. Its territory had been governed directly by the Communist Party of the Soviet Union, which also controlled the Communist Parties of the other republics.

57. A conservative gathering of several hundred thousand people for the annual Armed Forces Day on February 23, 1991, prompted demonstrations in Moscow by democrats and radicals the next day and over the next few weeks. Hundreds of thousands of people attended despite the fact that such events were prohibited by the authorities.

58. Armenia, Azerbaidzhan, Belorussia, Kazakhstan, Kirghizia, Moldavia, Uzbekistan, Russia, Tadzhikistan, Turkmenistan, and Ukraine.

59. Christmas Day was, of course, not celebrated during the Soviet era. The Nativity began to be celebrated in Russia in 1991, but December 25 on the Julian calendar used by the Orthodox Church corresponds to January 7 on the Gregorian calendar.

60. The Provincial Party Committee, the highest political authority in a given province (*oblast*). Actually, the administrative division of Stavropol was not a province but a territory (*krai*). Gorbachev was thus the head of a *kraikom*. The territories, of which there were six, differed from the provinces only by the fact that an autonomous region, or oblast, was attached to them. There was no real hierarchical difference between the first secretary of a province and the first secretary of a territory.

61. Most Soviet institutions had the equivalent of a post exchange for the exclusive use of their members. These outlets were supplied, according to their importance, with hard-to-find, high-quality items offered at heavily subsidized prices.

62. Sergei Medunov, a favorite of Brezhnev's, was first Party secretary of Krasnodar *krai* beginning in 1973, during the period when Gorbachev was first secretary of Stavropol *krai*. Accused of corruption, he was removed from office in 1982 and expelled from the Party seven years later, in 1989, but was never proven guilty of any criminal acts.

63. Nikolai Shchelokov was then Soviet minister of the interior.

About the Book and Author

As press secretary to Mikhail Gorbachev, Andrei Grachev witnessed and recorded many events unobserved by the general public. In this engaging and compelling book, he recounts these episodes in vivid detail, interpreting them in the context of the time. Highlighted are top-level meetings with Western leaders; State Council debates on a new treaty of union (promising, until Gorbachev and Yeltsin sparred over Russia's policy toward the Chechen republic); and Gorbachev's private talks with leading members of government, business, and religious and cultural circles from around the world.

Andrei S. Grachev was a foreign policy adviser to Mikhail Gorbachev from 1985 until the autumn of 1991, when he became press secretary. He is currently a *Moscow News* columnist and a senior research fellow at the Institute of World Economy and International Relations (IMEMO) in Moscow.

Index